Favorites from

THE LUNCH BELL

Family and Friends

BETTY SWAIN
RESEARCHED AND WRITTEN WITH BARBARA HOLLAND EBY

All recipes herein represent favorite recipes of
The Lunch Bell, family and friends.

Brand names have been used only when necessary.

First Edition

First Printing   May 2010   4,000 copies

To order additional copies of "Favorites from The Lunch Bell, Family and Friends", please contact **The Lunch Bell**:

The Lunch Bell
694 Town Center Drive
Newport News, VA 23606
(757) 873-1839
www.thelunchbell.com
thelunchbell@gmail.com

WIMMER
COOKBOOKS
A CONSOLIDATED GRAPHICS COMPANY
800.548.2537   wimmerco.com

The photographs on the following pages are courtesy of Barb Spencer Photography: 1, 13, 41, 75, 109, 137, 183 and 215

The photograph on the back cover is courtesy of Ann Efimetz, Williamsburg Magazine.

FEATURED RECIPE ON FRONT:

Aunt Della's Pineapple Cake, page 239

INTRODUCTION

I have been cooking and baking for over 60 years. My mother taught me to cook while raising me in the Shenandoah Valley of Virginia. To her, and to me, cooking shows your love for others.

Over the years, I have collected many recipes that I adore from my family and friends. Many have been in our family for generations.

I have taken my recipes, your recipes and found some other good ones along the way and put them all into "Favorites from The Lunch Bell, Family and Friends". **My secret recipes, recipes that are used at the restaurant and for catering or recipes that I just love are denoted with a "bell."** There are over 150 recipes that have my blessing since I have made and eaten them numerous times! I greatly appreciate the other recipes submitted and guarantee that they are just as wonderful as my own.

So after many years of cooking and almost 30 years in the restaurant business, the time has come to share my recipes with you!

Enjoy!
BETTY SWAIN

In 2007, Bill and Betty Swain
had their 50th Wedding Anniversary.

TABLE OF CONTENTS

My secret recipes, recipes that are used at the restaurant and for catering or recipes that I just love are denoted with a "bell."

ACKNOWLEDGMENTS

I would like to dedicate this cookbook to my husband, Bill Swain. Without his support, I could not have achieved all that I have achieved. He has been willing to do any and everything that needs to be done. He has sacrificed over the years to ensure the success of the business, and he has done every job imaginable — from host to dishwasher. His gentle demeanor has welcomed almost every customer who has walked through our doors, and he knows most customers by name. I truly appreciate everything that Bill has done, and I am happy to have been his wife for over 50 years.

"What do you need me to do now?"

My special family has made my life complete. A woman could not ask for more respectable, sincere, loving children and grandchildren. Blair, our oldest daughter, has taken on a love for the restaurant and has been managing it since 2005. Shelah, our youngest daughter, is always willing to help and has contributed immensely to the restaurant's success. Although Billy, our oldest, has not worked day to day at the restaurant, his support has always been there. All of our grandchildren, Jay, Tyler, Jennie, Mallory, Grae, Annie Kate and Ashley hold a special place in our hearts. Almost all of them have played a role at the restaurant. A sincere thank you to all of you!

I also want to thank some of my dedicated employees who have been with me for many years. Ruby Binder helped me open the restaurant in July of 1981. She worked full-time for many years, and she still makes an appearance in the kitchen and dining room. Bernice Kosier started working with us in August of 1981 and stayed with us through the 1990's until she retired. Carrie Osmondson started waitressing in January of 1986 and to this day still entertains our customers now and then. Audrey McCord was an integral part of the restaurant from 1986 to the late nineties. Patsy Taylor began helping in 1991 and still works the cash register today. Terry Barnes, Bridgette Brown, Bea Hoal, Lewis, LaTria Hebbons, Shirley Phillips and Will Reaves have all been outstanding employees over the years. These employees make the restaurant a family. They have made the customers feel welcome and like they are dining at home. Thanks to all of my wonderful employees!

continued on next page

Acknowledgments continued

Barbara Holland Eby has been instrumental in getting this cookbook printed. Barbara started working with me in the summer of 1989, when she was 17 years old. I almost didn't hire her, as I thought she was too young, but when I told her, "No", she said, "Will you give me a week and then decide?" She worked summers and holidays for the next few years. She moved to Charlotte, Baltimore and New York City for her career, but stayed in touch with us. Then she moved back to Virginia a few years ago and recently found herself with some spare time. So, she offered to help write the cookbook. She spent many days pulling recipes from my head so that they could be enjoyed by you. I appreciate all of your help, Barbara, in making this cookbook a reality.

And lastly, thank you to everyone who contributed a favorite recipe to help make this cookbook possible. Thank you for sharing your stories and thoughts about **The Lunch Bell**. We appreciate your support of our restaurant, as well as the cookbook.

BETTY SWAIN

THE HISTORY OF *THE LUNCH BELL*

Bernice Kosier, Bill Swain and Ruby Binder at the original *Lunch Bell*, which opened in February, 1981.

Whether you eat at **The Lunch Bell** regularly or you've never had the opportunity to eat there, we'd like to take this opportunity to thank you for purchasing "Favorites from The Lunch Bell, Family and Friends" cookbook. Before you set out to make some of the delicious recipes in this book, we'd like to share with you how **The Lunch Bell** began.

My husband, Bill, and I set out to fulfill the "All-American Dream" for our family — to work for ourselves by establishing a new business. We realized that the best way to accomplish this goal was to find a need in the community, and then determine a way to satisfy it. At that time, in January of 1981, Oyster Point Business Park in Newport News, Virginia, employed about 700 people who needed a convenient place to enjoy lunch. Thus, there was a need for a restaurant within the business park. We saw a way to serve this special business community and fulfill our dream at the same time.

And so it was that February 18, 1981, **The Lunch Bell** began as a sandwich shop with 52 seats, including seating at an old drug store style counter. We thought about omitting the counter section several times until a salesman said he never felt alone eating at a counter where he could talk to the waitress. Then we knew we would keep it. The restaurant also expanded outside the limit of the current facility to include business and corporate catered lunches and affairs. In January of 1986, **The Lunch Bell** relocated across the street to 703 Thimble Shoals Boulevard, and a second dining room was added for private meetings, business lunches and afternoon meetings. We enjoyed that location for 17 years.

The second *Lunch Bell* was located on Thimble Shoals Boulevard in Oyster Point.

We relocated and expanded once again in June, 2003 to a new building in a beautiful area known as "City Center" and are located at 694 Town Center Drive. This area houses some of the stalwart businesses of Newport News, as well as some of the city offices. We have been serving the entire Peninsula for about 7 years from this new location and don't see an end in sight!

Thank you for helping us to fulfill our American Dream for almost 30 years!

Sincerely,

BETTY SWAIN, WITH HUSBAND, BILL

The ribbon cutting for the third *Lunch Bell* was held in June, 2003.

7

The City of Newport News is located in Southeastern, Virginia, where the James River meets the Chesapeake Bay. The City runs approximately 23 miles along the James River and the Hampton Roads Harbor and is in the area known as the Peninsula, a portion of the larger metropolitan area known as Hampton Roads. Newport News was named for Christopher Newport, captain of the Susan Constant, the lead ship that carried the Jamestown settlers to the new world in 1607.

The Lunch Bell is located in City Center, Newport News, Virginia.

Newport News is the fourth largest independent city in Virginia and is home to more than 175,000 people. For the last 200 years, Newport News has been known as the provider of the nation's finest, technologically advanced military ships. In more recent years, Newport News has also become a center for international commerce, research and technology. The local economy is strengthened by a strong military presence and is home of the U.S. Army Transportation Center at Fort Eustis. The City's historic sites, museums and cultural facilities compliment the quality of life for Newport News residents and businesses. There are more than 20 public parks, as well as public boat ramps and recreation facilities.

The first **Lunch Bell** opened in a business park of Newport News, known as Oyster Point. The park was developed with a nautical theme and Thimble Shoals Boulevard, where the first and second restaurants were located, was named after a local lighthouse. The Thimble Shoal Light signals shallow waters that can be hazardous to shipping traffic.

Oyster Point expanded to include "City Center" in 2003. It is designed as an open-air gathering place and shopping district, landscaped in a southern living fashion with grand vistas to the gorgeous five acre fountain. City Center at Oyster Point is a vibrant community of luxurious apartments, distinctive condominiums, modern office buildings, and exciting and unique retail shops and restaurants. City Center is touted as the "new downtown" of Newport News because it is centrally located on the Peninsula. **The Lunch Bell** is happy to call City Center home.

BETTY'S APPLE BUTTER

The one recipe you won't find in this cookbook is the one for Betty's Apple Butter. It is currently served at **The Lunch Bell** and is also sold in jars at the store and at some local grocery stores. The apple butter contains a "secret ingredient" which gives the butter a rich red color and memorable flavor and Betty is not ready to share it yet!

The customers at **The Lunch Bell** have always commented on its unique flavor. They use the butter on toast and biscuits. Some put it in their oatmeal or on grits. Others enjoy it on a sandwich with peanut butter, instead of jelly. It has a nice balance of spices.

Betty started making jars of it in the fall of 2008 due to the demand by her customers. People kept asking to buy it in quantity. Now, Betty prepares the apple butter in large batches at Rowena's, a gourmet manufacturing facility in Norfolk, Virginia. Apple butter is traditionally made outside in big copper pots. The process takes hours to heat and cook the apples to produce the sweet taste. It is usually made with cinnamon and other spices.

Betty's Apple Butter carries the "Virginia's Finest" label and has always been a favorite at **The Lunch Bell**. The "Virginia's Finest" Trademark Program has been around for 20 years, promoting the development of Virginia agriculture and specialty food products. Betty is shown with the apple butter on the back cover of this cookbook.

You can purchase Betty's Apple Butter at **The Lunch Bell** or go to www.thelunchbell.com.

Betty's Apple Butter is a customer favorite at **The Lunch Bell**.

THE THANKSGIVING DAY FEAST
AT *THE LUNCH BELL*

Thanksgiving dinner has been served at **The Lunch Bell** for the past 12 years, starting in 1997. There are two seatings; one at 12:30 pm and one at 3:00 pm with about 150 to 200 people at each seating. Everyone makes reservations and there usually is not an empty seat in the house! Extra amenities, such as tablecloths and fresh flowers are added to make this a special occasion for all.

Many customers enjoy the variety of foods at the Thanksgiving buffet.

Every year, Stuart Bateman travels from New Mexico to have Thanksgiving dinner at *The Lunch Bell* with his friends, Lynn Sawyer and Patsy Murphy.

THE THANKSGIVING DAY MENU

APPETIZERS:
Hot Crab Dip
Deviled Eggs
Sweet Pickles

SOUPS & SALADS:
Cream of Potato Soup
Tomato, Cucumber and Onion Salad
Potato Salad
Macaroni Salad
Orange Thanksgiving Salad
Strawberry Cream Gelatin

VEGETABLES & SIDE DISHES:
Dressing
Mashed Potatoes
Senator Russell's Sweet Potatoes
Corn Pudding
Collards
Green Beans
Butter Beans with Corn
Betty's Cranberry Sauce
Cranberry Relish
Corn Bread
Hot Rolls

MAIN DISHES:
Turkey with gravy
Pot Roast with gravy
Ham
Baked Flounder
Hot Chicken Salad

DESSERTS:
Chocolate Cream Pie
Coconut Cream Pie
Lemon Meringue Pie
Pecan Pie
Pumpkin Pie
Sweet Potato Pie
Tollhouse Pie
Apple Pie
Pound Cake
Chocolate Cream Cake

Breakfast

Sandwiches

Featured Sandwich
"Sandwich in the Round": Egg*, ham and cheese on a toasted
English Muffin. 4.49

Sausage or Ham Biscuit 3.99

Egg* Sandwich
Toast or Biscuit 3.79
Add cheese 4.29

Country Ham Biscuit 4.99

Bacon or Sausage & Egg* Sandwich 4.99
Add cheese 5.49

Waffles

Malt Waffles
Sprinkled with powdered sugar and butter. 6.99
Add sausage, bacon or ham 8.99
Add Sausage, Bacon or Ham & Two eggs*
Cooked the way you like. 9.99

With Fruit Topping and Whipped Cream
Fruit topping may vary with season availability. 7.99
Add sausage, bacon or ham. 8.99

New **Multi-Grain Waffles** 6.99

Pancakes

Sweet Potato Pancakes
With honey pecan butter and powdered sugar. 6.49

New **Buttermilk Pancakes**
Served with butter. 6.49
Add sausage, bacon or ham. 7.99
Add sausage, bacon or ham and 2 eggs*. 8.99

Additional Items

Danish 3.49	Bagel 2.49
Grits 2.59	With cream cheese 2.99
Jumbo Assorted	Biscuit
Muffins 3.19	Butter & jelly 2.29
Hash Browns 2.29	Cereal Assorted
Oven Chips 2.99	hot & cold 2.79 and up
Toast & Jelly 1.99	Cereal with fruit 4.99
English Muffin 1.99	Breakfast Meats 2.99
	Side of Fresh Fruit 2.99

Plates

New Served with toast or biscuit and
choice of potatoes or grits.

"Egg Beaters"
Two eggs 6.29

One Egg* Breakfast
Served with sliced tomato. 3.99

**One Egg*, Bacon or Sausage or
Corned Beef Hash**
Served with sliced tomato. 5.99

Two Eggs* 4.99

**Two Eggs* Bacon or Sausage or
Corned Beef Hash**
Served with sliced tomato. 7.99

French Toast with Maple Syrup 6.79
With sausage or Bacon 8.79

Creamed Chipped Beef
Served on a biscuit or toast. 6.99

New **Sausage Gravy**
Served on a biscuit or toast. 6.99

New **Steak & Eggs***
Ribeye cooked to your desired temperature. 10.99

Omelettes

Omelettes are made with two eggs and your
choice of cheese; American, Cheddar or Swiss.

Meat & Cheese Omelette
Your choice of sausage, bacon or ham. 7.99

Western
Cheese, tomatoes, ham, onions,
and green peppers. 8.99

Spanish
Cheese, tomatoes, ham, onions, green
peppers and jalapenos. 8.99
Add an additional egg .99

Beverages

*12 oz. in house. 16 oz. to go.
Coffee, Hot Tea, Milk, Chocolate Milk, Hot Chocolate 2

Juices
Tomato, orange, apple, cranberry and grapefruit 2.29

*Contain (or may contain) raw or under cooked ingredients. Consuming raw or under cooked meats,
poultry, seafood, shellfish, or eggs may increase your risk of food borne illness.

Soup & Salad

Soup
Homemade Each Day!
Cup 3.79   Bowl 4.99   Chili 5.99

Monday & Wednesday   Vegetable Beef
Tuesday & Friday   Navy Bean
Thursday   Homemade Chili
Saturday   Chef Special

Bowl of Soup & Tossed Salad
9.49

Cup of Soup & ½ Cold Sandwich
7.99

Cup of Soup & Whole Cold Sandwich
Choose from Chicken, Tuna, Egg salad, Pimiento Cheese,
Cream Cheese and Olive or Cheese. 9.79

Tossed Salad
A combination of lettuce, cucumbers, radishes and tomato wedges,
served with your choice of dressing and crackers. 4.99

Fruit & Cottage Cheese
A generous portion of cottage cheese served on a bed of lettuce topped
with a peach half and a pineapple slice. 5.99
With seasonal fresh fruit add 1.29

Lunch Bell's Favorite Fruit Salad
A peach half, a pineapple slice on a bed of lettuce, topped
with house dressing and shredded cheddar cheese. 4.49

Chef's Salad
Fresh bed of lettuce, tomato wedges, diced cucumber, sliced radishes topped with
julienne ham or turkey, cheddar cheese and wedges of hard boiled egg. Your choice
of dressing. 9.79   Substitute ham or turkey with grilled chicken add 1.29

Grae's Chef
Chef salad with fried chicken fillet, bacon bits and
parmesan pepper dressing. 9.99

Luncheon Plates

Lobster Salad
With fresh fruit, one half deviled egg, lettuce and tomato. 11.99

Lobster Roll
Grilled roll, fresh fruit and potato salad. 11.99

Grilled Chicken Breast
With fresh fruit cup, lettuce and tomato. Roll upon request. 9.49

Fried Bologna Sandwich
With mustard, onions, relish and cheese. 6.99

Fried Fish Sandwich
Served with French fries and slaw, lettuce and tomato. 9.79

Fried Fillet of Chicken
Served with French fries and slaw, lettuce and tomato. 9.79

Chicken Salad Cold Plate
One generous scoop of homemade chicken salad, one scoop of potato salad or
macaroni salad, tomato, one half deviled egg and pickle slices. 8.99

Tuna Salad Cold Plate
One generous scoop of homemade tuna salad, one scoop of potato salad or
macaroni salad, tomato, one half deviled egg and pickle slices. 8.99

Hamburger Plate*
Ground fresh daily, one large scoop of potato or macaroni salad, sliced tomato,
one half deviled egg and pickle slices. 9.99

B.B.Q. Plate
B.B.Q. with cole slaw, scoop of potato or macaroni salad, sliced tomato, one half
deviled egg and pickle slices. Bun upon request. 9.99

Hot Dog Plate
Two hot dogs, scoop of potato or macaroni salad, sliced tomato, one half of
deviled egg and pickle slices. Bun upon request. 8.99

*Contain (or may contain) raw or under cooked ingredients. Consuming raw or under cooked me
poultry, seafood, shellfish, or eggs may increase your risk of food borne illness.

Lunch Bell Sandwich Board

Hot Sandwiches

*Add French fries, cole slaw
or macaroni salad for 1.99*

Hamburger 7.29
Cheeseburger 7.99
Hot Dog 3.79
Rueben (on rye bread only) 9.49
Large B.B.Q. (with slaw) 7.49
Small B.B.Q. (with slaw) 6.49
Rib Eye Steak Sandwich 9.79
Fried Bologna Sandwich 6.99

Cold Sandwiches

Our cold sandwiches are prepared fresh to order and are
dressed with mayonnaise and fresh lettuce. Choice of
breads: White, Whole Wheat, Rye or Sour Dough.
Available on homemade rolls add $0.69.

Homemade Chicken Salad 6.99
Homemade Tuna Salad 6.99
Egg Salad 6.99
Egg Salad & Ham 8.49
Pimiento Cheese (we make our own) 6.99
Cream Cheese & Olive 6.99
Bacon, Lettuce & Tomato 6.99
Cheese (grilled or cold) 6.99
Ham 6.99
Breast of Turkey 7.49
Roast Beef & Swiss Cheese 7.99
Corned Beef & Swiss Cheese 7.99
Pimiento Cheese & Bacon 7.99

Lunch Bell's House Special Club
Choice of turkey, ham or chicken
salad, served on club white toast
with mayonnaise, lettuce, bacon,
tomato, cheese, a pile of chips
with pickle slices. 8.99

Sides

Cottage Cheese	2.99
Potato Salad	2.99
Cole Slaw	2.99
Deviled Egg (two halves)	2.99
Macaroni Salad	2.99
Chicken Salad	4.99
Tuna Salad	4.99
Egg Salad	4.99
French Fries	2.49
Onion Rings	4.99

Desserts

Pie 4.89
Pie with Ice Cream 5.49
Cake 4.99
Banana Pudding 3.99
Cobbler 4.89
Cobbler with Ice Cream 5.49
Scoop of Ice Cream .99
Cookie .99
Whole Pie 25.00
(Special Order)

Beverages

Juices 2.29
Coke, Diet Coke, Sprite, Barqs Root
Beer, Pibb Extra, Pink Lemonade 2.29
One Refill
Milk 2.29
Chocolate Milk 2.29
Coffee 2.29
Iced Tea 2.29
Hot Chocolate 2.29
Lemonade 2.29 One refill
Carry Out Soft Drinks (16 oz.) 2.29

*Contain (or may contain) raw or under cooked ingredients. Consuming raw or under cooked meats, poultry, seafood,
shellfish, or eggs may increase your risk of food borne illness.

APPETIZERS
AND BEVERAGES

APPETIZERS AND BEVERAGES

**FEATURED RECIPES
ON FRONT:**

*Deviled Eggs,
page 15*

*Betty's Breakfast Punch,
page 35*

DEVILED EGGS

12 hard-boiled eggs
5 tablespoons sweet relish
4 tablespoons Duke's® mayonnaise

¼ teaspoon salt
Paprika for garnish

Slice eggs in half, setting aside the yolk. In a food processor, purée the egg yolks. Add mayonnaise and sweet relish and stir well. Add salt. Spoon egg yolk mixture into the egg white halves. Sprinkle with paprika.

Makes 6 servings

PARTY CHEESE BALL

16 ounces cream cheese, softened
2 cups shredded sharp Cheddar cheese
1 teaspoon finely chopped onion
1 teaspoon lemon juice

2 teaspoons Worcestershire sauce
Couple dashes of hot sauce
Sprinkle of garlic salt
½ cup crushed pecans
Crackers

Blend the cream cheese and Cheddar cheese together. Add the onion, lemon juice, Worcestershire sauce, hot sauce and garlic salt. Blend well. Shape into a ball and chill. Roll in crushed pecans and refrigerate until ready to serve. Enjoy with your favorite crackers.

Makes 10 to 12 servings

"The Lunch Bell is the perfect place for good friends to eat and to enjoy good food and fellowship with wonderful service."
Jean Beckerdite

TURKEY CHEESE BALL

1 (12.5 ounce) can turkey
⅔ cup mayonnaise
12 ounces cream cheese, softened
2 ounces sliced almonds

½ teaspoon curry powder (or more to taste)
Salt, pepper to taste
Dried parsley
Crackers

Drain turkey and mix with mayonnaise, cream cheese, almonds, curry powder, salt and pepper. Roll into a ball; roll in dried parsley. Refrigerate until ready to serve. Enjoy with your favorite crackers.

Makes 8 to 10 servings

CAROLYN CHRISTENBURY

PINEAPPLE CHEESE BALL

16 ounces cream cheese, softened

¼ cup finely chopped green pepper

2 tablespoons finely chopped onion

1 tablespoon seasoned salt

1 (8.5 ounce) can crushed pineapple, drained, reserving juice

2 cups chopped walnuts or pecans, divided

Crackers

Combine cream cheese, green pepper, onion and salt; mix well. Fold in pineapple and 1 cup nuts. If the mixture seems too firm, add a little pineapple juice and mix well. Chill for 1 hour. Shape into a ball and roll in remaining nuts. Serve with your favorite crackers.

Note: This cheese ball is much better if made a couple of days before serving.

Makes 10 to 12 servings

MARILYN HOLLAND

Betty's children, Shelah, Billy and Blair, have always enjoyed the holidays with their family.

Homemade Boursin Cheese

8   ounces cream cheese, softened
1   tablespoon butter, softened
2   cloves garlic, finely minced
⅛   teaspoon each of the following dried herbs and seasonings: oregano, sweet basil, dill weed, marjoram, thyme, white pepper and kosher salt

1   teaspoon dried parsley
1   teaspoon dried chives
Crackers

In a large bowl cream together cream cheese and butter with an electric mixer on low speed. Add garlic and beat well. In a small bowl, combine all herbs. Sprinkle herb mixture over the cheese and then fold in. With the electric mixer on high speed, beat until light and fluffy. Place in airtight storage containers. Refrigerate at least 24 hours before serving. Serve with crackers.

Note: Doubling or tripling this recipe is easy, as it keeps well. Pack in nice containers and give as gifts!

Makes 8 to 10 servings

EDIE FOSTER

Chicken Cheese Ball

2   (12.5 ounce) cans chicken
16 ounces cream cheese, softened

1   (1 ounce) package dry Ranch dressing mix
Crackers

Drain chicken and mix with cream cheese and Ranch dressing. Roll into a ball. Refrigerate until ready to serve. Enjoy with your favorite crackers.

Makes 10 to 12 servings

SHRIMP MOLD SPREAD

1   (10.5 ounce) can tomato
    soup
24 ounces cream cheese
2   envelopes (1 tablespoon
    each) unflavored gelatin
½   cup cold water
1   cup mayonnaise
2   cups cleaned, cooked and
    mashed shrimp

1   small grated onion
½   cup finely chopped celery
½   cup finely chopped green
    bell pepper
1   slice of black or green olive
    for garnish
Crackers

In a large saucepan, heat soup and dissolve cream cheese in soup until
well blended. Soften gelatin in water; add to soup and stir to dissolve.
Let cool. Add mayonnaise, shrimp, onion, celery and green pepper.
Turn into well-greased fish shaped mold using a slice of olive for eye.
Refrigerate until firm. Serve with your favorite crackers.

Note: Can be made up to 2 days in advance.

Makes 30 servings

SHIRLEY CLEMENTS SWAIN

HOT CRAB DIP

1   pound fresh crabmeat
22 ounces cream cheese
1   stick butter

Dash Tabasco® sauce
Dash garlic powder
Crackers or Melba toast

Heat crabmeat, cream cheese, butter, Tabasco® sauce and garlic powder
together in top of double boiler until hot and smooth. Serve in chafing
dish with crackers or Melba toast.

Makes 10 to 12 servings

Maryland Hot Crab Dip

16 ounces cream cheese, softened
1 cup sour cream
4 tablespoons mayonnaise
2 tablespoons lemon juice
3 teaspoons Worcestershire sauce
3 shakes garlic salt
½ cup shredded Cheddar cheese
1 pound crabmeat
Paprika
Crackers or Melba toast

Preheat oven to 350 degrees. Beat together the cream cheese, sour cream, mayonnaise, lemon juice, Worcestershire sauce, garlic salt and cheese. Gently fold in the crabmeat, leaving crabmeat in lumps. Sprinkle with paprika. Bake for 30 minutes. Serve warm with your favorite crackers.

Note: This dip is good with stone ground wheat crackers.

Makes 10 to 12 servings

JALENE BREEGER

"Being from Maryland, this is one of those crab inspired recipes that I am proud of and I guarantee it will be a hit. It is a given that one of my family members will make this for every family gathering."
Jalene Breeger

Cold Crab Dip

8 ounces cream cheese, softened
½ cup mayonnaise
½ cup sour cream
¼ cup minced onion
Dash Tabasco® sauce
¼ teaspoon dry mustard
1 tablespoon Worcestershire sauce
Salt and pepper to taste
½ pound lump crabmeat
Crackers or Melba toast

Cream together cream cheese, mayonnaise and sour cream. Stir in onion, Tabasco® sauce, dry mustard, Worcestershire sauce, salt and pepper. Fold in crabmeat. Serve with crackers or Melba toast.

Makes 8 to 10 servings

CLAM DIP

1	(7 ounce) can minced clams	3	drops Tabasco® sauce
8	ounces cream cheese, softened	1	tablespoon minced fresh parsley
¼	cup mayonnaise	2	teaspoons grated onion
1½	teaspoons lemon juice	¼	teaspoon salt
1½	teaspoons Worcestershire sauce		Corn chips, potato chips and/or vegetable strips

Combine clams, cream cheese, mayonnaise, lemon juice, Worcestershire sauce, Tabasco® sauce, parsley, onion and salt. Top with a parsley sprig for garnish. Serve with corn chips, potato chips and/or vegetable strips.

Makes 10 to 12 servings

GRAY BOWDITCH

 # HOT ONION DIP

2	cups Duke's® mayonnaise	2	cups chopped onion
2	cups shredded Swiss or mozzarella cheese		Crackers

Preheat oven to 350 degrees. Mix together mayonnaise, cheese and onion. Put into a baking dish and bake for 20 minutes or until hot and lightly brown. Serve with crackers.

Makes 25 servings

PRETZEL DIP

1	egg	8	ounces cream cheese, softened
1	tablespoon vinegar		Pretzels
1	tablespoon sugar		
1	teaspoon minced onion		

In a small saucepan, combine egg, vinegar, sugar and onion. Cook on low heat until thick, stirring frequently. Cool. With an electric mixer, beat cream cheese with egg mixture. Serve with pretzels.

Makes about 1 cup

GALA PECAN DIP

1   cup chopped pecans
2   tablespoons butter
16   ounces cream cheese,
       softened
4   tablespoons milk

5   ounces dried beef, minced
1   teaspoon garlic salt
1   cup sour cream
4   teaspoons minced onion
Crackers or small bread sticks

In a small saucepan, sauté pecans in butter; set aside. In a medium bowl, mix together cream cheese, milk, dried beef, garlic salt, sour cream and onion. Place in a 1½-quart baking dish and top with pecans. Chill until serving time. Bake at 350 degrees for 20 minutes. Serve hot with crackers or small bread sticks.

Makes 10 to 12 servings

HOT ARTICHOKE DIP

1   (14 ounce) can artichoke
       hearts
½   cup mayonnaise
1   (4.5 ounce) can chopped
       green chiles

1   cup shredded Monterey Jack
       cheese with jalapeños
2   tablespoons freshly grated
       Parmesan cheese
Tortilla chips, crackers or soft
       bread

Preheat oven to 350 degrees. Drain artichokes and cut into quarters or slightly smaller; set aside. Mix mayonnaise, chiles, and cheeses together (saving a little Monterey Jack for the topping). Gently mix in artichokes. Place in a small baking dish and top with extra Monterey Jack cheese and bake for 20 minutes. Broil for a few minutes to brown if necessary. Serve with tortilla chips, crackers or fresh soft bread.

Note: If you want to dress up this dip for a fancy occasion, add lump crabmeat to taste.

Makes 10 to 12 servings

JULIE RUSS

MOLLY'S BEAN DIP

1   (16 ounce) can pinto beans
1   (15 ounce) can garbanzo
     beans
1   (16 ounce) can white corn
1   small green bell pepper,
     finely chopped
4   stalks celery, finely chopped
1   cup finely chopped red onion

1   (4.5 ounce) can jalapeño
     peppers or green chiles,
     finely chopped
½   cup oil
½   cup apple cider vinegar
½   cup sugar
1   teaspoon black pepper
1   teaspoon salt
Corn chips

Drain pinto and garbanzo beans and corn; place in a bowl with a lid. Add green pepper, celery, onion and jalapeño peppers. In a small saucepan, bring the oil, vinegar, sugar, pepper and salt to a boil; remove from heat. Allow to cool completely. Pour over bean mixture and stir. Cover and marinate overnight. Serve with corn chips.

Makes 8 to 10 servings

HELEN CVIK

KIMBERLY'S SALSA DIP

2   (8 ounce) packages low-fat
     cream cheese
2   (8 ounce) packages shredded
     Mexican style four cheeses

2   (15 ounce) jars thick and
     chunky salsa
Tortilla chips

Spread both packages of cream cheese evenly over the bottom of a microwavable baking dish. Top with ⅓ of the cheese, then ⅓ of the salsa. Repeat the process with two more layers of cheese and salsa, reserving some of the cheese to put on top. Refrigerate until ready to heat and serve. Cover with a paper towel and heat in the microwave for 4 to 5 minutes or until cheese on top melts. You may also heat in the oven at 350 degrees until cheese on top melts. Serve with tortilla chips.

Note: It is important to use thick and chunky salsa so that when heated, the dip does not become too watery. If salsa is not thick, drain before using.

Makes 10 to 12 servings

JEAN BECKERDITE

SALSA FRESCA

5-6 diced fresh plum tomatoes
1   clove minced garlic
½   cup finely diced red or white
    onion
⅛   cup fresh lime juice
2   tablespoons mild vinegar
    such as apple cider vinegar
    or rice vinegar

2-3 fresh jalapeño peppers,
    seeded and finely chopped
    (may use Serrano chiles for
    extra heat)
1   small green bell pepper,
    finely diced (optional)
¼   cup coarsely chopped fresh
    cilantro
Salt
Tortilla chips

Put tomatoes, garlic, onion, lime juice, vinegar, peppers and cilantro in a bowl and mix well. Mixture may be coarsely puréed in a food processor or left intact for more texture. Add salt to taste. Let mixture set for 30 minutes to allow flavors to develop. Serve with tortilla chips.

Makes about 3 cups

BARBARA HOLLAND EBY

The herb, cilantro, is also known as Chinese parsley. It comes from the leaves of the coriander plant and is a key ingredient in Southwestern cuisine.

GUACAMOLE

2   medium ripe Hass avocados
2-3 tablespoons Salsa Fresca
    (see recipe above)

Salt
Fresh lime juice
Tortilla chips

Prepare avocados by peeling and removing the pits. Coarsely chop avocados. Mix together Salsa Fresca with avocados. Mash mixture with fork until avocado is fairly smooth and other ingredients are well combined. You may leave some chunks of avocado, if desired. Add salt and lime juice to taste. Use as a garnish on tacos, enchiladas or your favorite Mexican dish. Or just enjoy with fresh tortilla chips!

Note: Guacamole will discolor when exposed to air. When storing, ensure the mixture is well wrapped.

Makes about 2 cups

BARBARA HOLLAND EBY

Avocados are ripe when they are relatively firm, but will yield to gentle pressure when held in the hand and squeezed.

LAYERED MEXICAN DIP

1	(16 ounce) can refried beans	3	chopped green onions, including tops
1	(12 ounce) container guacamole (or homemade)	1	cup shredded Cheddar cheese
1	cup sour cream	1	(2.25 ounce) can sliced black olives
1	(1.25 ounce) package taco seasoning		Tortilla chips
1	cup chopped fresh tomatoes		

Put the ring of an 8-inch springform pan on a decorative plate of your choosing. Spread refried beans into the bottom of the pan. Cover with guacamole. Mix together sour cream and taco seasoning; spread over guacamole. Layer with tomatoes, green onion and cheese. Sprinkle with olives. Refrigerate for several hours; remove ring of springform pan. Serve with tortilla chips.

Makes 8 to 10 servings

ZESTY CHEESE DIP

¼	cup chopped onion	Dash paprika
1	tablespoon butter	1 (4 ounce) can chopped green chile peppers
¾	cup picante sauce	Dash Worcestershire sauce
3	ounces cream cheese	½ teaspoon salt
1	cup shredded Cheddar cheese	Tortilla chips

Sauté onion in butter until tender. Add picante sauce and stir. Gradually add the cream cheese and shredded cheese. Stir in paprika, peppers, Worcestershire sauce and salt; continue cooking and stirring until cheese is melted and mixture is well blended. Adjust seasonings to taste. Serve with tortilla chips. Keep warm in Crockpot or chafing dish, if desired.

Makes about 8 servings

Buffalo Chicken Dip

3 boneless, skinless chicken breasts
16 ounces cream cheese
12 ounces Texas Pete® hot sauce
¾ cup chunky blue cheese dressing
1¼ cups shredded Cheddar cheese, divided
Tortilla chips

Preheat oven to 400 degrees. Boil chicken breasts until done. Cool. While chicken is cooling, put cream cheese and hot sauce in a microwave-safe bowl. Mix well. Cover with a paper towel to prevent spatter and microwave on high for 3 minutes. Shred chicken and put in bowl with cream cheese and hot sauce. Mix well. Stir in blue cheese dressing and 1 cup of shredded Cheddar cheese. Spread in 7x11-inch glass baking dish. Bake for 25 minutes. Remove from oven, sprinkle remaining ¼ cup of cheese on top and bake another 5 minutes. Serve warm with tortilla chips.

Note: Tastes just as good, if not better, reheated.

Makes 8 to 10 servings

SANDY MAHONY

"This recipe came from a friend in Buffalo and is a twist to the original Buffalo wing, but it has no bones! Same great taste, same great flavor as the original wing!"
Sandy Mahony

Pizza Dip

1 pound ground beef
¼ cup chopped onion
2 cloves garlic, minced
1 (8 ounce) can tomato sauce
¼ cup ketchup
1 teaspoon sugar
1 teaspoon oregano
1 teaspoon salt
8 ounces cream cheese
¼ cup freshly grated Parmesan cheese
French bread or crackers

In a large skillet, sauté ground beef, onion and garlic until beef is browned. Drain fat. Add tomato sauce, ketchup, sugar, oregano and salt. Simmer for 10 minutes. Add cream cheese and Parmesan cheese; stir until melted. Serve warm with French bread slices or crackers.

Makes 10 to 12 servings

CINCINNATI CHILI DIP

12 ounces cream cheese
¼ cup diced onions
1 (13.25 ounce) package Skyline® chili, heated

12 ounces shredded mild Cheddar cheese
Tortilla or corn chips

Spread cream cheese evenly on the bottom of a 9x13-inch microwaveable baking dish. Sprinkle diced onion on top. Pour heated chili over onions and cream cheese. Cover with Cheddar cheese. Heat on high in the microwave for 2 minutes or until cheese is melted. Let stand 5 minutes before serving. Serve with tortilla chips or corn chips.

Makes 6 to 8 servings

PEANUT BUTTER SPREAD

Shelah is Betty's youngest daughter and has worked off and on over the years at **The Lunch Bell**. *She is an excellent cook and gets her love of cooking from her mother.*

1 (16 ounce) jar peanut butter
2 (7 ounce) jars marshmallow cream
½ cup firmly packed brown sugar

1 stick plus 2 tablespoons butter
½ cup corn syrup
½ cup water
Crackers, toast or pretzels

Mix together all ingredients and serve with crackers, toast or pretzels.

Makes 16 servings

SHELAH SWAIN

SUGAR AND SPICE PECANS

½ cup sugar
½ teaspoon salt
2 tablespoons ground cinnamon
1 egg white

3 cups pecans (or a combination of 1 cup each pecans, walnuts and peanuts)

Preheat oven to 300 degrees. In a small bowl, combine sugar, salt and cinnamon; set aside. Beat egg white until foamy. Add nuts to egg white and mix with hands to coat nuts evenly. Add sugar mixture to nuts, mixing well. Spread in a single layer on a baking pan. Bake for 30 minutes, stirring occasionally.

Makes 3 cups

CHEESE BALLS

2 sticks butter, softened	¼ teaspoon cayenne pepper
2 cups shredded sharp Cheddar cheese	2½ cups all-purpose flour
	2 cups Rice Krispies® cereal

Preheat oven to 400 degrees. Mix together butter, cheese, cayenne pepper and flour. Knead well. Gently fold in the Rice Krispies®. Roll the dough into 1-inch balls and place on an ungreased cookie sheet. Bake for 20 minutes.

Makes about 4 dozen balls

MARILYN HOLLAND

SAUSAGE CHEESE BALLS

1 pound hot pork sausage	2½-3 cups Bisquick® baking mix
1 pound mild Cheddar cheese, shredded	

Preheat oven to 400 degrees. In a large bowl, mix together the sausage and cheese. Gradually add the biscuit mix and blend thoroughly. Roll the dough into 1-inch balls and place on an ungreased cookie sheet. Bake for 15 to 20 minutes.

Note: These sausage balls may be made several weeks in advance and frozen prior to cooking. Cook frozen balls for 25 to 30 minutes.

Makes about 4 dozen balls

JENNIFER HERGET

SAUSAGE RING

2 pounds hot pork sausage	1½ cups cracker crumbs
2 eggs, beaten	Freshly chopped parsley
2 heaping tablespoons grated onion	Small party rolls

Preheat oven to 350 degrees. Mix together sausage, eggs, onion and cracker crumbs. Form a ring with the mixture and place on a wire rack in a shallow pan. Bake for 40 minutes. Place on a large plate, slice into ¼-inch slices and garnish with parsley. Serve with small party rolls.

Makes 10 to 12 servings

SANDI CVIK BREWER

# FINGER QUICHES

8 eggs
½ cup all-purpose flour
1 teaspoon baking powder
¾ teaspoon salt
⅛-¼ teaspoon black pepper
1½ cups shredded Cheddar cheese

1½ cups Monterey Jack or mozzarella cheese
1½ cups cottage cheese
2 (4 ounce) cans chopped green chiles, drained

Preheat oven to 350 degrees. In a large bowl, beat eggs with a wire whisk and stir in flour, baking powder, salt and pepper. Mix well. Fold in cheeses and chiles. Pour into a greased 9x13-inch baking dish. Bake for 40 minutes. Cut into small pieces. Can be served cold.

Makes 10 to 12 servings

MINI SIRLOIN BURGERS ON TOASTED ROLLS

1 pound ground sirloin
¼ cup grated red onion
½ cup whipping cream
1 teaspoon salt
¼ teaspoon ground black pepper
1 cup mayonnaise

2 tablespoons finely chopped fresh parsley
15 small dinner rolls
½ stick butter, melted
1 tablespoon canola oil
Sliced Cheddar cheese, cut into 15 thin 1½-inch squares

Preheat oven to 350 degrees. In a mixing bowl, gently combine the ground sirloin, onion, whipping cream, salt and pepper. Do not over mix. Form 15 mini-burgers into 1x1½-inch disks. Place in refrigerator. In a small bowl, combine the mayonnaise and parsley and mix well. Brush the rolls generously with the melted butter and toast on a baking sheet in the oven for 5 to 10 minutes or until golden brown and crisp. Remove to a baking sheet or paper towel and cool to room temperature.

In a nonstick pan over medium heat, heat the oil and brown the mini-burgers well on both sides. Remove them from the pan and place them on a baking sheet. Place the mini-burgers in the oven and cook to medium rare, about 10 minutes. Place a slice of Cheddar cheese on top of each mini-burger and return to the oven to melt the cheese and cook to desired doneness. To serve, place a small dollop of the herbed mayonnaise on the toasted roll and top with the mini-burger.

Makes 15 mini-burgers

COCKTAIL MEATBALLS

MEATBALLS

2-3	slices white bread, lightly toasted
1	medium onion, cut into chunks
¼	cup milk, or more to moisten
2½-3	pounds ground beef

SAUCE

32	ounces ketchup
16-18	ounces grape jelly
½	teaspoon garlic powder
½	cup dried parsley

Preheat oven to 350 degrees. In a blender, crumb bread. Remove and set aside. Put chunks of onion and milk in blender and blend until there are no large pieces. Mix bread and onion mixture with meat. Shape into ¾-inch balls. Bake on broiler pan for 10 to 12 minutes or until brown.

In a saucepan, heat ketchup and jelly over medium heat until melted. Add garlic powder and parsley. Mix well and simmer for 5 to 6 minutes. Add meatballs and simmer for 15 minutes. Put meatballs and sauce in a chafing dish. Serve warm.

Note: Meatballs and sauce can be covered with foil and frozen. Before serving, thaw and bake at 350 degrees for 30 minutes. Do not remove foil. Stir gently a few times while cooking.

Makes 12 servings

JENNIFER HERGET

Bill and Betty Swain in 1982.

HOT MAMAS

1	pound Cheddar cheese, shredded	2	eggs
1	pound Monterey Jack cheese, shredded	1	(12 ounce) can evaporated milk
1	(4 ounce) can jalapeño peppers, chopped	½	cup all-purpose flour

Preheat oven to 350 degrees. Layer cheese in a greased 9x13-inch baking dish. Sprinkle with jalapeños. In a small bowl, combine eggs, milk and flour and mix well. Pour milk mixture over cheese. Bake for 45 minutes. Cool; cut into squares.

Makes 24 to 32 squares, depending on the size of square

ASHLEY DARCY

HANKY PANKIES

1	pound hot pork sausage	1	tablespoon Worcestershire sauce
1	pound ground beef	1	teaspoon oregano
2	pounds Velveeta® cheese, cut into cubes	2	loaves Pepperidge Farm® Rye or Pumpernickel party bread

Preheat oven to 350 degrees. In a large skillet, brown sausage and ground beef. Drain. Add cheese and cook on medium, stirring until cheese is melted. Add Worcestershire sauce and oregano and stir until well blended. Place bread slices on a cookie sheet. Top with a spoonful of meat mixture. Bake for 10 to 15 minutes.

Note: You can freeze the Hanky Pankies on a cookie sheet before baking. Once frozen, place into a plastic bag and put back in the freezer. Remove a few at a time as needed for breakfast or a snack. Just reheat and serve.

Makes 24 servings

ASHLEY DARCY

Party Beef and Horseradish Sauce Sandwiches

Beef

1   (2 to 3 pound) filet of beef, trimmed and tied
Olive oil
1   tablespoon unsalted butter, softened

1   teaspoon Dijon mustard
2   teaspoons kosher salt
2   teaspoons coarsely ground black pepper

Mustard Horseradish Sauce

¾   cup mayonnaise
1½ tablespoons Dijon mustard
1   tablespoon whole grain mustard

½   tablespoon prepared horseradish, or more to taste
2   tablespoons sour cream
Kosher salt to taste

Sandwiches

4   dozen small party rolls
1   bunch arugula

Butter, softened

Let the beef come to room temperature. Preheat the oven to 500 degrees. Place the beef on a baking sheet and pat the outside dry with a paper towel. Rub the meat with olive oil. Mix together the unsalted butter and mustard in a small bowl and spread the mixture over the beef with your hands. Sprinkle evenly with salt and pepper. Roast in the oven for 22 minutes for rare and 25 minutes for medium rare. Remove the beef from the oven and cover tightly with aluminum foil; allow it to rest at room temperature for 20 minutes. Remove the strings and slice the filet into small, thin slices.

For the mustard horseradish sauce, whisk together the mayonnaise, mustards, horseradish, sour cream, and a pinch of salt in a small bowl.

To make the sandwiches, spread the bottom side of the rolls with the mustard horseradish sauce. Top with slices of beef and arugula and sprinkle with salt and pepper. Finish with buttered top side of the rolls.

Note: The mustard horseradish sauce is also excellent with Prime Rib.

Makes 4 dozen party-sized sandwiches

JEAN BECKERDITE

PARTY HAM BISCUITS

1 stick butter, softened	1 small onion, grated with juice drained
1½ tablespoons poppy seeds (optional)	2 packages party rolls
1½ teaspoons Worcestershire sauce	¾ pound paper-thin smoked ham
1½ teaspoons Dijon mustard	½ pound shredded Swiss cheese

Preheat oven to 350 degrees. Mix butter, poppy seeds, Worcestershire sauce, Dijon mustard and grated onion in a bowl. Slice entire package of rolls through the middle, creating a top half and a bottom half. Spread the inner side of each half of bread with the butter mixture. Using half of the ham, place a layer on the bottom half of the bread. Top with cheese and then the rest of the ham. Put the other half of bread on top. Bake for 15 to 20 minutes. Cut into separate rolls and serve while warm.

Note: Can be wrapped in foil and frozen until needed.

Makes 2 to 3 dozen party-sized sandwiches

MARILYN HOLLAND

 # SNOOKIE'S CRABMEAT TOAST POINTS

2 tablespoons mayonnaise	12 slices white bread, cut on the diagonal into 4 triangles
½ teaspoon Texas Pete® hot sauce	1 pound fresh backfin crabmeat
1 teaspoon Worcestershire sauce	1 cup shredded sharp Cheddar cheese
1 small onion, finely grated	

Preheat oven to 350 degrees. Combine mayonnaise, hot sauce, Worcestershire sauce and onion. Spread mayonnaise mixture onto bread, top with crabmeat and then sprinkle with cheese. Put onto a baking sheet and bake until edges of bread have browned.

Makes 24 servings

MEXICAN STYLE SHRIMP COCKTAIL

4 cups tomato juice or V-8® juice
⅓ cup fresh chopped cilantro
⅓ cup finely chopped onion
1 teaspoon salt
1 teaspoon black pepper

1 avocado, peeled, cored and cut into small chunks
1 cucumber, peeled and diced (optional)
½ pound cooked and cleaned shrimp
Juice of 1 lime

In a medium bowl, combine tomato juice, cilantro, onion, salt and pepper. Gently fold in avocado, cucumber and shrimp. Squeeze lime juice over shrimp and stir gently. Chill until ready to serve.

Makes 4 servings

JESUS SANCHEZ

Jesus is Blair's husband and Betty's son-in-law. He has been a recent and welcome addition to the family.

BETTY'S MARINATED SHRIMP

1 pound cooked and cleaned shrimp
½ cup sliced celery
¼ cup sliced stuffed olives
1 teaspoon minced onion
⅓ cup Duke's® mayonnaise

¼ cup French dressing (see Betty's recipe on page 107 for Homemade French Dressing)
Salt to taste
Lemon to taste
½ cup chopped walnuts (optional)
Mixed greens

Combine all ingredients, chill and serve on greens with assorted garnishes.

Note: Betty uses 30/40 count shrimp. Can also be used as a salad for lunch.

Makes 8 servings

Marinated Shrimp

3 pounds cooked and cleaned shrimp
1 cup vegetable oil
2 cups ketchup
1 large onion, sliced
1 cup vinegar
2 tablespoons sugar
2 tablespoons prepared mustard
2 tablespoons Worcestershire sauce
1 teaspoon salt
2 dashes Tabasco® sauce
Garlic powder to taste

Combine all ingredients and place in sealed container. Refrigerate.

Makes 16 to 20 servings

BETTY LASSEN

Easy Punch

1 (3 ounce) package lemon gelatin
1 cup boiling water
1 (46 ounce) can pineapple juice
1 cup sugar
1 (6 ounce) can frozen lemonade concentrate
Water, as needed
2 liters ginger ale

Dissolve gelatin in boiling water. In large container, combine pineapple juice, sugar and lemonade concentrate; add dissolved gelatin and stir to mix well. Add just enough water to bring to 1 gallon. Pour into containers and freeze. Remove from freezer and partially thaw. Add ginger ale just before serving.

Makes 16 servings

Orange Blossom Passion Punch

2 quarts orange juice
2 quarts lemonade
1 (46 ounce) can pineapple juice
1 liter lemon-lime soda
Orange slices and mint for garnish

Mix together orange juice, lemonade and pineapple juice. Chill. Add lemon-lime soda just before serving. Add ice to chill. Garnish with orange slices and mint.

Makes 50 servings

RAINBOW PUNCH

1 (46 ounce) can unsweetened pineapple juice, chilled
1 (46 ounce) can orange juice, chilled
1 pint lime sherbet

1 pint orange sherbet
1 pint raspberry sherbet
1 (32 ounce) bottle chilled ginger ale

Combine pineapple juice and orange juice in punch bowl. Add scoops of sherbet. Pour ginger ale over sherbet.

Makes approximately 35 servings

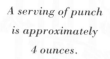

A serving of punch is approximately 4 ounces.

BETTY'S BREAKFAST PUNCH

1 (12 ounce) can frozen orange juice concentrate
1 (12 ounce) can frozen lemonade concentrate

1 cup pineapple juice
2 liters Mountain Dew®

Mix together orange juice concentrate, lemon juice concentrate, pineapple juice and Mountain Dew® and serve chilled.

Note: For a variation, add frozen strawberry margarita concentrate or another frozen concentrate. Use leftovers to make an ice ring with maraschino cherries. Place ring in the punch the next time it is served.

Makes approximately 25 servings

FROZEN PUNCH

2 (.13 ounce) packets unsweetened cherry or lime Kool Aid®
4 cups sugar
3 quarts water
1 (12 ounce) can frozen lemonade concentrate, thawed

1 (46 ounce) can pineapple juice
3 (12 ounce) cans frozen orange juice concentrate
3 quarts ginger ale

Mix together Kool Aid®, sugar, water, lemonade, pineapple juice and orange juice. Freeze overnight. Before serving, add ginger ale.

Makes 50 servings

MARILYN HOLLAND

COFFEE PUNCH

2	cups water	1	quart low-fat vanilla yogurt
3	heaping teaspoons of instant decaffeinated coffee	1	(16 ounce) container frozen whipped topping, thawed
½	cup sugar		

In a small saucepan, heat water, coffee and sugar until coffee and sugar are dissolved. Cool. Add cold coffee syrup mixture, a little at a time, to yogurt and whipped topping. Mix well. The punch should be about the thickness of a milkshake, and you may not need all of the coffee syrup. Add more yogurt or whipped topping to your liking.

Note: Tasters Choice® instant decaffeinated coffee is very good in this recipe.

Makes 12 servings

JUDYE HAFLING

RASPBERRY LEMONADE

| 13 | lemons (12 juiced, 1 for garnish) | 2 | cups sugar |
| 6 | cups water | 1 | cup fresh raspberries |

With a zester, remove the zest from 6 of the lemons; set aside. Squeeze the juice from 12 of the lemons to make approximately 2 cups of lemon juice. Combine juice, water, sugar and zest in a small saucepan (non-aluminum). Bring to a boil. Reduce heat and then simmer about 5 minutes. Remove from heat and chill. Purée raspberries in a food processor, adding a little of the lemonade to help purée. Add purée to lemonade and strain through a very fine strainer or through cheesecloth. Serve with ice and garnish with sliced lemon.

Makes 8 to 10 servings

Punch for 150

12 cups sugar	3 (12 ounce) cans frozen lemonade concentrate
18 cups water, divided	
6 (3 ounce) packages lime gelatin	3 quarts pineapple juice
3 (12 ounce) cans frozen orange juice concentrate	2 ounces almond extract

Add sugar to 6 cups water and boil until sugar is dissolved. Dissolve gelatin in 12 cups of hot water. Add to sugar mixture; let cool. When ready to serve, add juices and extract and stir well.

Makes 150 servings

Brunch Punch

1 (46 ounce) can pineapple juice, chilled	¼ cup lime juice
	Orange slices, lemon slices, lime slices and/or maraschino cherries for garnish
3 cups orange juice, chilled	
2 cups cranberry juice, chilled	
¾ cup confectioners' sugar	

Stir together pineapple juice, orange juice, cranberry juice, confectioners' sugar and lime juice. Serve immediately or cover and chill for 2 to 24 hours. Stir before serving. Garnish with fruit slices and/or cherries.

Makes 15 to 18 servings

Lemonade for 50

2 cups water	3½ cups crushed pineapple
4 cups sugar	4 sliced, seeded oranges
3¾ cups lemon juice	2 gallons water

Boil 2 cups water with sugar for 10 minutes. Add lemon juice. Stir in crushed pineapple. Add oranges and water and chill. Serve over ice.

Makes 50 servings

CHRISTMAS CRANBERRY PUNCH

2   (16 ounce) bottles cranberry
       juice or cocktail
1   (12 ounce) can frozen orange
       juice concentrate
1   (12 ounce) can frozen
       lemonade concentrate
4½ cups water
1   quart ginger ale
Lemon sherbet

Mix together cranberry juice, orange juice, lemonade and water. Chill.
Pour into a punch bowl. Add ginger ale and stir. Scoop lemon sherbet
into the punch bowl.

Makes 30 servings

PERCOLATOR WASSAIL

1   cup sugar
1   tablespoon whole cloves
1   tablespoon allspice
3   cinnamon sticks
1   quart clear apple cider
1   pint cranberry juice
2   cups orange juice
¾   cup lemon juice

Put sugar, cloves, allspice and cinnamon sticks in a filter or cheesecloth
and place in the basket of the percolator. Percolate using the apple cider,
cranberry juice, orange juice and lemon juice instead of water.

Note: Gives a wonderful fragrance to your home for the holidays.

Makes 10 to 12 servings

JUDYE HAFLING

RUDOLPH'S SPRITZER

*One medium lemon
should yield 3 tablespoons
of juice and 2 to 3
teaspoons of zest.*

5   cups orange juice
2   cups lemon-lime soft drink,
       chilled
½   cup maraschino cherry juice
¼   cup fresh lemon juice
Lemon slices, maraschino
       cherries for garnish

Stir together orange juice, soft drink, cherry juice and lemon juice. Serve
over ice. Garnish with lemon slices or maraschino cherries.

Makes 12 to 16 servings

INSTANT RUSSIAN TEA

1 cup Tang® powdered mix
4 tablespoons instant tea
½ cup sugar
6 tablespoons sweetened lemonade mix
½ teaspoon ground cinnamon
½ teaspoon ground cloves

Mix all ingredients in a bowl; add small amounts to blender and blend into a powder. Continue blending small amounts until mixture is a light orange powder. Store in a glass jar. To serve, put 2 heaping teaspoons in a cup and add 6 to 8 ounces boiling water.

Note: This tea makes a delightful gift. Make sure you label the jar with serving instructions.

Makes 16 servings

HOLIDAY MULL

1 (48 ounce) bottle cranberry juice or cocktail
2 (32 ounce) bottles apple juice
½ cup firmly packed brown sugar
½ teaspoon salt
4 cinnamon sticks
1½ teaspoons whole cloves
1 orange, thinly sliced
1 lemon, thinly sliced

Combine cranberry juice, apple juice, brown sugar and salt in a Crockpot or large saucepan. Over medium-low heat, stir until sugar is dissolved. Tie cinnamon sticks and cloves in cheesecloth and place in liquid. Add orange and lemon slices. Cover pot and cook on low for 2 hours. Do not boil. Remove spices and serve.

Note: Making this drink in a Crockpot works best and it makes your whole house smell wonderful!

Makes 28 servings

CHRISTMAS EGGNOG

2 eggs
1½ cups sugar
½ teaspoon salt
6 cups milk, divided

2 teaspoons pure vanilla extract
2 cups heavy whipping cream
Ground nutmeg

In a 4-quart heavy saucepan, beat eggs with a wire whisk. Gradually add the sugar and the salt, beating constantly. Over low heat, stirring constantly, gradually add half of the milk. Cook about 20 minutes, stirring constantly, until mixture thickens and coats the spoon. Do not boil or milk will curdle. Pour into separate container and add vanilla and remaining milk and mix well. Cover and refrigerate until well-chilled (about 3 hours). When ready to serve, beat whipping cream in a medium bowl with an electric hand mixer until soft peaks form. Gently fold whipping cream into custard mixture. Pour into chilled punch bowl and sprinkle with nutmeg.

Makes 16 servings

Harvey Lindsay hosted a holiday party for all of the tenants of City Center.
The Lunch Bell catered the desserts and coffee event.

BREAKFAST AND BREADS

BREAKFAST AND BREADS

**FEATURED RECIPES
ON FRONT:**

*Sweet Potato Pancakes,
page 51*

***The Lunch Bell**
Cheddar Cheese Biscuits,
page 72*

EGG AND CHEESE SPECIALTY STRATA

10	slices day-old bread	¼	teaspoon cornstarch
½	cup shredded Cheddar cheese	¼-½	cup cooking sherry
7	eggs	¼	teaspoon almond extract
2⅔	cups whole milk (or part cream)	4	tablespoons butter, melted
		½	cup slivered almonds

The secret ingredient that Betty puts in every dish is love, and it makes all the difference!

Remove crusts from bread and cut into cubes. Layer bread and cheese in a 9x13-inch baking dish. Beat eggs, milk, cornstarch, sherry and almond flavoring together in a blender. Pour over bread and cheese; pour melted butter over this. Refrigerate overnight or at least 8 hours before baking.

When ready to bake, sprinkle almonds on top of casserole. Place casserole in oven and put a pan of water on the rack below. Bake for 1 hour at 325 degrees or until brown on top.

Note: For a heartier version, add chipped beef, cubed ham or crisp bacon. Leave out almond flavoring and almonds when adding meat and top with more shredded cheese.

Makes 10 to 12 servings

BREAKFAST QUICHE

1	cup heavy whipping cream or half-and-half	½	pound bacon
5	eggs	1	cup cooked and cubed ham
Pinch salt, cayenne pepper and ground nutmeg		1	cup shredded Gruyère or Swiss cheese
		1	(9-inch) pie shell

Preheat oven to 375 degrees. In a blender or large bowl, beat the cream, eggs, salt, cayenne and nutmeg. Fry the bacon until crisp; drain and crumble. Spread bacon, ham and cheese into the bottom of the pie shell. Fill with egg mixture. Bake for 40 minutes.

Note: Can refrigerate up to 1 week. To freeze, cool quickly and wrap.

Makes 8 servings

DEBBIE RAPPOLD BRUCE

BREAKFAST BEFORE

1	pound pork sausage	½	teaspoon salt
12	slices bread	1	teaspoon dry mustard
8	eggs	1½-2	cups shredded Cheddar cheese
1½	cups milk		
1	(10.75 ounce) can cream of mushroom soup		

Brown the sausage in a frying pan until thoroughly cooked. Drain fat and place sausage on paper towels; set aside. Cut shapes out of the bread slices using cookie cutters or a beverage glass with a sharp edge. Take the remaining bread and tear into pieces. In a medium bowl, beat the eggs. Add the milk, mushroom soup, salt and dry mustard to the eggs and mix well. In a 9x13-inch glass baking dish, layer the pieces of bread, then the sausage, then the cheese, then place the bread shapes on top. Slowly pour the egg mixture over everything, being sure to saturate each piece of bread. Cover with tin foil and refrigerate overnight or at least 8 hours before baking.

When ready to bake, tent foil over casserole and bake at 350 degrees for 1 hour. Remove the foil the last 15 minutes to brown.

Makes 10 to 12 servings

JULIE RUSS

 ## BREAKFAST CASSEROLE

1	pound pork sausage	2	cups shredded Cheddar cheese
2	large baked potatoes, cooked and cooled	4	eggs, beaten
5⅓	tablespoons butter	¼	cup milk
			Ground black pepper

Preheat oven to 350 degrees. Brown the sausage in a skillet until thoroughly cooked. Drain fat and place sausage on paper towels; set aside. Grate potatoes. In a large skillet, melt butter and add potatoes. Cook until lightly browned. Place potatoes into an 8x8-inch baking dish. Cover with cheese; top with sausage. In a bowl, beat eggs with milk. Pour over sausage; sprinkle with pepper. Bake for 30 minutes or until set.

Makes 6 to 8 servings

DEBRA SWAIN

CREAMY SCRAMBLED EGGS

8	eggs	3	tablespoons fresh chopped chives, divided
¼	cup whole milk	1	tablespoon butter
¼	teaspoon salt	4	ounces cream cheese, cut into cubes
¼	teaspoon pepper		

In a large bowl, beat eggs, milk, salt, pepper and 1 tablespoon chopped chives. In a large non-stick pan, melt butter over medium heat. Add egg mixture and cook like standard scrambled eggs. When eggs are about half set, add cubes of cream cheese. The cream cheese should melt by the time the eggs are finished cooking. Divide eggs onto serving plates and sprinkle remaining chives around the plates.

Makes 4 to 6 servings

SAUSAGE AND EGG BAKE

1	pound pork sausage	1¼	cups baking mix
1½	cups sliced fresh mushrooms	1	cup milk
8	green onions, sliced	1½	teaspoons salt
2	medium tomatoes, chopped	½	teaspoon pepper
2	cups shredded mozzarella cheese	1½	teaspoons fresh chopped oregano (or ½ teaspoon dried oregano)
12	eggs		

Preheat oven to 350 degrees. Brown the sausage in a skillet until thoroughly cooked. Drain fat and place sausage on paper towels; set aside. Layer sausage, mushrooms, onion, tomatoes and mozzarella cheese in a greased 9x13-inch baking dish. In a medium bowl, whisk together eggs, baking mix, milk, salt, pepper and oregano. Pour egg mixture over ingredients in baking dish. Bake for 30 to 35 minutes or until golden brown and set.

Makes 10 to 12 servings

BAKED WESTERN OMELET

8 slices bread, crust trimmed and reserved
1½ cups shredded Cheddar cheese, divided
¼ cup chopped green bell pepper
¼ cup chopped red bell pepper
½ cup chopped onion
½ cup sliced fresh mushrooms
½ pound julienne ham or cooked and diced sausage
8 eggs
2 cups milk
Salt and pepper to taste
1-2 tablespoons prepared yellow mustard (optional)
4 tablespoons butter, melted

Preheat oven to 350 degrees. Grease a 9x13-inch baking dish and arrange bread slices over bottom. Sprinkle ¾ cup cheese over bread; top with peppers, onion, mushrooms and ham (or sausage). Finish with remaining cheese. In a separate bowl, combine eggs, milk, salt, pepper and mustard. Pour mixture slowly over ingredients in baking dish. Cube leftover bread crusts and toss with melted butter. Sprinkle over top of omelet. Bake for 1 hour or until a knife inserted into the center comes out clean.

Note: This dish may be prepared the night before. Cover with plastic wrap and refrigerate overnight. Remove casserole from refrigerator 1 hour prior to baking to prevent baking dish from cracking.

Makes 8 to 10 servings

OVEN-BAKED OMELET

6 eggs
½ cup low-fat cottage cheese
½ cup sour cream
½ cup mild salsa
1 cup shredded Monterey Jack cheese
1 cup shredded Cheddar cheese

Preheat oven to 350 degrees. In a medium bowl, whisk together eggs, cottage cheese and sour cream. Spread salsa over bottom of greased 9-inch pie plate. Sprinkle with shredded Monterey Jack and Cheddar cheeses. Pour egg mixture over cheese. Bake for 45 minutes.

Makes 4 servings

How to Cook a Perfect Omelet

2	eggs, at room temperature
2	tablespoons water
1	tablespoon margarine or olive oil (do not use butter)

Cheese, brought to room temperature

Ham, bacon or vegetables, cooked and warm

Lightly beat the eggs and add water; mix well. Heat a 10-inch pan to high heat. When adding the margarine or olive oil, it should bubble up and melt immediately. Add the egg and water mixture. With a spatula, draw the egg from the perimeter to the center. After about 15 seconds, add cheese and any other ingredients to half of the omelet. Fold the other half over your ingredients.

Makes 1 serving

 # How to Cook Link Sausage

Place link sausage in a skillet over medium heat. Cover with water and cook until water has evaporated. Roll in pan until sausage is browned.

Every Holiday Breakfast Casserole

1	pound pork sausage	1	(5.5 ounce) package seasoned croutons
8	eggs	1½	cups shredded Cheddar cheese
2	cups half-and-half	1	cup shredded Swiss cheese
1½	cups milk	1	cup shredded Monterey Jack or Pepper Jack cheese
1½	teaspoons dry mustard		
1	tablespoon minced onion		

Brown the sausage in a skillet until thoroughly cooked. Drain fat and place sausage on paper towels; set aside. In a bowl, beat together eggs, half-and-half, milk, dry mustard and minced onion. In a 9x13-inch baking dish, layer the croutons, then the cheese, then the sausage. Pour egg mixture over top. Cover with tin foil and refrigerate overnight or at least 8 hours before baking.

When ready to bake, tent foil over casserole and bake at 350 degrees for 50 to 60 minutes. Remove the foil the last 15 minutes to brown.

Makes 10 to 12 servings

One tip that Betty gives to all who enter her kitchen is to always use the proper equipment for the job. Wet ingredients should be measured with liquid measuring cups and dry ingredients need the dry measuring cups. Proper size pans should be utilized too.

SPINACH FRITTATA

½	cup sliced onion	¼	teaspoon black pepper
1	garlic clove, minced	¼	teaspoon ground nutmeg
1-2	tablespoons olive oil	10	eggs
1	cup sliced mushrooms	½	teaspoon salt
2	cups fresh baby spinach	4	tablespoons fresh grated Parmesan cheese
¼	cup fresh lime juice		
1	teaspoon fresh basil, cut into thin strips	2	tablespoons chopped green onion, including tops

Preheat oven to 350 degrees. In a large skillet over medium heat, sauté onion and garlic in olive oil until tender. Add mushrooms and cook for 2 to 3 minutes. Add spinach, lime juice, basil, pepper and nutmeg and cook for 3 to 4 minutes. In a large bowl, beat eggs and add salt. Add spinach mixture to eggs and stir well. Pour egg mixture into a greased 9x13-inch glass baking dish. Sprinkle with cheese and green onion and bake for 15 to 20 minutes or until eggs are set. Remove from oven and allow to cool for a few minutes before cutting.

Makes 6 to 8 servings

HOT TOMATO GRITS

3	bacon slices	2	large tomatoes, peeled and chopped
2	(14.5 ounce) cans chicken broth	2	tablespoons canned, chopped green chiles
½	teaspoon salt		
1	cup uncooked, quick-cooking grits	1	cup shredded Cheddar cheese

In a large skillet, cook bacon over medium-high heat until crisp. Remove bacon, reserving the drippings in the pan. Drain bacon on paper towels and set aside. Gradually add chicken broth to bacon drippings, stirring constantly. Add salt; bring to a boil. Stir in grits, tomatoes and green chiles. Return to a boil, stirring often. Reduce heat, cover and simmer for 15 to 20 minutes, stirring frequently. Add Cheddar cheese and stir until melted. Top with crumbled bacon. Serve immediately.

Makes 6 servings

THE LUNCH BELL GRITS

3   cups water
1   cup quick cooking grits

¼   teaspoon salt
½   stick butter

In a heavy saucepan, bring water to a boil. Slowly stir in grits, salt and butter. Reduce heat to medium-low and cover. Cook for 5 to 7 minutes or until thickened, stirring occasionally. Remove from heat.

Makes 4 servings

CHEESE GRITS

4   cups water
1½ teaspoons salt, divided
1   cup hominy grits (not instant)
2   sticks butter, divided
1   cup milk
4   eggs, beaten

1   (6 ounce) roll garlic cheese, slivered
¼   teaspoon cayenne pepper
3   tablespoons freshly grated Parmesan cheese

Bring water to a rolling boil and add 1 teaspoon salt. Slowly pour in grits, stirring constantly. Cover, reduce heat to low and cook for 45 minutes, stirring occasionally. Remove from heat and cool slightly. Preheat oven to 350 degrees. Stir in 1 stick butter, milk, eggs, garlic cheese, cayenne pepper and ½ teaspoon salt. Turn into a well-buttered baking dish (using about ½ stick butter). Sprinkle with Parmesan cheese and bake for 1 hour. With the side of a serving spoon, make 4 to 5 ruts in the grits. Pour ½ stick melted butter on top of the grits. Serve immediately.

Note: Casserole may be frozen prior to putting Parmesan cheese on top. Thaw before heating frozen casserole.

Makes 6 to 8 servings

GRAY BOWDITCH

CHEESE GRITS WITH SAUSAGE

8 ounces pork sausage	1½ cups shredded sharp Cheddar cheese, divided
4 cups water	½ stick butter
½ teaspoon salt	4 eggs, lightly beaten
1 cup uncooked, quick-cooking grits	½ cup milk

Preheat oven to 350 degrees. Brown the sausage in a frying pan until thoroughly cooked. Drain fat and place sausage on paper towels; set aside. Place water and salt in a large saucepan and bring to a boil over medium-high heat. Slowly stir in grits. Reduce heat to low and cover pan. Simmer for 5 minutes or until grits are cooked, stirring occasionally. Remove from heat. Mix in 1 cup of the cheese; add butter. Stir until cheese and butter are thoroughly melted. Add eggs, milk and sausage and mix well. Pour grits mixture into greased 9x13-inch baking dish. Sprinkle with remaining cheese. Bake for 45 to 50 minutes or until casserole bubbles and is lightly browned. Let cool for 15 minutes before serving.

Note: Casserole may be prepared the day before serving and refrigerated until baking.

Makes 10 to 12 servings

APPLESAUCE BLITZENS

1½ cups all-purpose flour	1 cup milk
1 teaspoon salt	Vegetable oil
1¼ cups water	Applesauce
4 eggs	Confectioners' sugar

Mix together flour, salt and water with a wire whisk. Then add eggs one at a time, mixing well after each egg. Stir in milk.

Heat a 10-inch skillet with a teaspoon of oil. Pour ¼ cup of mix into center and roll pan in a circle to just coat bottom of the pan. Allow batter to cook until edges pull away from pan; slide spatula about ⅓ of way under crêpe, pick up and flip over. Allow to cook 1 minute longer; then slide onto a dinner plate. Put 2 to 3 tablespoons of applesauce into center and spread in a circle to make a thin layer. Start at one end and roll into a crêpe. Sprinkle lightly with confectioners' sugar and serve.

Makes 8 to 10 crêpes

TAMMY LAWSON

"I couldn't cook these fast enough for my little brother and sister when I had to cook for them. Occasionally I had to make another batch."

Tammy Lawson

SWEET POTATO PANCAKES

PANCAKES

2¼ cups all-purpose flour
¾ cup sugar
2 teaspoons baking powder
¼ teaspoon salt
¼ teaspoon ground cinnamon

¼ teaspoon ground nutmeg
1½ cups whole milk
3 eggs, beaten
6 tablespoons vegetable oil
1½ pounds mashed sweet
    potatoes

HONEY PECAN BUTTER

1 stick butter, softened
¼ cup honey

¼ cup chopped, toasted
    pecans

In a large bowl, mix together flour, sugar, baking powder, salt, cinnamon and nutmeg. Stir in milk and eggs. Add oil and whisk until smooth. Fold in the sweet potatoes. When griddle is hot, grease lightly and pour ¼ cup of batter per pancake on griddle. Cook until top is covered with bubbles. Turn pancakes and finish cooking.

While pancakes are cooking, mix together butter, honey and pecans. Serve on top of pancakes.

Note: When you fold in sweet potatoes, batter will be somewhat lumpy.

Makes 6 to 8 servings

*"Saturday morning is always a pleasure to relax and read the newspaper at **The Lunch Bell**. We enjoy dining with fellow friends, chatting about life and world affairs! We like everything from eggs to pancakes to waffles. It is a great way to start your weekend after a long week!"*
Paula Maria Orphanidys

THE LUNCH BELL FRENCH TOAST

4 eggs
1 cup French Vanilla coffee
    creamer

6-8 slices Texas toast
Butter

Beat together eggs and cream. Dredge the toast in the egg mixture until it is well coated. Cook toast on a hot buttered griddle until golden brown on each side.

Makes 2 to 3 servings

Baked Caramel Apple Pancakes

5   tablespoons butter
6   tablespoons brown sugar
¼   teaspoon ground cinnamon
1-2 baking apples
1   cup all-purpose flour
1   tablespoon sugar

1   teaspoon baking powder
½   teaspoon baking soda
Dash of salt
1   cup buttermilk
1   egg
3   tablespoons butter, melted

If you don't have buttermilk, you can add 1 tablespoon of lemon juice or vinegar to 1 cup of milk. Let the mixture stand for 10 minutes before using.

Preheat oven to 400 degrees. To make the caramel, melt butter in a small saucepan and add brown sugar. Cook on medium high until sugar melts, about 4 minutes. Stir in cinnamon. Pour caramel into a greased 9-inch pie plate or baking dish. Slice apples with apple slicer and quarter. Arrange apple slices evenly on top of the caramel; set aside. In medium bowl combine flour, sugar, baking powder, baking soda and salt. Sift together. Add buttermilk and egg and whisk until blended. Stir in melted butter. Pour onto caramel and apples in the pan, covering evenly. Bake for 25 minutes or until golden brown around edge. Remove from oven and let set for 10 minutes. Invert onto a serving dish.

Makes 4 servings

Pumpkin Pancakes

1½ cups all-purpose flour
1   teaspoon baking powder
1½ teaspoons pumpkin pie spice
¼   teaspoon baking soda
¼   teaspoon salt

1   egg
¼   cup canned pure pumpkin
1½ cups milk
3   tablespoons vegetable oil

In a medium bowl, combine flour, baking powder, pumpkin pie spice, baking soda and salt. In a separate bowl, beat together egg, pumpkin, milk and oil. Add flour mixture to milk mixture, stirring until just blended but still lumpy. When griddle is hot, grease lightly and pour ¼ cup of batter per pancake on griddle. Cook until top is covered with bubbles. Turn pancakes and finish cooking.

Makes 10 pancakes

Cinnamon Waffles with Pecan Syrup

Waffles

2	cups biscuit mix	½	teaspoon ground cinnamon
½	cup oil	1⅓	cups club soda
1	egg, beaten		

Pecan Syrup

1	cup maple syrup	1	tablespoon butter
1	cup dark corn syrup	2	cups finely chopped pecans, toasted
2	tablespoons bourbon		

Preheat waffle iron. In a medium bowl, combine biscuit mix, oil, egg, cinnamon and club soda. Mix well. Pour batter into hot waffle iron and cook until golden brown. For pecan syrup, combine maple syrup, corn syrup, bourbon and butter in a medium saucepan. Bring to a boil over medium-high heat. Stir in toasted pecans and let cool slightly. Pour over hot waffles.

Note: Syrup can be stored in the refrigerator in an airtight container for up to 1 week.

Makes 4 to 6 waffles, depending on the size of the waffle iron

To toast pecans, place them in a single layer on a baking sheet. Bake at 350 degrees for 10 minutes or until golden brown.

Caramel French Toast

1	stick butter	1½	cups milk
1	cup firmly packed brown sugar	1	teaspoon pure vanilla extract
1	loaf French bread	2	tablespoons sugar
5	eggs	¼	teaspoon salt

To make the caramel, melt butter in a small saucepan and add brown sugar. Simmer over medium heat until mixture becomes syrupy. Pour caramel into a 9x13-inch glass baking dish. Slice French bread into ¾-inch thick slices and remove crusts. Place slices of bread over caramel. In a large bowl, beat eggs, milk, vanilla, sugar and salt. Pour over bread. Cover and refrigerate overnight. Preheat oven to 350 degrees. Bake, uncovered, for 35 minutes.

Makes 4 to 6 servings

French Toast Stuffed with Bananas and Walnuts

6 eggs
¼ cup half-and-half
1 teaspoon pure vanilla extract
¼ teaspoon ground cinnamon
4 ripe bananas, peeled and mashed
¼ cup coarsely chopped walnuts
⅛ teaspoon ground nutmeg
8 slices egg bread
2-4 tablespoons butter
Confectioners' sugar and walnut halves for garnish

In a medium bowl, beat eggs and stir in half-and-half, vanilla and cinnamon. In a separate bowl, combine mashed bananas, chopped walnuts and nutmeg. Spread banana mixture generously onto 4 slices of egg bread and cover each slice with remaining 4 slices of bread. In a medium saucepan, melt butter over medium heat. Dip sandwiches into egg mixture, turning until saturated on both sides. Place sandwiches into hot butter in saucepan and fry for about 2 minutes on each side or until golden brown. If desired, sprinkle with confectioners' sugar and garnish with walnut halves.

Makes 4 servings

Jennie Swain, Jesus Sanchez and Bernie Gervais
enjoy a meal together at **The Lunch Bell**.

OVERNIGHT APPLE FRENCH TOAST

1 cup firmly packed brown
  sugar
1 stick butter
2 tablespoons light corn syrup
2 large tart apples, peeled and
  sliced ¼-inch thick
3 eggs
1 cup milk

1 teaspoon pure vanilla extract
9 slices day old French bread,
  cut ¾-inch thick
1 cup applesauce
1 (10 ounce) jar apple jelly
½ teaspoon ground cinnamon
⅛ teaspoon ground cloves

In a small saucepan over medium heat, combine brown sugar, butter and corn syrup. Cook for 5 to 7 minutes or until thickened. Pour mixture into an ungreased 9x13-inch baking dish. Arrange apple slices over mixture in baking dish. In a medium bowl, combine eggs, milk and vanilla; mix well. Dip bread slices into egg mixture, letting soak for 1 minute. Place bread slices over apples in baking dish. Cover and refrigerate overnight.

Remove from refrigerator 30 minutes before baking. Preheat oven to 350 degrees. Bake, uncovered, for 35 to 40 minutes. In a medium saucepan over medium heat, combine applesauce, apple jelly, cinnamon and ground cloves. Cook until thoroughly heated. To serve, place French toast on serving plates and cover with hot applesauce mixture.

Makes 9 servings

Firm apples are best for baking. Some good varieties are Rome, Granny Smith, Cortland and Gala.

CINNAMON SWEET ROLLS

ROLLS

4½	cups whole milk	3	teaspoons salt
⅔	cup butter plus 1 stick butter, divided	4	packages dry yeast
8	cups all-purpose flour, divided	2	eggs
1	cup sugar	1	cup firmly packed light brown sugar
		4	teaspoons cinnamon

FROSTING

2	tablespoons butter	½	teaspoon ground cinnamon
4	tablespoons whole milk	2	cups confectioners' sugar
2	teaspoons pure vanilla extract		

In a small saucepan heat milk and ⅔ cup butter until butter is almost melted. In a large mixing bowl, mix together 4 cups flour, sugar, salt and dry yeast. Add eggs and warm milk/butter mixture to flour mixture. Beat until well blended. Slowly add more flour until you have a soft, firm dough (about 4 additional cups of flour). Knead for approximately 10 minutes. Place in a greased bowl and set in a warm place until dough is doubled in size (about 35 to 40 minutes). Punch dough down and cut into quarters (4 sections). Roll each quarter into a rectangle approximately ½-inch thick.

Preheat oven to 350 degrees. Mix together brown sugar and cinnamon; set aside. Spread melted butter over each roll quarter (about ¼ stick per quarter). Sprinkle cinnamon mixture over top of buttered quarters. Roll up and seal edges. Cut into 1-inch slices with a serrated knife. Place in a well-buttered pan. Again, place in a warm location to rise (about 35 to 40 minutes). Bake for 20 to 30 minutes or until golden brown.

While rolls are baking, make the frosting by beating together the butter, milk, vanilla, cinnamon and confectioners' sugar with an electric mixer. Cool rolls approximately 15 minutes in pan and drizzle with the frosting.

Note: These rolls can be made a day or two in advance and can be frozen. Keep them in an airtight container or cover them securely with plastic wrap to seal in freshness.

Approximately 60 rolls

LORETTA ZEITZ

DANISH PUFFS

CRUST
1	cup all-purpose flour	2	tablespoons water
1	stick butter, softened		

DANISH
1	stick butter	1	cup all-purpose flour
1	cup water	3	eggs, beaten
1	teaspoon almond extract		

ICING
1½	cups confectioners' sugar	1-2	tablespoons warm water
2	tablespoons butter, softened	¼	cup slivered almonds
1½	teaspoons pure vanilla extract		

Preheat the oven to 350 degrees. Place flour in a medium bowl. Cut in butter using a fork or a pastry blender. Sprinkle water over flour, and stir with a fork until dough comes together. Divide into two balls. Pat dough into two long strips on an ungreased baking sheet, about 14 inches long and 3 inches wide; set aside.

In a saucepan, combine butter and water. Bring to a rolling boil. Add almond extract and remove from the heat. Immediately stir in flour until the mixture pulls away from the sides of the pan. Gradually stir in the eggs until well blended. Divide evenly, and spread over the two crusts on the baking sheet. Bake for 1 hour. Allow to cool almost to room temperature before frosting.

For icing, mix together confectioners' sugar, butter, vanilla and warm water until smooth. Spread over cooled Danish. Sprinkle with slivered almonds.

Note: You may also make 3 smaller ones by making the crusts short ways on the baking sheet. Bake at 350 degrees for 50 minutes.

Makes 2 Danish, 8 to 10 servings each

TAMMY LAWSON

BAKED BLUEBERRY OATMEAL

4 eggs, beaten
1 cup oil
2 cups milk
1 teaspoon pure vanilla extract
2 cups sugar
1 teaspoon salt
4 heaping teaspoons baking powder
6 cups s rolled oats (do not use quick oats)
1 (16 ounce) bag frozen blueberries

Preheat oven to 350 degrees. Mix eggs, oil, milk and vanilla together. Add sugar, salt, baking powder and oats to the liquid ingredients and stir well. Gently fold in frozen blueberries. Do not stir excessively, as the batter will turn blue, making the final dish less visually appealing. Pour into a 9x13-inch glass baking dish sprayed with cooking spray. Cover with tin foil and bake for 1 hour, removing the foil about 15 minutes before oatmeal is done. Oatmeal should look "cakey" with no liquid pooling in the middle.

Note: Canned, fresh or frozen fruit can be used. Peaches and strawberries also work well. Try pouring a little cold milk on top of the oatmeal!

Makes 8 to 10 servings

JULIE RUSS

Betty Swain in February, 1957

BAKED APPLE OATMEAL

3 cups quick cooking oats
½ cup firmly packed brown sugar
2 eggs
2 cups milk
¼ teaspoon salt
½ cup vegetable oil
1 teaspoon pure vanilla extract
1 teaspoon ground cinnamon
¼ teaspoon ground nutmeg
1 teaspoon baking powder
½ cup raisins
½ cup pecans
½ cup diced apples

Preheat oven to 350 degrees. In a large bowl, combine oats, brown sugar, eggs, milk, salt, oil, vanilla, cinnamon, nutmeg and baking powder. Mix well. Add raisins, pecans and diced apples and stir until well combined. Pour mixture into a 1-quart baking dish. Bake for 45 minutes or until set.

Makes 8 servings

MOIST AND RICH PINEAPPLE COFFEE CAKE

CAKE

2	cups all-purpose flour	2	cups crushed pineapple, undrained
1½	cups sugar	½	cup firmly packed brown sugar
1	teaspoon baking soda		
½	teaspoon salt	1	cup chopped pecans
2	eggs, beaten		

TOPPING

1	stick butter	1	cup evaporated milk
¾	cup sugar	1	teaspoon pure vanilla extract

Preheat oven to 325 degrees. Combine flour, sugar, baking soda and salt in a large mixing bowl; stir together. Add eggs and pineapple. Stir until well combined. Pour batter into a greased and floured 9x13-inch baking dish or for a thicker cake use a 7x11-inch baking dish. Mix together brown sugar and pecans. Sprinkle over the batter. Bake for 30 minutes.

Begin making the topping about 10 minutes before the cake is done. Put butter, sugar and evaporated milk in a saucepan and bring to a boil. Boil for 2 minutes. Stir in vanilla. When the cake is taken out of the oven, spoon the topping over it, covering entire cake. Cool slightly and serve or serve later at room temperature.

Note: There is no butter or shortening in the batter of this cake. The topping **must** be used on this coffee cake in order for it to be complete.

Makes 12 to 15 servings

*In the aftermath of Hurricane Isabel, Betty and her staff served over 2,600 meals to the utility workers who came from all over the East Coast to help Hampton Roads. For almost a week, they would wake up at 2:00 a.m. to prepare breakfast for between 100 and 275 people. They also served countless lunches and dinners to the utility workers and to many hungry locals without power. **The Lunch Bell** was the only restaurant in the local vicinity with electricity in the first few days after the hurricane.*

SHELAH'S CINCINNATI COFFEE CAKE

CAKE

2	sticks butter, softened	1½	teaspoons baking powder
1¾	cups sugar	½	teaspoon salt
4	eggs	¼	cup milk
1	teaspoon pure vanilla extract	1	(21 ounce) can pie filling (blueberry, strawberry, cherry or raspberry)
3	cups all-purpose flour		

ICING

1	cup confectioners' sugar	2	tablespoons milk or more to mix
½	teaspoon pure vanilla extract		

Preheat oven to 350 degrees. In a medium bowl, cream together the butter and sugar with an electric mixer. Add the eggs and vanilla and beat until fluffy. In a separate bowl, sift together flour, baking powder and salt. Add dry ingredients to butter mixture alternately with milk and mix well. Spread half of batter into a greased 10x15-inch jelly-roll pan. Spread pie filling over batter. Then drop remaining batter by spoonfuls over pie filling. Using a fork, gently rake batter with pie filling. Bake for 30 minutes or until cake is fully cooked.

For icing, mix together confectioners' sugar, vanilla and milk until smooth. Drizzle over warm cake. Serve warm.

Makes 24 servings

SHELAH SWAIN

Betty's children, Billy and Shelah, graduated from Cincinnati Bible College in Cincinnati, OH. Shelah's roommate shared this coffee cake recipe with Shelah, and Betty has been making it ever since. They also fell in love with "Cincinnati Chili" while living there.

SOUR CREAM COCONUT COFFEE CAKE

COFFEE CAKE

1	box Duncan Hines® yellow cake mix	½	cup vegetable oil
1	(3.4 ounce) box coconut cream instant pudding mix	1	cup sour cream
		1	teaspoon coconut extract
4	eggs	⅓	cup grated coconut (optional)

CRUMB TOPPING

½	cup sugar	½	cup chopped pecans
1	tablespoon ground cinnamon		

Preheat oven to 350 degrees. In a large mixing bowl, combine cake mix, pudding mix, eggs, oil and sour cream and mix well. Add coconut extract and mix. Add grated coconut and stir well. In a separate bowl, mix together sugar, cinnamon and pecans.

Pour ½ of the batter into a greased and floured angel cake pan. Sprinkle ½ of the topping mixture over the batter. Pour remaining batter on top; sprinkle again with crumb topping, saving 1 teaspoon of topping. Marbleize by pulling a knife through the batter mix while turning the pan. Use the last teaspoon of topping to cover the spot where the knife is removed. Pat down top of cake gently with back of spoon.

Bake for 55 minutes or until a toothpick inserted into the center of the cake comes out clean. Let cool and remove exterior of pan. Run knife around bottom of pan to loosen cake. To retain topping, place a paper plate over top and turn cake upside down and remove bottom of pan. Turn cake right side up again onto a serving plate.

Note: Recipe can be cut in half and baked in 2 small angel cake pans. If doing this, set aside 2 teaspoons of topping to cover where marbleizing knife is removed and reduce cooking time to 45 minutes. May be frozen.

Makes 16 servings

JAY MUSSER

"This recipe was originally in our church cookbook, but was adopted by my family over 30 years ago and has become a tradition for reunions, holidays and as gifts for friends and neighbors."
Jay Musser

WELLESLEY COFFEE CAKE

CAKE

2	sticks butter, softened	½	teaspoon almond extract
2	cups sugar	2	cups sifted all-purpose flour
2	eggs	1	teaspoon baking powder
1	cup sour cream	¼	teaspoon salt
½	teaspoon pure vanilla extract		

FILLING

4	teaspoons sugar	1	teaspoon ground cinnamon
1	cup chopped pecans		

Preheat oven to 350 degrees. With an electric mixer, cream together butter and sugar. Add eggs, one at a time, beating with each addition. Add sour cream, vanilla and almond extract; beat well. In a separate bowl, combine flour, baking powder and salt. Add to mixture and beat. In a small bowl, combine sugar, pecans and cinnamon for filling. Place ⅓ of batter in a greased and floured tube pan. Sprinkle with ¾ of filling mixture. Spoon in rest of batter and sprinkle with remaining filling. Bake for 1 hour.

Makes 10 to 12 servings

Bridgette Brown, Bill Swain, Betty Swain, Carrie Osmondson and
Audrey McCord celebrate Christmas with Santa!

Brown Sugar Coffee Cake

COFFEE CAKE

1   stick butter, softened
2   cups sugar
1   teaspoon pure vanilla extract
4   eggs, beaten

3   cups all-purpose flour
½   teaspoon salt
2   teaspoons baking powder
1   cup milk

FILLING

1   cup firmly packed brown
    sugar
2   tablespoons butter, softened

2   tablespoons all-purpose flour
1   teaspoon ground cinnamon
1   cup chopped pecans

Preheat oven to 350 degrees. With an electric hand mixer, cream together butter and sugar. Add vanilla and eggs and beat well. In a separate bowl, sift together the flour, salt and baking powder. Add dry ingredients alternately with milk to the butter mixture.

For the filling, combine brown sugar and butter. Add flour, cinnamon and mix well. Fold in pecans. Pour a third of the cake mixture into the bottom of a greased tube pan. Sprinkle on a third of the filing. Repeat twice, ending with the filling on top. Bake for 30 to 40 minutes or until a toothpick inserted into the center of the cake comes out clean.

Makes 16 to 20 servings

APPLE COFFEE CAKE

COFFEE CAKE

4	tablespoons butter	2	cups all-purpose flour
1	cup sugar	1	teaspoon baking powder
¼	cup applesauce	1	teaspoon baking soda
2	eggs	1	cup sour cream
1	teaspoon pure vanilla extract	1	medium apple, peeled and thinly sliced

TOPPING

½	cup chopped pecans	¾	cup firmly packed brown sugar
2	teaspoons ground cinnamon		

Preheat oven to 375 degrees. In a large bowl, cream together butter and sugar; blend in applesauce. Add eggs and vanilla; blend well. In a separate bowl, mix together flour, baking powder and baking soda. Gradually add flour mixture and sour cream to butter mixture, being sure to start and end with the flour mixture. When blended, spoon half of batter into a greased and floured Bundt pan. Layer apple slices on top of batter. Combine pecans, cinnamon and brown sugar and sprinkle half on top of apples. Top with remaining batter and sprinkle with remaining topping. Bake for 40 minutes or until a toothpick inserted into the center of the cake comes out clean.

Makes 16 to 20 servings

Fresh Blueberry Coffee Cake

Coffee Cake

2	cups all-purpose flour		2	eggs
3	teaspoons baking powder		¾	cup milk
½	teaspoon salt		1	teaspoon pure vanilla extract
1	stick butter, softened		1	cup fresh or frozen
½	cup sugar			blueberries, well drained

Topping

½	teaspoon cinnamon		2	tablespoons all-purpose flour
½	cup firmly packed brown sugar			

Preheat oven to 350 degrees. In a medium bowl, mix together flour, baking powder and salt; set aside. In a large bowl, mix together butter, sugar and eggs with an electric hand mixer on high. Beat until fluffy. Add dry ingredients alternately with the milk using low speed. Stir in vanilla. Fold in blueberries. Pour batter into a greased and floured 8x8-inch glass baking dish. Combine cinnamon, brown sugar and flour and sprinkle on top of batter. Bake for 30 to 35 minutes or until a toothpick inserted into the center of the cake comes out clean.

Makes 10 to 12 servings

Pumpkin Bread

4	eggs		½	teaspoon ground cloves
1	cup vegetable oil		½	teaspoon ground nutmeg
1	cup pumpkin		1	teaspoon ground cinnamon
1	cup water		2	teaspoons baking soda
3	cups all-purpose flour		¼	teaspoon salt
3	cups sugar			

Preheat oven to 350 degrees. In a large bowl with an electric mixer, beat together eggs, oil, pumpkin and water. In a separate bowl, stir together flour, sugar, ground cloves, nutmeg, cinnamon, baking soda and salt. Add dry ingredients in 3 parts to batter, mixing thoroughly in between. Pour batter into 2 greased and floured loaf pans. Bake for 1 hour or until toothpick inserted into the center of the bread comes out clean. Cool bread in pan on wire rack for 10 minutes; remove and cool completely on wire rack.

Makes 2 loaves, 10 to 12 servings each

"The Lunch Bell is very convenient for me, and I eat there because I love the food and admire and respect the owners."
Lt. Col. Jay Musser

BANANA NUT BREAD

5	tablespoons butter	1½	cups mashed ripe bananas
½	cup sugar	1¾	cups all-purpose flour
½	cup firmly packed light brown sugar	1	teaspoon baking soda
1	egg	½	teaspoon salt
2	egg whites	¼	teaspoon baking powder
1	teaspoon pure vanilla extract	½	cup heavy whipping cream
		⅓	cup chopped pecans

Preheat oven to 350 degrees. With an electric mixer, beat together butter, sugar and brown sugar. Add egg, egg whites and vanilla and combine well. Then add the mashed bananas and beat on high for 30 seconds. In a separate bowl, combine flour, baking soda, salt and baking powder. Add dry ingredients to banana mixture alternately with the cream, ending with the flour. Fold in pecans. Pour batter into a greased loaf pan. Bake for 1 hour and 15 minutes or until a toothpick inserted into the center of the bread comes out clean. Cool bread in pan on wire rack for 10 minutes; remove and cool completely on wire rack.

Makes 1 loaf, 10 to 12 servings

PATSY TAYLOR

 # QUICK AND EASY BANANA NUT BREAD

¼	cup vegetable shortening	1	cup mashed ripe bananas (2 to 3 medium)
¾	cup sugar	⅓	cup chopped pecans
2	eggs		
2	cups baking mix		

Preheat oven to 350 degrees. With an electric mixer, cream together shortening and sugar on medium speed. Add eggs and baking mix and mix well. Fold in the bananas and nuts. Pour batter into a greased loaf pan. Bake for 55 minutes or until a toothpick inserted into the center of the bread comes out clean. Cool bread in pan on wire rack for 10 minutes; remove and cool completely on wire rack.

Makes 1 loaf, 10 to 12 servings

CHRISTMAS CRANBERRY BREAD

2   cups all-purpose flour
1   cup sugar
½   teaspoon salt
½   teaspoon baking powder
½   teaspoon baking soda
1   cup raw cranberries, cut in half

½   cup chopped pecans
1   egg, beaten
½   cup orange juice
2   tablespoons butter, melted
2   tablespoons hot water

Preheat oven to 350 degrees. Sift together flour, sugar, salt, baking powder and baking soda. Stir in cranberries and nuts. Add egg, orange juice, butter and water; stir lightly until moistened. Pour into a greased and floured loaf pan. Bake for 50 minutes or until a toothpick inserted into the center of the bread comes out clean. Cool bread in pan on wire rack for 10 minutes; remove and cool completely on wire rack.

Makes 1 loaf, 10 to 12 servings

MARILYN HOLLAND

And He directed the people to sit down on the grass. Taking the five loaves and the two fish and looking up to Heaven, He gave thanks and broke the loaves.
Matthew 14:19

BANANA BLUEBERRY BREAD

1   cup sugar
½   cup vegetable oil
1   cup mashed (2 medium) bananas
½   cup plain yogurt
1   teaspoon pure vanilla extract

2   eggs
2   cups all-purpose flour
1   teaspoon baking soda
½   teaspoon salt
1   cup fresh or frozen blueberries

Preheat oven to 350 degrees. Beat together sugar and oil with an electric mixer. Add bananas, yogurt, vanilla and eggs and blend well. In a separate bowl, sift together flour, baking soda and salt and add to sugar mixture. Stir until just moistened. Fold in blueberries. Pour into 1 large or 3 small loaf pans. Bake for 60 to 70 minutes for the large loaf or 40 to 50 minutes for the small loaves. Cool in pan for 5 minutes; remove to a wire rack and cool completely.

Note: Good with whipped cream cheese

Makes 1 large loaf or 2 small loaves,

BETTY FREEMAN KELLY

ZUCCHINI BREAD

⅔ cup vegetable shortening
2 cups sugar
3 eggs
2½ cups packed shredded raw zucchini with skin on
⅔ cup water
1½ teaspoons pure vanilla extract

¾ teaspoon butter extract
2½ cups all-purpose flour
1½ teaspoons baking soda
½ teaspoon baking powder
1 teaspoon salt
1 teaspoon ground cinnamon
1 teaspoon powdered cloves
½ cup chopped nuts (optional)

Preheat oven to 350 degrees. Mix together shortening and sugar. Add eggs, zucchini, water, vanilla and butter extract. Mix well. In a separate bowl, stir together flour, baking soda, baking powder, salt, cinnamon and cloves. Add dry ingredients in 3 parts to batter, mixing thoroughly in between. Fold in nuts.

Pour batter into 2 small greased and floured loaf pans or into 1 large greased and floured loaf pan. Bake for 45 to 60 minutes or until a toothpick inserted into the center of the bread comes out clean. Cool bread in pan on wire rack for 10 minutes; remove and cool completely on wire rack.

Makes 1 to 2 loaves, 10 to 12 servings each

TAMMY LAWSON

LEMON BLUEBERRY BREAD

BREAD

¾ cup sugar
½ cup milk
½ stick butter, softened
1 egg
½ teaspoon lemon extract
2 cups all-purpose flour

2 teaspoons baking powder
¼ teaspoon salt
3 cups fresh or frozen blueberries
1½ tablespoons lemon zest

TOPPING

½ cup sugar
¼ cup firmly packed brown sugar
⅓ cup all-purpose flour

½ stick butter, softened
1 teaspoon lemon zest
¾ teaspoon ground cinnamon

Preheat oven to 375 degrees. In a medium bowl, mix together the sugar, milk, butter and egg until smooth. Stir in lemon extract. In another bowl, sift together the flour, baking powder and salt. Stir the dry ingredients into the milk mixture and mix until just moistened. Fold in the blueberries and lemon zest. Pour into a greased 9x5-inch loaf pan.

For topping, combine sugar, brown sugar, flour, butter, lemon zest and cinnamon in a small bowl. Stir until smooth. Sprinkle on top of batter. Bake for 50 minutes or until topping is golden brown and has formed a thick crust. Cool in pan for 5 minutes; remove to a wire rack and cool completely.

Makes 1 loaf, 10 to 12 servings

CRANBERRY ORANGE MUFFINS

2	cups all-purpose flour	½	cup orange juice
1	cup sugar	1	teaspoon grated orange peel
1½	teaspoons baking powder	2	eggs, beaten
½	teaspoon baking soda	1	cup coarsely chopped fresh cranberries
1	teaspoon salt		
½	stick butter	½	cup chopped pecans
⅓	cup vegetable oil		

Preheat oven to 350 degrees. In a medium bowl, sift together flour, sugar, baking powder, baking soda and salt. Cut in butter until mixture resembles cornmeal; set aside. In a small bowl, combine oil, orange juice, orange peel and eggs. Stir into flour mixture, mixing until just moistened. Gently fold in cranberries and pecans. Pour batter into greased muffin tins about ⅔ full. Bake for 15 to 20 minutes or until a toothpick inserted into the center of a muffin comes out clean. Cool and wrap overnight to allow flavors to ripen.

Makes 12 to 16 muffins, depending on the size of the muffin tins

SWEET POTATO MUFFINS

1	stick butter, softened	¼	teaspoon salt
1¼	cups sugar	1	teaspoon ground cinnamon
2	eggs	¼	teaspoon ground nutmeg
1¼	cups cooked and mashed sweet potatoes	1	cup milk
		¼	cup chopped pecans
1½	cups flour	½	cup golden raisins
2	teaspoons baking powder		

Preheat oven to 400 degrees. In a large bowl, cream together butter and sugar. Add eggs, sweet potatoes, flour, baking powder, salt, cinnamon, nutmeg and milk. Mix until just moistened. Fold in pecans and raisins. Pour batter into greased muffin tins about ⅔ full. Bake for 15 to 20 minutes.

Makes 8 to 10 muffins, depending on the size of the muffin tins

BLUEBERRY MUFFINS

MUFFINS

1   cup blueberries, washed and well drained
2   cups all-purpose flour, divided
3   teaspoons baking powder
½   teaspoon salt

⅛   teaspoon ground cinnamon
½   cup sugar
2   eggs, room temperature
1   cup milk, room temperature
½   stick butter, melted
1   teaspoon pure vanilla extract

TOPPING

3   tablespoons sugar

1   teaspoon ground cinnamon

Preheat oven to 400 degrees. In a small bowl, dredge blueberries in 4 tablespoons of the flour; set aside. In a medium bowl, sift together remaining flour, baking powder, salt, cinnamon and sugar. In another bowl, beat together eggs, milk, butter and vanilla. Add egg mixture to flour mixture all at one time. Mix together, until batter is just moistened. Do not over mix. Gently fold in blueberries. Pour batter into greased muffin tins about ⅔ full. Combine sugar and cinnamon and sprinkle on top of muffins. Bake for 15 to 20 minutes or until a toothpick inserted into the center of a muffin comes out clean.

Makes 12 to 16 muffins, depending on the size of the muffin tins

Betty also recommends Duncan Hines® Blueberry Streusel Muffins. Just make according to package directions and enjoy!

GARLIC CHEESE BISCUITS

2   cups Bisquick® baking mix
⅔   cup milk
½   cup shredded Cheddar cheese

2   tablespoons butter, melted
¼   teaspoon garlic powder

Preheat oven to 450 degrees. Stir together baking mix, milk and cheese until soft dough forms. Drop by spoonfuls onto ungreased baking sheet. Bake for 8 to 10 minutes or until golden brown. Stir together butter and garlic powder; brush over warm biscuits.

Makes 8 to 9 biscuits

Betty uses frozen Bridgford® white rolls at the restaurant. They are excellent — just bake according to package directions and serve!

Parker House Rolls

1	packet active dry yeast	2	tablespoons sugar
¼	cup warm water	1	teaspoon salt
1	cup milk	1	beaten egg
2	tablespoons vegetable shortening	3½	cups sifted all-purpose flour
			Melted butter

Put yeast in warm water. In a saucepan, scald milk (do not boil) and pour into large glass bowl. Add shortening, sugar and salt. Stir until dissolved. Cool to lukewarm. Add yeast. Add the egg and gradually stir in flour to form soft dough. Beat vigorously with spoon. Cover and let rise in warm place until dough has doubled in size (approximately 1½ hours). Turn dough onto lightly floured surface. Knead well. Form rolls using biscuit cutter. Brush with butter and fold over. Let rise (approximately 1½ hours). Preheat oven to 400 degrees. Place rolls on well-greased baking sheet. Bake for 15 minutes or until golden brown.

Makes 3 dozen rolls

BETTY VARNER

The Lunch Bell Cheddar Cheese Biscuits

5⅓	tablespoons butter, cold	⅔	cup whole milk
2½	cups Bisquick® baking mix		Melted butter
½	cup shredded Cheddar cheese		

Preheat oven to 450 degrees. Cut cold butter into small pieces and place into a medium bowl. Add Bisquick® and cheese and toss until coated. Add milk and stir until just absorbed. Turn dough onto a floured surface and roll to coat. Fold and knead dough 5 times and pat to ½-inch thick. Cut with 3-inch round cutter. Place on ungreased cookie sheet. Bake for 9 minutes. Brush with melted butter.

Makes 10 to 12 biscuits

BROCCOLI CORNBREAD

4 eggs
1 tablespoon mayonnaise
1 tablespoon sour cream
⅓ cup milk
1 (8.5 ounce) box corn muffin mix

2 tablespoons sugar
1 (10 ounce) package frozen chopped broccoli, cooked and drained
½ cup chopped onion
2 cups shredded Cheddar cheese

Preheat oven to 425 degrees. In a large bowl, combine eggs, mayonnaise, sour cream and milk. Stir in corn muffin mix and sugar. Add broccoli, onion and cheese; mix well. Pour batter into a greased 9x9-inch baking dish or cast-iron skillet. Bake for 25 to 35 minutes or until edges are crispy and brown.

Makes 8 to 10 servings

Only one pan of rolls, bread or biscuits should be baked at a time. There should be nothing else in the oven when baking these items.

BACON AND CHEESE MUFFINS

8 slices bacon
1¾ cups flour
1 teaspoon baking powder
½ teaspoon salt
1 tablespoon sugar
½ teaspoon baking soda

⅛ teaspoon garlic powder
1 cup shredded Cheddar cheese
1 cup sour cream
1 egg, beaten
2 tablespoons milk

Preheat oven to 400 degrees. In a large skillet, cook bacon until crisp. Crumble bacon and set aside. Reserve 2 tablespoons of bacon drippings. In a large bowl, sift flour, baking powder, salt, sugar, baking soda and garlic powder. Stir in cheese and crumbled bacon. In a small bowl, beat together bacon drippings, sour cream, egg and milk. Stir sour cream mixture into dry ingredients. Mix until batter is well blended. Pour batter into greased muffin tins about ⅔ full. Bake for 20 to 25 minutes or until golden brown.

Makes 10 to 12 muffins, depending on the size of the muffin tins

Corn Spoon Bread

2 eggs, beaten (or 4 egg whites, beaten)
1 (8 ounce) can cream style corn
1 (8 ounce) can drained whole kernel corn
1 cup sour cream
1 stick butter, melted
1 (8.5 ounce) package corn muffin mix
1 cup shredded Swiss cheese (optional)

Preheat oven to 350 degrees. Combine eggs, corn and sour cream and mix well. Add butter, muffin mix and cheese and stir until blended. Spread into a greased 1½ to 2-quart baking dish and bake for 35 minutes or until a toothpick inserted into the center comes out clean.

Makes 10 servings

MALLORY MCKEE

Mallory is Shelah's daughter and one of Betty's 7 grandchildren.

 # The Lunch Bell Corn Bread

2 eggs, beaten
½ cup vegetable oil
1 cup sour cream
2 tablespoons sugar
1 (14.75 ounce) can cream style corn
1 (8.5 ounce) boxes Jiffy® corn muffin mix

Preheat oven to 350 degrees. Mix together eggs, vegetable oil, sour cream, sugar and corn. Fold in corn muffin mix. Pour into a greased 8x8-inch baking dish. Bake for 1 hour or until golden brown.

Makes about 12 servings

Italian Bubble Bread

2 frozen loaves bread dough
1 stick butter, slightly melted
1 tablespoon Italian dry seasoning
1 teaspoon garlic powder
1 egg, beaten

Thaw frozen loaves of bread slightly; cut each loaf into 16 small pieces. Beat together butter, Italian seasoning, garlic powder and egg. Dip bread pieces in egg mixture; put into a greased tube or Bundt pan. Let bread rise, approximately 2 hours. Bake at 350 degrees for 20 to 25 minutes.

Makes 10 to 12 servings

MARILYN HOLLAND

SOUPS, SALADS AND DRESSINGS

SOUPS, SALADS AND DRESSINGS

FEATURED RECIPES

ON FRONT:

The Lunch Bell
Potato Salad,
page 93

The Lunch Bell
Pimento Cheese Spread,
page 96

Sweet and Sour Pickles,
page 136

VEGETABLE SOUP WITH HAMBURGER

½ pound ground beef
½ medium onion, chopped
½ cup diced celery
1½ teaspoons salt or more to taste
1 teaspoon black pepper or more to taste
Water

1 (28 ounce) can crushed tomatoes
2 (29 ounce) cans whole potatoes, drained and diced
4 (15 ounce) cans mixed vegetables, drained
½ tablespoon sugar

Place ground beef, onion, celery, salt and pepper in a large stockpot. Cover with water. Bring to a boil; reduce heat and cook until hamburger is brown, stirring occasionally to break up hamburger. Add crushed tomatoes, potatoes, mixed vegetables and sugar and bring to a boil. Reduce heat and simmer for 1 hour. Add additional water if needed.

Makes 18 to 20 servings

RUBY BINDER

*Ruby Binder has been with Betty at **The Lunch Bell** since the initial opening in 1981. She worked full-time for about 8 years and has continued on an "as needed" basis to this day. Her recipes for a variety of soups and salads have been enjoyed by many at **The Lunch Bell** and other places, including **Hidenwood Pharmacy** and **Bruton Park Pharmacy**.*

The Lunch Bell ladies who make everyone feel welcome. Ruby Binder, Carrie Osmondson, Audrey McCord, Beverly Sigler and Bernice Kosier.

Vegetable Beef Soup

1½ pounds stew beef, cut into bite-sized pieces
1 tablespoon vegetable oil
2 (16 ounce) bags frozen mixed vegetables
1 (28 ounce) can crushed tomatoes
1 (28 ounce) can diced tomatoes
2 (29 ounce) cans whole potatoes, drained and diced
½ cup diced celery
½ cup diced onion
8 cups water
Salt and pepper to taste
½ cup sugar

In a stockpot, brown stew beef in vegetable oil. Add mixed vegetables, tomatoes, potatoes, celery, onion and water. Add salt and pepper to taste. Bring to boil; reduce heat, cover and simmer for 4 to 6 hours. About 1 hour prior to serving, add sugar and simmer.

Makes 15 to 18 servings

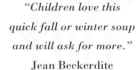

For the vegetable soups, feel free to adjust the seasonings and amounts of vegetables to your liking.

Ann's No Name Soup

1½ pounds ground beef
1 small onion, diced
½ cup chopped celery
3 (19 ounce) cans minestrone soup
2 (28 ounce) cans ranch style beans
2 (14.5 ounce) cans Mexican-style stewed tomatoes
1 (15.25 ounce) can corn
1 (14 ounce) can chicken broth
Salt, pepper and chili powder to taste

In a large skillet, brown ground beef; drain fat. Add onion and celery and sauté until onion is translucent. Pour soup, beans, tomatoes, corn and chicken broth into a 6-quart stockpot. Add meat, onion and celery; add salt, pepper and chili pepper to taste. Cook slowly for 1 hour.

Note: Extra vegetables may be added to this dish. Ranch style beans are spicy and are typically found near the pinto and baked beans at your local grocery store.

Makes 10 to 12 servings

JEAN BECKERDITE

"Children love this quick fall or winter soup and will ask for more."
Jean Beckerdite

CREAMY POTATO SOUP

4	pounds potatoes, peeled and diced	¾	cup all-purpose flour
1	cup finely chopped celery	2.5	ounces chicken base (about 3 tablespoons)
1	medium onion, finely chopped	4	cups water
½	stick butter	1	gallon whole milk, heated
		¼	teaspoon white pepper

In a large stockpot, cover potatoes with salted water and boil until fork tender. Drain and set aside. In the cleaned stockpot, sauté celery and onion in butter until onion is translucent. Add flour and chicken base, stirring until well blended. Cook about 5 minutes, stirring frequently. Slowly add water and stir with a whisk until mixture thickens. Stir in heated milk and bring to a simmer. Do not boil. Reduce heat to low and add potatoes. Cover and simmer for 10 minutes, stirring occasionally. Before serving, add white pepper and stir.

Makes 25 servings

"We love the friendliness of the people, the excellent service and the quality of the down-home food at **The Lunch Bell**. *We've been eating there regularly since they moved into City Center. The Creamy Potato Soup is one of my favorites!"*
Cephise Overby

EASY POTATO SOUP

3	medium potatoes (about 1 pound), peeled and diced	½	cup milk
2	cups water	¼	cup sour cream
2	chicken bouillon cubes		Salt and pepper

Place potatoes in stockpot with water and bouillon cubes. Bring to a boil. Stir; reduce heat to a simmer. Cook about 15 minutes or until potatoes are fork tender. Remove pan from the heat. Using a fork, slightly mash the potatoes (the mixture should be lumpy). Stir in milk and return to heat. Bring to a simmer, but do not boil. Pour into bowls; top each bowl with a spoonful of sour cream. Sprinkle with salt and pepper.

Makes 3 to 4 servings

DEBRA SWAIN

NAVY BEAN SOUP

2 pounds dried navy beans
½ medium onion, chopped
1½ teaspoons salt or more to taste

1 teaspoon black pepper or more to taste
2 tablespoons sugar
2 sticks margarine
1½ gallons water or more to thin

Soak navy beans in water overnight. In the morning, drain the water and wash the beans, discarding any discolored beans. Put navy beans, onion, salt, pepper, sugar and margarine in a large stockpot. Cover with water and bring to a boil. Reduce heat and simmer at least 1 hour. More water may be added if beans are too thick.

Note: If unable to soak beans overnight, you may wash beans and then cover and boil them in water for 1 hour or longer. Then simmer them for 1 hour. When reheating this soup, it is best to put it in a Crockpot and heat for at least 1 hour on high or until it is warmed.

Makes 15 to 18 servings

RUBY BINDER

RUBY'S CHILI

2 pounds ground beef
1 medium onion, chopped
1½ teaspoons salt or more to taste
1 teaspoon black pepper or more to taste
2 tablespoons chili powder

1 (28 ounce) can crushed tomatoes
1 (28 ounce) can diced tomatoes
2 (15 ounce) cans large red kidney beans, undrained
4 cups water

In a stockpot, brown ground beef with onion. Add salt, pepper, chili powder and tomatoes, stirring well. Add kidney beans and water; bring to a boil. Reduce heat and simmer for 1 hour. More water may be added if chili is too thick.

Makes 15 to 18 servings

RUBY BINDER

CINCINNATI CHILI

2 pounds ground beef
1 quart water
2 (8 ounce) cans tomato sauce
2 medium onions, chopped
4 cloves garlic, minced
4 tablespoons chili powder
4 tablespoons vinegar
2 teaspoons Worcestershire sauce
1½ tablespoons cocoa powder

1½ teaspoons salt
1 teaspoon ground cumin
1 teaspoon ground cinnamon
1 teaspoon ground cloves
1 teaspoon allspice
½ teaspoon cayenne pepper
Cooked thin spaghetti
Finely shredded Cheddar cheese
Oyster crackers

Cincinnati chili is a regional style of chili characterized by the unusual ingredients, including chocolate, cloves and allspice.

Place the ground beef in a large stockpot; cover with cold water. Bring to a boil, stirring and breaking up the beef with a fork to a fine texture. Boil for 30 minutes. Stir in the tomato sauce, onion, garlic, chili powder, vinegar, Worcestershire sauce, cocoa, salt, cumin, cinnamon, cloves, allspice and cayenne pepper. Bring to a boil; reduce heat to a simmer, and cook, stirring occasionally, for 3 hours. Add water if necessary to prevent the chili from burning. Serve over thin spaghetti with shredded Cheddar cheese and oyster crackers.

Note: For a healthier version, refrigerate the ground beef after boiling and skim off the solid fat.

Makes 8 to 10 servings

SHELAH'S CHILI

1 medium onion, chopped
2 pounds ground beef
1 (16 ounce) jar Rotel® salsa, medium heat
3-4 (15.5 ounce) cans tomato sauce
1 (14.5 ounce) can diced tomatoes

1 (14.5 ounce) can tomatoes seasoned with garlic, basil and oregano
1 (14.5 ounce) can tomatoes with green chiles
5 big dashes chili powder, or more to taste
Shredded Cheddar cheese

In a large stockpot, sauté the onion. Add the ground beef and cook until browned. Drain off part of the fat. Add the salsa, tomato sauce, tomatoes and chili powder. Cook for at least 30 minutes over medium-low heat. Serve with shredded Cheddar cheese.

Makes 8 to 10 servings

SHELAH SWAIN

CREAMY TOMATO BASIL SOUP

To easily peel tomatoes, remove the core and blanch them in scalding water for 30 seconds. The skin will fall right off!

4   fresh tomatoes, peeled, seeded and diced
3   cups tomato juice
1   (6 ounce) can tomato paste
14 leaves fresh basil
½   cup heavy whipping cream, or more to taste
½   stick butter
Salt and pepper to taste

Place tomatoes, juice and tomato paste in a stockpot over medium heat. Simmer for at least 30 minutes. In a food processor, purée the tomato mixture with the basil leaves. Return the purée to the stockpot. (You may use an immersion blender instead of a food processor to purée the tomatoes and basil.) Over medium heat, stir in the cream and butter. Season with salt and pepper. Heat until butter is melted, stirring continuously. Do not boil.

Note: If you can't find good quality fresh tomatoes, you can substitute with 1 (15 ounce) can of crushed tomatoes and 1 teaspoon of lemon juice.

Makes 4 to 6 servings

BARBARA HOLLAND EBY

ONION SOUP

5   cups thinly sliced onion
3-4 tablespoons olive oil
¼   teaspoon black pepper
½   teaspoon salt
¼   teaspoon garlic powder
¼   teaspoon sugar
3   tablespoons all-purpose flour
3   cups boiling water
2   (10.5 ounce) cans beef broth
1   (10.5 ounce) can chicken broth
½   cup dry white wine (optional)
8   slices French bread, toasted
8   slices mozzarella cheese
½   cup freshly grated Parmesan cheese

In a large stockpot, sauté onion in olive oil over medium heat until golden, but not brown. Sprinkle onion with pepper, salt, garlic powder and sugar and stir. Sprinkle flour on onion and stir. Add hot water and both broths. Stir in wine. Cover stockpot and simmer gently for 20 minutes. When soup is almost ready, toast bread. Place toasted bread in 8 ovenproof bowls. Pour soup over bread and top with a slice of mozzarella. Sprinkle with Parmesan. Place in oven on broil about 6 inches from heat. Broil until cheese melts and is lightly browned.

Makes 8 servings

CREAMED ASPARAGUS SOUP

½ cup diced celery
¼ cup diced onion
½ stick margarine
½ cup all-purpose flour
1.5 ounces chicken base (about 2 tablespoons)

2 (14 ounce) cans chicken broth
½ gallon whole milk, heated
1½ pounds asparagus, chopped into ½-inch pieces
¼ teaspoon white pepper

In a stockpot, sauté celery and onion in margarine until onion is translucent. Add flour and chicken base, stirring until well blended. Cook for 5 minutes, stirring frequently. Slowly add chicken broth and stir with a whisk until mixture thickens. Stir in heated milk and bring to a simmer. Do not boil. Reduce heat to low and add asparagus. Cover and simmer for 15 minutes or until asparagus has reached desired tenderness; stir occasionally. Before serving, add white pepper and stir.

Makes 8 to 12 servings

Chicken base is a concentrated, moister version of chicken bouillon and can be found in jars near the chicken bouillon cubes at the grocery store.

CREAM OF BROCCOLI SOUP

¾ cup finely chopped onion
1 stick margarine
8 tablespoons all-purpose flour
1 tablespoon chicken base
¾ teaspoon salt
¼ teaspoon black pepper
¼ teaspoon garlic powder
⅛ teaspoon dry mustard
Pinch of cayenne pepper

4 cups whole milk
2 (14 ounce) cans chicken broth
12 ounces processed or American cheese, cubed
1 pound broccoli florets, steamed and coarsely chopped

Sauté onion in margarine until soft. Whisk in flour, chicken base, salt, pepper, garlic powder, dry mustard and cayenne pepper. Cook over low heat until flour is smooth. Allow flour to cook until lightly browned. Remove from heat and slowly add milk and chicken broth. Mix well. Return to low heat and cook until it is fairly thick. Add cheese, stirring until melted. Add chopped broccoli and let soup cook on low heat for 15 to 30 minutes or until broccoli is tender and flavors blend.

Note: You may use frozen broccoli, coarsely chopped, instead of fresh. Soup may be made a day ahead and reheated over low heat when ready to serve.

Makes 8 to 12 servings

Virginia Kale Soup

½ pound Surry smoked
   sausage, sliced
1 garlic clove, chopped, or
   more to taste
1 (10 ounce) package frozen
   chopped kale (or 1 pound
   fresh kale, chopped)

1 medium onion, coarsely
   chopped
3 medium potatoes (about
   1 pound), cubed
6 cups water or broth
Salt and Tabasco® sauce to taste

In a medium skillet, sauté sliced sausage slowly until it renders fat; add garlic until sausage is browned and garlic is soft; set aside. Cook kale, onion and potatoes in 6 cups water or stock for an hour in a large saucepan or Dutch oven. Add sausage and garlic mixture. Partially mash potatoes to thicken soup and heat together for 10 minutes more. Season with salt and Tabasco® sauce to taste and serve.

Note: This dish is best served the following day. You may also add a can of great Northern beans, if desired.

Makes 4 to 6 servings

MARY SHERWOOD HOLT

*"A great winter supper
with cornbread. Place
Tabasco® bottle on table
and enjoy!"*
Mary Sherwood Holt

Zesty Pumpkin Soup

1 small onion, finely chopped
2 tablespoons butter
1 tablespoon curry powder
1 tablespoon ground coriander

1 (22 ounce) box low sodium
   chicken broth
1 (16 ounce) can pumpkin
Sour cream, chopped chiles

In a 2-quart saucepan over medium heat, sauté onion in butter until translucent and soft. Add curry powder and coriander and stir for 30 seconds. Deglaze the pan by slowly adding the chicken stock and then add the pumpkin. Simmer for 10 minutes. Garnish with sour cream and chopped chiles.

Makes 4 servings

CHIP TIFFANY

BUTTERNUT SQUASH SOUP

3-4 tablespoons unsalted butter

3 large leeks, washed and sliced (white and light green parts only)

2 pounds (about 3 small) butternut squash, peeled, seeded and cubed

4 cups chicken broth

Salt and pepper to taste

Sour cream (optional)

In a large stockpot, melt butter. Add leeks and sauté until translucent. Add squash and broth. Bring to a boil, reduce heat and simmer for 30 to 40 minutes or until squash is tender. Remove from heat and cool slightly. Puree squash mixture in a food processor or blender, leaving some small pieces for texture. Season with salt and pepper to taste. Reheat gently and serve with a dollop of sour cream if desired.

Makes 4 to 6 servings

Blair Swain Sanchez and Bridgette Brown always have a smile on their face!

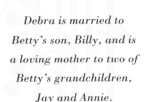

SIMPLE AND DELICIOUS CHICKEN SOUP

1   cup sliced carrots
½   cup chopped onion
⅓   cup sliced celery
6   chicken bouillon cubes
6   cups water
½   pound diced chicken breast, cooked and cubed
1   teaspoon dill weed
¼   teaspoon black pepper
½   cup egg noodles

In a large saucepan over medium heat, combine carrots, onion, celery, chicken bouillon, water, chicken breast, dill weed and pepper. Bring to a boil, stirring occasionally. Add egg noodles and simmer 20 minutes.

Makes 6 servings

DEBRA SWAIN

Debra is married to Betty's son, Billy, and is a loving mother to two of Betty's grandchildren, Jay and Annie.

CHICKEN AND SAUSAGE GUMBO

2   tablespoons all-purpose flour
2   tablespoons butter
1   medium onion, chopped
1   medium green bell pepper, chopped
2   stalks celery, chopped
4   large skinless and boneless chicken breasts, cooked, then diced or shredded
2   cups diced smoked sausage, andouille
2   cups sliced kielbasa
4   cups chicken broth
1   (28 ounce) can diced tomatoes
2   cups diced okra
1   teaspoon thyme
1   teaspoon filé powder
1   teaspoon salt
1   teaspoon black pepper
1   bay leaf
2   cups cooked rice
Hot sauce

In a 5-quart pot, combine flour and butter and cook over medium heat, stirring constantly, until the roux is light brown in color. Add onion, pepper and celery and sauté until translucent. Add cooked chicken and pre-cooked sausage and kielbasa. Add chicken broth, tomatoes and okra. Add thyme, filé powder, salt, pepper and bay leaf, adjusting seasonings to your liking. Simmer for 45 to 50 minutes. Remove bay leaf. Serve over rice. Add hot sauce to taste.

Note: This recipe tastes better each time it is reheated. Seafood may be added for a truly Cajun flavor.

Makes 10 servings

JEAN BECKERDITE

Filé powder is a necessary spice in authentic Cajun cooking. It is the powdered leaves of the sassafras tree and can be found in the spice aisle at your local grocery store.

Hearty White Chili

The Beans

1	pound dried navy beans or dried great Northern beans
8	cups water
1	medium onion, chopped
2	fresh garlic cloves, minced
	Freshly ground black pepper
1	teaspoon salt

The Chili

1	(12 ounce) can beer, not dark
2	cups diced onion
1½	tablespoons minced garlic
1	red bell pepper, diced
2	jalapeño peppers, seeded and finely diced
3	(4.5 ounce) cans green chiles
1	tablespoon dried oregano
1	tablespoon crushed cumin
4	boneless, skinless chicken breasts
1	(14.5 ounce) can chicken broth
½	teaspoon cayenne pepper, or more to taste
1	pound tomatillos, husks removed by soaking
1	cup fresh minced cilantro
1	tablespoon rice vinegar
1	teaspoon salt or more to taste
2	cups shredded sharp white Cheddar cheese

Look over the beans and discard any discolored ones; rinse well. Place beans in a large stockpot. Add the water, onion, garlic and black pepper; bring to a boil. Reduce heat and simmer for 2 to 3 hours or until the beans are tender. Add the salt during the last 30 minutes of cooking.

About half way through cooking the beans, pour the beer into a 4-quart stockpot. Add the onion, garlic, bell pepper, jalapeños, green chiles, oregano and cumin. Simmer for 10 minutes. Cut the chicken into strips; dice and add to the chili along with the chicken broth. Sprinkle the cayenne pepper over the top and simmer for 15 minutes.

Combine tomatillos, cilantro, vinegar and salt in a food processor and process to a salsa consistency. Stir into the chili. Add the drained, cooked beans and simmer for another 20 minutes. Season with salt to taste. Serve with shredded cheese on top of each bowl of chili.

Makes 6 to 8 servings

BARBARA HOLLAND EBY

CREAM OF CRAB SOUP

1½-2	cups finely chopped onion	¼	teaspoon seafood seasoning
2	cups finely chopped celery	1	(14 ounce) can chicken broth
2	cups finely chopped carrots	1	cup water
½	stick butter	1	quart half-and-half
3	tablespoons all-purpose flour	1	quart heavy whipping cream
1	teaspoon salt	1	pound crabmeat
⅛	teaspoon black pepper	2-3	ounces sherry (optional)
Cayenne pepper to taste		Parsley flakes for garnish	

In a 4-quart cooking pan, sauté onion, celery and carrots in butter until tender. Blend in flour, salt, pepper, cayenne and seafood seasoning. Add chicken broth and water and cook over medium-low heat for 15 to 20 minutes. Gradually add half-and-half and whipping cream, stirring constantly until mixture thickens enough to coat spoon. Add crabmeat and heat; do not boil. Add a touch of sherry if desired. Add parsley flakes for garnish.

Note: Soup improves upon standing, allowing flavors to blend. Prepare the day ahead or early in the morning. Reheat over very low heat, stirring often, until soup is hot.

Makes 10 to 12 servings

DONNA WEST

 # CRAB BISQUE

1	stick butter	1	cup whole milk
1	tablespoon all-purpose flour	2	cups half-and-half
½	teaspoon salt	½	cup sherry
¼	teaspoon ground nutmeg	2	cups crabmeat
1	small onion, finely chopped		

Melt butter in large saucepan and add flour, mixing well. Add salt, nutmeg, onion, milk and half-and-half, stirring continuously. Bring to a boil. Reduce heat to simmer and add sherry. Simmer about 20 minutes, stirring occasionally. Just prior to serving, stir in crabmeat.

Makes 4 servings

CLAM CHOWDER

4 pounds potatoes, peeled and diced	4 cups water
1 cup finely chopped celery	1 gallon whole milk, heated
1 medium onion, finely chopped	1 (15 ounce) can clams, undrained
½ stick butter	2 tablespoons lemon juice
¾ cup all-purpose flour	Freshly chopped parsley (optional)
2.5 ounces chicken base (about 3 tablespoons)	¼ teaspoon white pepper

In a large stockpot, cover potatoes with salted water and boil until fork tender. Drain and set aside. In the cleaned stockpot, sauté celery and onion in butter until onion is translucent. Add flour and chicken base, stirring until well blended. Cook about 5 minutes. Slowly add water and stir with a whisk until mixture thickens. Stir in heated milk and bring to a simmer, but do not boil. Reduce heat to low and add potatoes, clams, lemon juice and parsley. Cover and simmer for 10 minutes, stirring occasionally. Before serving, add white pepper and stir.

Makes 25 servings

White pepper has a milder flavor and aroma than black pepper and is used in many light-colored dishes for aesthetic reasons.

CROCKPOT CLAM CHOWDER

1 tablespoon minced onion	2 cans half-and-half
½ cup chopped celery	1 (15 ounce) can clams, undrained
2 tablespoons butter	
2 (10.75 ounce) cans potato soup	

In a skillet, sauté onion and celery in butter until translucent. Pour soup in a Crockpot. Using the soup can, measure out the half-and-half and add to pot. Stir in onion, celery and clams. Heat on low for 4 to 6 hours.

Makes 4 to 6 servings

PAT TUCK

Oyster Bisque

2 cups fresh oysters, undrained
½ stick butter
2 (10 ounce) cans chicken and rice soup
½ cup soft bread, cubed
1 small onion, chopped
2 stalks celery, chopped
1 bay leaf
1 tablespoon chopped fresh parsley or ½ teaspoon dried parsley
2 teaspoons salt
½ teaspoon black pepper
2 cups milk, heated

In a 4-quart saucepan, simmer oysters and butter for 3 minutes. Add soup, bread, onion, celery, bay leaf, parsley, salt and pepper. Simmer 10 minutes; remove bay leaf. Drain through a colander, reserving all liquid. Put drained ingredients in the food processor and chop coarsely. Return all to soup pan. Add heated milk. If bisque is not thick enough, make a roux of 1 tablespoon water and 1 teaspoon flour. Add to soup. Simmer over very low heat, stirring occasionally. Do not boil.

Makes 8 to 10 servings

GRAY BOWDITCH

Oysters are only in season in the months that contain the letter "R". September, October, November, December, January, February, March and April.

Cold Avocado Soup

2 ripe avocados, peeled, seeded and cut into ½-inch cubes
2 tablespoons fresh lemon juice
2 cups chicken broth
1 cup heavy whipping cream
2 tablespoons sliced green onion
2 tablespoons canned, chopped green chiles
1 tablespoon fresh lime juice
1 cucumber, peeled and seeded
1 tablespoon fresh chopped chives for garnish

Combine avocados, lemon juice, chicken broth, cream, green onion, green chiles, lime juice and cucumber. Put into a food processor and blend until smooth. Remove and chill. To serve, pour into chilled bowls and garnish with fresh chives.

Makes 6 servings

CALVIN HEBBONS

COLD STRAWBERRY SOUP

1 pound strawberries, with tops removed
1 pound frozen strawberries in syrup
1 teaspoon pure vanilla extract
1 cup plain yogurt
Strawberry slices for garnish

Combine all strawberries, vanilla extract and yogurt. Put into a food processor and blend until smooth. Remove and chill. To serve, pour into chilled bowls and garnish with a slice of strawberry.

Makes 8 servings

CALVIN HEBBONS

*Calvin Hebbons is a chef at the Tide's Inn resort located in Irvington, Virginia. His daughter, LaTria Hebbons, is a cook at **The Lunch Bell**.*

LAYERED SALAD

SALAD

1 head lettuce, chopped
4 carrots, shredded
6 green onions including tops, shredded
1½ cups frozen green peas, thawed but not cooked
4 hard-boiled eggs, sliced thin (optional)
½ pound bacon, fried crisp and crumbled

DRESSING

3 tablespoons sugar
3 tablespoons vinegar
3 tablespoons milk
3 tablespoons mayonnaise

In a clear bowl, layer ingredients in the following order — lettuce, carrots, green onion, peas, eggs and then bacon. In a separate bowl, mix together sugar, vinegar, milk and mayonnaise to make dressing. Serve dressing separately.

Note: Dressing may be doubled.

Makes 10 servings

SPINACH SALAD

SALAD

2   (6 ounce) bags baby spinach
1   teaspoon fresh dill or
      1 teaspoon dried dill weed

2   teaspoons toasted sesame
      seeds
1   pint of fresh strawberries
      (or 1 cup dried cranberries)

DRESSING

¼   cup red wine vinegar
¼   cup sugar
½   cup vegetable oil
1   teaspoon dry mustard

¼   teaspoon garlic powder
¼   teaspoon onion powder
¼   teaspoon black pepper
¼   teaspoon salt

Wash spinach; dry and place in a large bowl. Sprinkle with dill weed and sesame seeds. Slice strawberries over spinach. Combine all dressing ingredients in a bottle and shake well. Let dressing set for 30 minutes. Just before serving, pour dressing over spinach and strawberries. Toss and serve.

Makes 8 to 10 servings

GRETCHEN QUANT

CRAB SALAD

1   pound lump crabmeat
1   tablespoon capers
2   stalks celery, chopped
¾   cup Duke's® mayonnaise or
      more to moisten

2   teaspoons lemon juice
½   teaspoon salt
½   teaspoon white pepper

Put all ingredients together and mix gently with a fork. Chill for several hours before serving.

Makes 4 servings

POTATO SALAD

5-6 large red potatoes, peeled and diced
2 eggs, boiled and mashed
5-6 celery stalks, chopped
1 medium onion, chopped
1½ cups sweet gherkins pickle, chopped

Pimentos, chopped (optional)
2¼ cups mayonnaise
4 squirts prepared yellow mustard
1 teaspoon sugar

Put potatoes into a stockpot of boiling water and cook for approximately 10 minutes or until potatoes are fork tender. Drain and cool slightly. Place in bowl and add eggs, celery, onion, pickles and pimento; mix well. In a small bowl, mix mayonnaise, mustard and sugar together and then fold into potato mixture.

Makes 6 to 8 servings

PAULA MARIA ORPHANIDYS

"This recipe was given to me by my mother, Edith Lewis Orphanidys, and was handed down from my grandmother, Lillian Hancock Lewis. My grandmother always had it on Thanksgiving and Christmas. It was also a favorite at horseshows when I was a teenager, along with her fried chicken and deviled eggs!"
Paula Maria Orphanidys

THE LUNCH BELL POTATO SALAD

7 pounds all-purpose or chef potatoes, peeled and diced (not baking potatoes)
¼ cup salt
1½ cups finely chopped celery, drained
1½ cups sweet relish, drained

½ cup finely chopped onion
1 cup Duke's® mayonnaise, more if necessary
3 tablespoons prepared yellow mustard, more if necessary
½ cup sugar
1 teaspoon black pepper

In a large stockpot, cover potatoes with salted water and boil until fork tender. Drain and let set until almost cool. In a large bowl, toss celery, relish and onion together; add potatoes. With your hands, gently fold in mayonnaise; add mustard, sugar and pepper. Add more mayonnaise and mustard to your liking.

Makes 6 pounds or 20 to 24 servings

CAJUN POTATO SALAD

When boiling potatoes, place them in cool water, then bring to a boil. Starting with cool water ensures that the potatoes will cook evenly. Potatoes are done when a fork can gently break apart the potato.

8-10 medium size redskin potatoes
½ cup diced white onion
½ cup diced green onion
½ cup diced red bell pepper
½ cup diced green bell pepper
½ cup diced celery
¼ cup spicy brown mustard
1 cup mayonnaise
Salt to taste
¼ teaspoon cayenne pepper
¼ teaspoon red pepper flakes
¼ cup cored and diced jalapeño peppers (optional)

Clean potatoes, but do not remove skins. Cut potatoes into bite-sized chunks and boil for 8 to 10 minutes until fork tender. Drain; refrigerate until cold. Combine potatoes, onion, bell pepper, celery, mustard and mayonnaise in large bowl and mix thoroughly. Salt to taste. Mix in cayenne pepper and red pepper flakes. Taste and adjust heat to your satisfaction. Gently stir in jalapeños if additional heat is desired.

Makes 8 to 10 servings

JIM CARGILE

WILLIAM'S PASTA SALAD

3 cups cooked pasta
¼ cup celery, chopped finely
1 large cucumber, seeded and chopped
¼ cup shredded cheese
¼ cup ham, cut into cubes
1 head broccoli florets, separated
¼ cup olives, sliced ¼-inch thick
6 tablespoons mayonnaise
1 teaspoon lime juice
Dash salt and pepper to taste

Prepare pasta according to package directions; drain and allow to cool. Combine remainder of ingredients in bowl and fold in pasta until completely mixed. Add seasonings to taste.

Note: This recipe can be prepared ahead of time and refrigerated until ready to serve.

Makes 10 to 12 servings

JEAN BECKERDITE

Judy, Kimberly and William Beckerdite enjoy Thanksgiving at **The Lunch Bell**.

THE LUNCH BELL MACARONI SALAD

16 ounces elbow macaroni, uncooked
1 tablespoon salt
1 cup diced celery
1 cup sweet relish
½ cup chopped pimento
4 tablespoons sugar
1 cup Duke's® mayonnaise or more to taste

Cook macaroni in salt water according to package directions or until soft. Let cool. Add celery, relish, pimento and sugar. Stir in mayonnaise, adding more to taste.

Makes 8 to 10 servings

RUBY BINDER

"The Lunch Bell is like Cheers without the beers. Everyone knows your name!"
William Beckerdite

COUNTRY KITCHEN MACARONI SALAD

1 tablespoon salt
3 quarts boiling water
2 cups elbow macaroni, uncooked
½ cup Miracle Whip® Salad Dressing or mayonnaise
1 tablespoon prepared mustard
½ teaspoon black pepper
½ teaspoon horseradish (optional)
½ cup grated carrot
½ cup chopped cucumber
¼ cup chopped green bell pepper (or celery)
1 (16 ounce) package frozen peas, thawed

Add 1 tablespoon salt to rapidly boiling water. Gradually add macaroni so that the water continues to boil. Cook uncovered, stirring occasionally, until tender. Drain; rinse with cold water and drain again. In a large bowl, combine salad dressing (or mayonnaise), mustard, pepper and horseradish. Mix thoroughly. Add carrots, cucumber, green pepper and peas to dressing mixture. Mix thoroughly. Add macaroni to vegetable and dressing mixture and toss lightly but thoroughly. Chill well. Garnish with parsley or bell pepper rings and paprika.

Note: If you don't like peas, substitute cooked and cooled Edamame beans.

Makes 4 to 6 servings

CEPHISE OVERBY

"I've had this recipe for at least 35 years and have taken it to an untold number of pot luck suppers and church sales, as well as serving it to my family."
Cephise Overby

*The amounts of mayonnaise for many of **The Lunch Bell** salads are not exact. Please adjust to your liking.*

THE LUNCH BELL EGG SALAD

12   hard-boiled eggs
2   tablespoons Duke's®
     mayonnaise, with more to
     thin

Salt to taste

Grate the hard-boiled eggs. Mix with mayonnaise and salt to taste. Add more mayonnaise if desired.

Makes 6 servings

THE LUNCH BELL PIMENTO CHEESE SPREAD

2½   pounds sharp Cheddar
     cheese, shredded
¼   cup chopped pimento

¾   cup sugar, with more to taste
1   cup Duke's® mayonnaise,
     with more if needed

In a medium bowl, mix together cheese and pimento. Add sugar and mix well. Slowly add mayonnaise until you get your desired consistency. Let set for at least 24 hours to allow the flavors to blend. You may need to add more mayonnaise prior to serving.

Makes about 4 cups

PIMENTO CHEESE

8   ounces cream cheese
1   (4 ounce) jar diced pimento,
     drained
1   (5 ounce) jar pimento cheese
     spread
½   cup mayonnaise
¼   teaspoon garlic powder

¼   teaspoon ground chipotle
     chili pepper
¼   teaspoon salt
Dash ground black pepper
3   cups shredded sharp
     Cheddar cheese

In a medium bowl, microwave cream cheese for 1 minute or until melted and smooth. Stir in rest of ingredients. Serve immediately or chill and serve later.

Note: May store in an airtight container in the refrigerator for up to 4 days. Serve on crackers, bread, celery sticks, etc.

Makes about 4 cups

LINDA CARSON

TEAROOM PIQUANT CHEESE

1 (10 ounce) package
shredded extra sharp
Cheddar cheese
1 small onion, finely chopped

1 small green bell pepper,
finely chopped
Dash of cayenne pepper
2-3 dashes Worcestershire sauce
Ketchup

In a medium bowl, mix together cheese, onion and green pepper. Add cayenne pepper, Worcestershire sauce and enough ketchup to make it spreadable, but not soupy.

Makes about 2½ cups

SYLVIA WEINSTEIN

This cheese spread was served at the old Tearoom in the Smith & Welton department store in Norfolk, Virginia.

THE LUNCH BELL
CREAM CHEESE AND OLIVE SPREAD

16 ounces cream cheese,
softened
4 tablespoons Duke's®
mayonnaise, with more to
taste

1 cup chopped pimento-
stuffed green olives

With an electric mixer, mix together cream cheese and mayonnaise until fluffy. Stir olives into cream cheese mixture.

Makes 8 to 10 servings

THE LUNCH BELL COLE SLAW

1 medium head cabbage
1 large carrot

Marzetti's® cole slaw dressing

In a food processor, finely chop (do not pulverize) cabbage and carrot. Place in separate bowl, add Marzetti's® cole slaw dressing to taste.

Makes 8 to 10 servings

Broccoli Salad

1	cup mayonnaise	1	cup raisins
¼	cup sugar	1	cup chopped pecans
1	tablespoon red wine vinegar	¼	cup bacon bits
4	cups fresh broccoli florets		

In a medium bowl, whisk together mayonnaise, sugar and vinegar until thoroughly mixed. Stir in broccoli, raisins, pecans and bacon bits.

Makes 8 servings

MARGARET SWAIN

Four Bean Salad

¾	cup sugar	1	(14.5 ounce) can green beans, drained
⅔	cup vinegar	1	(14.5 ounce) can yellow wax beans, drained
⅓	cup vegetable oil		
1	teaspoon salt	1	(15 ounce) can green lima beans, drained
1	teaspoon freshly ground black pepper		
		1	(15 ounce) can red kidney beans, drained and rinsed
½	cup chopped green bell pepper		
½	cup chopped onion	1	(4 ounce) jar chopped pimento

Combine sugar, vinegar, oil, salt and pepper in a large bowl. Add bell pepper, onion, drained beans and pimento; stir well. Cover. Marinate in refrigerator for at least 24 hours, stirring occasionally.

Makes 8 to 12 servings

BENITA EDWARDS

Strawberry Cream Gelatin

Mayonnaise		1	cup crushed pineapple, partially drained
1	(6 ounce) package strawberry gelatin		
		10	ounces frozen strawberries, thawed
1½	cups hot water		
		1	cup sour cream

Grease a 6-cup mold lightly with mayonnaise. Dissolve gelatin in hot water. Add pineapple and strawberries. Fill mold with half of gelatin mixture. Chill until firm. Spread sour cream over gelatin. Add remaining gelatin mixture to mold; chill.

Makes 8 servings

Blueberry Salad

1 (20 ounce) can crushed
   pineapple
1 (15 ounce) can blueberries
   (not pie filling)
About 1 cup water
1 (5.1 ounce) box wild cherry
   gelatin

8 ounces cream cheese,
   softened
1 cup sour cream
1 cup sugar
1 cup chopped pecans

Drain juices from pineapple and blueberries and add water to make 1½ cups liquid. Bring liquid to a boil and add gelatin to dissolve. Remove from heat and add fruit. Pour into an 8x12-inch baking dish and chill until firm.

Mix together cream cheese, sour cream, sugar and pecans. Put on top of firm gelatin mixture and refrigerate overnight.

Note: This salad can be prepared a couple of days ahead of time.

Makes 12 servings

MYRNA ALDERFER

 # Glazed Fruit

1½ cups pineapple juice, or
   more if desired
1 (5.1 ounce) box of
   unsweetened instant vanilla
   pudding
2 (20 ounce) cans pineapple
   chunks, drained
2 (29 ounce) cans chunky
   tropical fruit salad, drained

2 (11 ounce) can Mandarin
   oranges, drained
3 medium bananas, sliced into
   ½-inch rounds
1 pint fresh strawberries, tops
   removed and cut in half

Mix together pineapple juice and vanilla pudding; set aside. In a large bowl combine pineapple, fruit salad and Mandarin oranges. Stir in glaze until well coated; add more pineapple juice if desired. When ready to serve, fold in bananas and strawberries. Garnish with fresh strawberries.

Makes 10 to 12 servings

GRANNY'S GREEN PINEAPPLE SALAD

This was Billy Swains's favorite salad for holidays and he would always ask his granny to make "that green salad." Billy is Betty's oldest child.

1   (20 ounce) can crushed pineapple
About 2 cups of water
1   (3 ounce) box lemon gelatin
1   (3 ounce) box lime gelatin

1   cup mayonnaise
1   cup cottage cheese
1   cup pecans
Dash of salt

Drain pineapple, reserving liquid, and put pineapple aside. Measure pineapple juice and add water to make 2½ cups of liquid. Heat juice and water to boiling point; add lemon and lime gelatins and stir until gelatin has dissolved. Place gelatin in decorative bowl and put in refrigerator. In a separate bowl, mix together pineapple, mayonnaise, cottage cheese, pecans and salt. When gelatin is partially set, fold in pineapple mixture. Chill.

Makes 12 servings
SHELAH HARRIS

CHERRY SALAD SUPREME

1   (3 ounce) package cherry gelatin
2   cups boiling water, divided
1   (21 ounce) can cherry pie filling
1   (3 ounce) package lemon gelatin
3   ounces cream cheese, softened

⅓   cup mayonnaise
1   (8 ounce) can crushed pineapple, undrained
1   (2.6 ounce) package Dream Whip® whipped topping mix
1   cup miniature marshmallows
2   tablespoons chopped nuts

Dissolve cherry gelatin in 1 cup boiling water; stir in cherry pie filling. Turn into 9x9x2-inch baking dish and chill until partially set. Dissolve lemon gelatin in 1 cup boiling water; chill until just beginning to gel. Beat together cream cheese and mayonnaise. Add to partially gelled lemon gelatin. Stir in undrained pineapple. Make Dream Whip® according to package directions; fold into lemon mixture. Add marshmallows. Spread lemon mixture on top of cherry mixture. Sprinkle with nuts. Chill until set.

Makes 8 to 10 servings

Frozen Fruit Salad — "The Pink Stuff"

1 (21 ounce) can cherry pie filling

1 (20 ounce) can crushed pineapple, undrained

1 (14 ounce) can sweetened condensed milk

1 (16 ounce) container frozen whipped topping, thawed

Mix together cherries, pineapple and condensed milk. Fold in whipped topping. Pour into muffin tins or a glass baking dish. Freeze until solid.

Note: Fruit salad can also be served without freezing and is just as good.

Makes 12 servings

Growing up, Betty and her family used to "analyze" the food during every meal! They would discuss what was good and what could be changed about the dishes.

Gelatin Salad

2 (3 ounce) packages lemon or mixed fruit gelatin

1 cup boiling water

8 ounces cream cheese, softened

1 (8 ounce) can crushed pineapple, undrained

1 cup whole milk

1 cup chopped black walnuts

Dissolve gelatin in boiling water. With an electric mixer, mix cream cheese until soft, gradually adding pineapple and milk. Add gelatin and mix until well blended. Fold in nuts. Pour into a small gelatin mold or an 8x8-inch baking dish. Chill before serving.

Makes 6 to 8 servings

SYLVIA BLAIR

Cherry Coke Salad

1 (20 ounce) can crushed pineapple

½ cup water

2 (3 ounce) packages cherry gelatin

1 (21 ounce) can cherry pie filling

¾ cup coca cola

Drain pineapple, reserving juice; set aside pineapple. In a saucepan or microwave, bring pineapple juice and water to boil. Add gelatin; stir until dissolved. Stir in pie filling and coke. Pour into serving bowl. Refrigerate until slightly thickened. Fold in reserved pineapple. Refrigerate until firm.

Makes 10 to 12 servings

ROSEMARY MURPHY

Orange Thanksgiving Salad

This salad is served at
The Lunch Bell's
Thanksgiving dinner,
but it is good any time
of the year.

1   (11 ounce) can Mandarin oranges
1   cup drained crushed pineapple, reserving juice
1   (3 ounce) box orange gelatin
1   (3 ounce) box lemon gelatin
1   pint orange sherbet

Drain juices from oranges and pineapple and add water to make 1½ cups liquid. Boil and add to gelatins to dissolve. Stir in orange sherbet. Pour into 6 cup mold. Chill until partially set and fold in fruit. Chill until firm.

Makes 8 to 10 servings

White Holiday Salad

3   ounces cream cheese
1   (3 ounce) box lemon gelatin
10 large marshmallows or 1 cup small marshmallows
2   cups boiling water
8   ounces heavy whipping cream
1   cup drained crushed pineapple
6   decorative lettuce leaves
¼   cup red maraschino cherries for garnish
¼   cup green maraschino cherries for garnish

Put cream cheese, gelatin and marshmallows in a large bowl; pour boiling water over top. Beat with an electric mixer until smooth. Chill until partially set. Beat whipping cream until it is light and fluffy. Remove gelatin mixture from refrigerator and beat again until smooth. Fold in whipped cream. Stir drained pineapple into gelatin mixture. Pour salad into a 1½-quart salad mold or 6 to 8 individual molds or a decorative glass bowl. Chill until firm. Unmold on a bed of lettuce and garnish with red and green maraschino cherries.

Note: This salad may be made a day or two ahead.

Makes 6 to 8 servings

PRETZEL SALAD

2	cups boiling water	2	cups crushed pretzels
1	(6 ounce) box strawberry gelatin	1½	sticks butter, melted
		3	tablespoons sugar
20	ounces frozen strawberries	8	ounces cream cheese
15	ounces crushed pineapple, drained	8	ounces frozen whipped topping, thawed

Place boiling water in a glass bowl. Pour in gelatin and mix until completely dissolved. Add frozen strawberries, stirring to loosen chunks. Add drained pineapple. Place in refrigerator until firm. Mix together pretzels, butter and sugar. Place pretzel mixture in 9x13-inch glass baking dish and pat down. Bake at 400 degrees for 7 minutes. Cool completely. With an electric hand mixer, beat together sugar and cream cheese. Fold in whipped topping. Spread onto pretzel crust. Using a fork, scoop gelatin mixture over the whipped topping.

Note: This salad is worth the work!

Makes 6 servings

DEBRA SWAIN

THE LUNCH BELL TUNA SALAD

Canned or bag light tuna, packed in water, drained
Finely shredded celery

Duke's® mayonnaise
Black pepper

In a bowl, stir together tuna and celery. Add mayonnaise and black pepper to taste.

THE LUNCH BELL LOBSTER SALAD

2	pounds lobster meat, coarsely chopped	1	cup Duke's® mayonnaise
1	cup finely chopped celery	½	teaspoon salt
1	teaspoon finely minced onion	¼	teaspoon black pepper

Mix together lobster, celery, onion, mayonnaise, salt and pepper in a medium bowl. Chill for at least 30 minutes.

Makes 6 servings

> *"A good memory of **The Lunch Bell** was in September of 2003 when Hurricane Isabel hit the area and many were without power for several days. Betty and Bill were one of the only restaurants open and they provided delicious food for the utility workers."*
> **Margie Stallings**

THE LUNCH BELL CHICKEN SALAD

Canned cooked chicken, drained
Finely shredded celery

Duke's® mayonnaise
Salt

In a bowl, stir together chicken and celery. Add mayonnaise and salt to taste.

*Note: **The Lunch Bell** chops their celery in a food processor.*

Only the ingredients are listed for the chicken and tuna salad recipes, since they are typically made in large batches. Add mayonnaise and celery to taste.

TARRAGON CHICKEN SALAD

¾ cup mayonnaise
1 tablespoon chopped fresh tarragon (or 1½ teaspoons dried crushed tarragon)
1 teaspoon grated lemon rind
1 tablespoon fresh lemon juice
1 teaspoon salt
½ teaspoon freshly ground pepper

3 cups chopped, cooked chicken
2 celery stalks, finely chopped
½ small sweet onion, finely chopped
½ cup chopped almonds
2 cups seedless red grapes, cut in half (optional)

Whisk together mayonnaise, tarragon, lemon rind, lemon juice, salt and pepper. Gently stir in chicken, celery, onion and almonds and mix until just blended. Stir in grape halves, if desired. Cover and refrigerate until time to serve.

Makes 4 to 6 servings

CHICKEN SALAD WITH DRIED CRANBERRIES

1 cup mayonnaise
2½ tablespoons whole grain mustard
1 tablespoon chicken broth
⅛ teaspoon each of the following dried herbs and seasonings: white pepper, thyme, oregano, sage, rosemary, marjoram and basil

Pinch ground nutmeg
2 teaspoons chopped fresh dill
5 chicken breasts, cooked and chopped
3 stalks celery, finely chopped
⅓ cup finely chopped onion
⅓ cup chopped pecans
⅓ cup dried cranberries

Combine mayonnaise, mustard, chicken broth, herbs and seasonings, including the nutmeg and dill. Mix in the chicken, celery, onion, pecans and cranberries. Cover and refrigerate until time to serve.

Makes 6 to 8 servings

Fruity Chicken Salad

4 chicken breasts, cooked and diced
2 apples, diced
½ box white raisins
16 ounces crushed pineapple, drain off half of juice
1½ cups chopped celery
¾ cup walnuts
⅓ cup honey
Mayonnaise

In a large bowl, mix together chicken, apples, raisins, pineapple, celery, walnuts and honey. Add just enough mayonnaise for the mixture to hold together. Refrigerate overnight before serving.

Note: Serve on croissants with lettuce.

Makes 8 to 10 servings

DEBRA SWAIN

"These sandwiches look beautiful and taste great!"
Debra Swain

Debra Swain is married to Betty's son, Billy.

Chicken Waldorf Salad

¼ teaspoon unflavored gelatin
2 tablespoons cold water
3 tablespoons white wine vinegar
2½ tablespoons unsweetened apple juice
2 teaspoons vegetable oil
½ teaspoon sugar
¼ teaspoon salt
¼ teaspoon dry mustard
Dash of black pepper
2 cups skinned, cooked chicken breast, shredded
1½ cups cubed, unpeeled Red Delicious apples
½ cup sliced celery
½ cup halved seedless red grapes
3 tablespoons raisins
2 tablespoons chopped walnuts
4 cups torn romaine lettuce

In a small saucepan, sprinkle gelatin over cold water. Let stand for 1 minute. Cook over low heat, stirring until gelatin dissolves. Pour gelatin mixture into a jar and add vinegar, apple juice, oil, sugar, salt, dry mustard and pepper. Cover and shake vigorously. In a bowl, combine chicken, apples, celery, grapes, raisins and walnuts and stir gently. Add gelatin mixture and toss gently. Arrange 1 cup of lettuce on each of 4 salad plates; top with 1½ cups of chicken mixture.

Makes 4 servings

Grace's Walnut Chicken Salad

1	(3½ to 4 pound) whole chicken	½	cup coarsely chopped walnuts
1	gallon water	½	cup diced celery
1	tablespoon salt	1	teaspoon tarragon
1½	cups mayonnaise	2	teaspoons celery salt

Boil chicken in water and salt until thoroughly cooked, approximately 45 minutes. The internal temperature of the chicken should be at least 165 degrees. While warm, pull chicken meat off the bones and cut large pieces into ½-inch cubes; set aside. Combine mayonnaise, walnuts, celery, tarragon and celery salt. Toss chicken with mayonnaise mixture. Cover and refrigerate until time to serve.

Note: This salad is good when served with fresh pineapple or fruit salad.

Makes 8 servings

CALVIN HEBBONS

Peanut Butter Dressing

¼	cup creamy peanut butter	5	tablespoons white vinegar
1	teaspoon salt	2	teaspoons soy sauce
5	teaspoons sherry	1	teaspoon sesame oil
5	tablespoons sugar		

Mix all ingredients well. Add more vinegar or sugar to taste.

Note: Serve with a fresh salad.

Makes about ½ cup

Homemade Mustard

1	cup dry mustard	1	tablespoon salt
1	cup vinegar	2	eggs, beaten
1	cup white sugar		

Combine dry mustard and vinegar and place in a double boiler; let set overnight. Add sugar, salt and eggs to mustard mixture. Heat in double boiler until thickened. Store in jars in the refrigerator.

Makes about 2 to 3 small jars

BETTY LASSEN

THE LUNCH BELL
FAVORITE FRUIT SALAD DRESSING

1   cup Duke's® mayonnaise   ½   cup pineapple juice

Mix together mayonnaise and pineapple juice with a wire whisk. Serve over your favorite fruit.

Makes 1½ cups

*At **The Lunch Bell**, this dressing is served over a sliced pineapple and half a peach on a bed of lettuce. A little Cheddar cheese is sprinkled over the dressing and it's topped with a maraschino cherry!*

HOMEMADE FRENCH DRESSING

⅔   cup sugar   1   teaspoon paprika
⅔   cup vinegar   1   teaspoon black pepper
⅔   cup ketchup   1   teaspoon salt
1   cup vegetable oil   1   small onion, finely minced

Combine all ingredients in blender and mix well.

Makes about 3 cups

PARMESAN PEPPER DRESSING

1½   cups oil   1   teaspoon prepared yellow
½   cup white wine vinegar   mustard
Juice of 1½ lemons   ¼   cup freshly grated Parmesan
½   teaspoon Worcestershire   cheese
     sauce   Salt and freshly ground black
3   tablespoons chili sauce   pepper to taste

Combine oil, vinegar, lemon juice, Worcestershire sauce, chili sauce, mustard, Parmesan cheese, salt and pepper in an electric blender or food processor. Blend well. Cover and chill at least 1 hour before serving.

Makes about 2½ cups

ROQUEFORT DRESSING

2 cups olive oil	1 teaspoon grated onion
1 cup vinegar	⅛ teaspoon cayenne pepper
Juice of 1 lemon	1 teaspoon salt
2 teaspoons paprika	8 ounces Roquefort cheese,
Dash of Worcestershire sauce	mashed

Place oil and vinegar in a quart jar. Add lemon juice, paprika, Worcestershire sauce, onion, cayenne pepper, salt and Roquefort cheese. Mix well. Refrigerate indefinitely. Shake well before serving.

Note: Flavor improves over time. Bleu cheese may be substituted for the Roquefort.

Makes 4 cups

This picture has been in the Swain family living room since 1917. The poem, written by
James Whitcomb Riley, was one of Bill's mother's experiences after she met her future husband.

VEGETABLES AND SIDE DISHES

VEGETABLES AND SIDE DISHES

**FEATURED RECIPES
ON FRONT:**

*The Lunch Bell
Pot Roast, page 155*

*The Lunch Bell
Green Beans, page 113*

*The Lunch Bell
Mashed Potatoes,
page 126*

*The Lunch Bell
Cabbage, page 113*

ITALIAN GREEN BEANS

1½ pounds fresh green beans	2 small tomatoes, chopped
1 cup water	¼ teaspoon dried oregano, divided
1 tablespoon bacon drippings	¼ teaspoon dried basil, divided
¼ teaspoon salt	¼ teaspoon dried rosemary, divided
¼ teaspoon black pepper	2 tablespoons freshly grated Parmesan cheese
1 medium onion, diced	
1 garlic clove, crushed	
2 tablespoons olive oil	

Wash beans. Trim ends and remove strings. Cut into 1½-inch pieces. In a large saucepan, combine beans, water, bacon drippings, salt and pepper. Bring to a boil. Cover, reduce heat and simmer for 25 to 30 minutes. Drain and set aside. In a medium skillet, sauté onion and garlic in olive oil until onion is translucent.

Preheat oven to 350 degrees. In a lightly greased 1½-quart baking dish, layer half each of beans, onion mixture and chopped tomatoes. Sprinkle with ⅛ teaspoon of oregano, basil and rosemary. Layer with remaining beans, onion and chopped tomatoes; sprinkle with remaining herbs. Top with Parmesan cheese. Cover and bake for 15 minutes.

Makes 4 to 6 servings

GREEN BEAN TOMATO SPECIAL

1 (16 ounce) can stewed tomatoes	1 teaspoon salt
1 (16 ounce) can cut green beans, drained	Dash of cayenne pepper
2 tablespoons mayonnaise	Dash of black pepper
1 teaspoon Worcestershire sauce	½ cup crushed potato chips or 1 cup seasoned croutons

Preheat oven to 350 degrees. Combine tomatoes, beans, mayonnaise, Worcestershire sauce, salt, cayenne pepper and black pepper in a 2-quart baking dish. Sprinkle crushed potato chips on top. Bake uncovered for 30 minutes.

Makes 4 to 6 servings

GREEK STYLE GREEN BEANS

½	cup olive oil	¼	teaspoon oregano
1	medium onion, finely diced	¼	teaspoon thyme
1	garlic clove, finely minced	2	cups chicken broth
1½	cups diced tomatoes	1½-2	pounds green beans, fresh
⅓	cup chopped fresh parsley		or frozen
¼	teaspoon cumin		

Heat oil in saucepan; sauté onion and garlic until translucent. Add tomatoes, parsley, cumin, oregano and thyme and cook approximately 5 minutes, stirring occasionally to avoid sticking. Add chicken broth and green beans; reduce heat to simmer. Cook until beans are tender and sauce thickens, approximately 45 minutes to 1 hour. If using frozen green beans, thicken sauce before adding green beans. Garnish with fresh parsley and serve.

Makes 6 to 8 servings

WILLIAM BECKERDITE

"Our daughter loves to attend the Greek Festival in Newport News and her favorite vegetable is green beans. This recipe represents our family's version to an old Greek favorite."
William Beckerdite

FANCY GREEN BEANS

2	tablespoons teriyaki sauce	2	slices bacon
1	tablespoon honey	½	cup red bell pepper strips
1	tablespoon butter	½	cup onion wedges
1	tablespoon lemon juice	½	cup whole cashews
1½	pounds fresh green beans		

In a small bowl, stir together teriyaki sauce, honey and butter. Fill a bowl with cold water and ice cubes; set aside. Bring a large pot of water to a boil and add the lemon juice. Drop in the beans and cook for 4 to 5 minutes, or until beans are bright green. Drain the beans in a colander and then plunge them into the iced water. Drain again and set aside.

In a skillet, cook the bacon until crisp; crumble and set aside. Sauté the bell pepper and onion in the hot bacon fat for 2 minutes. Add the beans, bacon and cashews to the skillet. Add the teriyaki-honey sauce and toss gently.

Makes 6 to 8 servings

BARBARA HOLLAND EBY

THE LUNCH BELL GREEN BEANS

1 (38 ounce) can Hanover®
green beans, drained and
rinsed

1½ cups water
1 (32 ounce) can chicken broth
1 stick butter

In a large saucepan, combine green beans and water. Bring to a boil, reduce heat and simmer for 15 minutes. Drain. Add chicken broth and bring to a rapid boil; reduce heat and simmer for 20 minutes. Add butter and simmer another 10 minutes.

Makes 6 to 8 servings

RANCH BEANS

1 pound ground beef
1 medium onion, diced
1 package onion soup mix
1 cup water
1 cup ketchup
1 teaspoon vinegar

1 tablespoon mustard
½ cup firmly packed brown
sugar
3 (1 pound) cans pork and
beans
1 (15 ounce) can kidney beans

Preheat oven to 350 degrees. In a large skillet, cook ground beef and onion until beef is browned. Drain fat. Add onion soup mix. Add water, ketchup, vinegar and mustard and mix well. Add brown sugar and beans and mix together. Pour into a medium baking dish and bake for 30 minutes to 1 hour.

Makes 8 to 10 servings

JANET BLEAKLEY

THE LUNCH BELL CABBAGE

1 medium head cabbage,
coarsely chopped
3 cups salted water
1 carrot, peeled and shredded

2 cups chicken broth
1 teaspoon salt
¼ teaspoon black pepper
1 stick butter

In a medium stockpot, place cabbage in salted water and bring to a boil. Cook 10 to 15 minutes; drain. Put cabbage back in pot and add carrot, chicken broth, salt, pepper and butter and bring to a boil over medium-high heat. Cover; turn off heat. Let set at least 1 hour before serving.

Makes 6 to 8 servings

PINTO BEAN CASSEROLE

2   (15.5 ounce) cans pinto
    beans, rinsed and drained
1   (15.25 ounce) can whole
    kernel yellow corn, drained
1   (8 ounce) can tomato sauce

1   (14.5 ounce) can diced
    tomatoes
1   (1.25 ounce) package taco
    seasoning
Tortilla chips
Shredded Cheddar cheese

Preheat oven to 350 degrees. Mix pinto beans, corn, tomato sauce, tomatoes and taco seasoning. Crumble enough tortilla chips to cover the bottom of a 9x13-inch pan. Pour mixture over chips and sprinkle cheese on top. Bake for 25 minutes or until hot.

Makes 6 to 8 servings

VIANA DIAL

MILDRED MATTHEW'S CORN PUDDING

3   eggs, beaten
1   cup milk
½   cup sugar
2   tablespoons all-purpose flour

1   (14.75 ounce) can cream
    style corn
¼   teaspoon salt
½   stick butter, melted

Preheat oven to 375 degrees. Mix together all ingredients with a fork being sure to break up any clumps of flour. Pour into medium baking dish. Bake for 35 to 45 minutes.

Makes 6 servings

NANCY MILLER BOUTEILLER

CORN, LIMAS AND TOMATOES

1   medium onion, chopped
1   green pepper, chopped
Oil
1   (16 ounce) can whole kernel
     white corn, drained
1   (17 ounce) can lima beans,
     drained
1   (8 ounce) can tomato sauce

1   (16 ounce) can stewed
     tomatoes
1   tablespoon Worcestershire
     sauce
Salt and pepper
Seasoned salt to taste
4   slices bacon

Preheat oven to 350 degrees. In a skillet, sauté onion and green pepper in oil until onion is translucent. Combine the corn, lima beans, tomato sauce, tomatoes, Worcestershire sauce, salt, pepper and seasoned salt in a large bowl. Add onion and green pepper. Pour into an 8x8-inch baking dish. Lay bacon slices across top. Bake covered for 1 hour. Uncover for last 10 minutes to crisp bacon.

Makes 8 servings

To make this dish with fresh vegetables, cover the bottom of the baking dish with bacon slices. Place a layer of fresh lima beans, sliced, peeled fresh tomatoes, chopped onion, chopped green pepper, fresh white corn cut off cob and then a second layer of tomatoes; cover with more bacon slices. Salt and pepper liberally between the layers. Cover and bake for 1 hour or until lima beans are tender.

 # THE LUNCH BELL COLLARD GREENS

3   pounds fresh collard greens,
     washed
4   cups salted water, or more if
     necessary

4   cups chicken broth
1   stick butter
Salt and pepper to taste

With a knife, strip stalk from collard greens. Place collard greens in a medium stockpot with salted water. Bring to a boil; reduce heat and simmer 15 minutes. Drain. Put collards back in pot and add chicken broth, bring to a gentle boil; simmer for 20 minutes or until tender. Stir in butter until melted. Check seasoning and add salt and pepper if desired. Place collards into serving bowl and cut into bite-sized pieces.

Makes 6 to 8 servings

CABBAGE CASSEROLE

1	medium head cabbage, cut into small wedges	½	cup green bell pepper, chopped
½	stick butter	½	cup red bell pepper, chopped
¼	cup all-purpose flour	2	teaspoons red pepper relish
2	cups milk	4	tablespoons grated onion
	Salt to taste	1	cup shredded sharp Cheddar cheese
½	teaspoon black pepper		

Preheat oven to 350 degrees. Bring a large pot of salted water to a boil. Cook cabbage in boiling water until barely tender, about 8 minutes; drain. Meanwhile, melt butter in a small saucepan over low heat. Blend in flour, milk, salt and pepper. Cook and stir until slightly thickened. Layer cabbage in a greased 8x8-inch baking dish. Pour half of the cream sauce over the cabbage and bake for 15 minutes. While cabbage is cooking, combine green pepper, red pepper, relish and onion. Spread over cooked cabbage and top with cheese; pour the remaining cream sauce on top. Return to oven for 20 minutes.

Makes 6 servings

JO ANN JONES

 # THE LUNCH BELL CORN PUDDING

2	(16 ounce) bags frozen corn, thawed	1	teaspoon salt
5	eggs yolks, beaten	¼	teaspoon white pepper
1¼	cups whole milk	2	tablespoons butter, melted
3	tablespoons sugar	5	egg whites

Preheat oven to 325 degrees. In a large bowl, combine corn, egg yolks, milk, sugar, salt and pepper. Slowly add butter, stirring constantly. Beat egg whites until stiff; fold into corn mixture. Pour into medium baking dish. Put baking dish in a large roasting pan. Add enough hot water to roasting pan to reach halfway up side of baking dish. Bake for 30 to 45 minutes or until set.

Makes 10 to 12 servings

BAKED CORN PUDDING

2	tablespoons cornstarch	1	(16 ounce) can cream style
1	(12 ounce) can evaporated		corn
	milk	½	cup sugar
4	eggs, beaten	2	tablespoons butter

Preheat oven to 350 degrees. In a medium bowl, mix together cornstarch with a little of the evaporated milk until smooth. Add eggs, corn, sugar and rest of milk. Pour into a medium baking dish. Top with bits of butter. Bake for 35 to 40 minutes.

Makes 6 servings

RUTH BREEGER

"This corn pudding recipe is from Tangier Island in the Chesapeake Bay. It is from a lifelong friend whose father was born on Tangier Island."
Ruth Breeger

BAKED CORN

1	(15 ounce) can whole kernel	1	cup sour cream
	corn	1	(8.5 ounce) box corn muffin
1	(15 ounce) can cream style		mix
	corn	1	stick butter, melted

Preheat oven to 350 degrees. Drain ¼ cup water from whole kernel corn. In a small bowl, mix together corns, sour cream and muffin mix. Pour melted butter into a 2-quart baking dish. Add corn mixture and mix well. Bake for 1 hour or until set.

Makes 4 to 6 servings

DEBRA SWAIN

Romans 8:28, is Debra's favorite scripture verse. "And we know that all things work together for good to them that love God, to them who are the called according to his purpose."

CARROTS AND SNOW PEAS

1½	cups baby carrots	1	tablespoon butter
Water		½	teaspoon dried dill weed
1½	cups fresh snow peas		

In a small saucepan, cover carrots with water. Once carrots are fork tender, add snow peas. Bring to a boil and boil uncovered 2 to 3 minutes. Drain; return to saucepan. Add butter and stir until melted. Add dill weed.

Makes 4 servings

DEBRA SWAIN

ASPARAGUS CASSEROLE

1	cup crushed Ritz® crackers	1½	sticks butter, cut into thin slices
2	(14.5 ounce) cans cut green asparagus, drained	1	cup blanched almonds, toasted and finely ground
1	cup shredded sharp Cheddar cheese	1	cup milk

Line an 8x8-inch baking dish with a few cracker crumbs. Alternate layers of asparagus, cheese, cracker crumbs, butter and almonds. Pour the milk in one side of the dish. Let set in the refrigerator overnight or for at least 2 hours. When ready to bake, preheat oven to 350 degrees and bake for 1 hour.

Makes 6 servings

ASPARAGUS BUNDLES WITH HOLLANDAISE

6	thin slices Swiss cheese	1	stick plus 1 tablespoon butter, melted, divided
6	slices cooked ham	3	egg yolks
1	(10 ounce) can asparagus spears, drained	2	tablespoons lemon juice
½	(17.5 ounce) package frozen puff pastry, thawed		

Preheat oven to 425 degrees. Place 1 slice Swiss cheese over each slice of cooked ham. Top cheese slices with drained asparagus spears. Roll each bundle up, trimming asparagus if necessary. Cut puff pastry into 6 equal triangles. Brush pastry lightly with 1 tablespoon melted butter. Wrap each pastry around cheese, ham and asparagus bundles, sealing at the seam. Place bundles, seam side down, inn a shallow lightly greased baking dish. Make sure bundles do not touch each other or the sides of the pan. Brush tops of pastry with some of the melted butter. Bake for 18 to 20 minutes or until golden brown.

For Hollandaise sauce, combine egg yolks and lemon juice in a blender. Puree for 30 seconds. Slowly pour in 1 stick hot melted butter while blending. Blend until sauce thickens slightly. Place asparagus bundles on serving plate and drizzle with Hollandaise sauce.

Makes 6 servings

Yellow Squasherole

Casserole

2 pounds yellow squash, sliced
1 small onion, chopped
Salted water
½ cup mayonnaise
2 eggs, beaten

1 cup shredded Cheddar or Velveeta cheese
½ stick butter, melted
1 tablespoon sugar
2 tablespoons all-purpose flour

Topping

¾ sleeve of Town House® or Ritz® crackers, crushed

½ cup chopped walnuts
½ stick butter, melted

Preheat oven to 350 degrees. Place sliced squash and onion in a medium saucepan and cover with lightly salted water. Bring to a boil; reduce heat and simmer for 5 to 10 minutes or until squash is tender. Drain and set aside. Combine mayonnaise, eggs, cheese, butter, sugar and flour and mix well. Add mixture to squash and onion and stir well. Spoon into a medium, greased baking dish. Toss crackers with nuts and butter; sprinkle over squash. Bake for 35 to 45 minutes or until lightly browned.

Makes 4 to 6 servings

CAROLYN WHITTEN

"The Lunch Bell is an icon for quality food prepared to perfection with eye appeal. It is also served in a family friendly atmosphere."
Carolyn Whitten

Marinated Carrots

5 cups cooked sliced carrots
1 medium green bell pepper, chopped
¾ cup chopped onion
1 (10.75 ounce) can tomato soup
¾ cup vinegar

1 cup sugar
½ cup vegetable oil
1 teaspoon Worcestershire sauce
1 teaspoon salt
1 teaspoon black pepper
1 teaspoon prepared mustard

Place carrots in a large bowl. Mix together green pepper, onion, soup, vinegar, sugar, oil, Worcestershire sauce, salt, pepper and mustard. Pour over carrots and let stand overnight. Drain and serve.

Note: You can store the leftover sauce in the refrigerator and use to marinate another batch of carrots at a later date.

Makes 8 to 10 servings

FRANCES HOGGE

HEARTY SQUASH CASSEROLE

6	small yellow squash, sliced	1	(10.5 ounce) can cream of chicken soup
2	medium onions, chopped	1	(8 ounce) package herb stuffing
2	medium carrots, peeled and shredded	1	stick butter, melted
	Salted water		
1	cup sour cream		

Preheat oven to 350 degrees. Place sliced squash, onion and carrots in a medium saucepan and cover with salted water. Bring to a boil; reduce heat and simmer for 5 to 10 minutes or until squash is tender. Drain and mash. Add sour cream and cream of chicken soup. In a separate bowl, mix stuffing with melted butter. Place a thin layer of stuffing mix into a greased 9x13-inch baking dish. Spread half of the squash mixture over the stuffing. Add half of the remaining stuffing; top with the remaining squash. Finish with the remaining stuffing. Bake for 30 minutes or until bubbly.

Makes 8 to 10 servings

SQUASH PUDDING

3	small yellow squash, sliced	½	stick butter, melted
3	eggs	3	tablespoons all-purpose flour
1	(12 ounce) can evaporated milk	⅔	cup sugar
1	tablespoon pure vanilla extract		Ground nutmeg

Preheat oven to 350 degrees. Place sliced squash in a medium saucepan and cover with water. Bring to a boil; reduce heat and simmer for 10 minutes or until tender. Drain squash well. Put squash in blender with eggs, milk, vanilla, butter, flour and sugar. Blend well. Pour into a greased 8½x8½-inch baking dish. Sprinkle with nutmeg and bake for 35 to 45 minutes or until lightly browned.

Makes 6 to 8 servings

ARNOLD WALKER

CHEESY SQUASH CASSEROLE

6   cups sliced yellow squash
1   cup chopped onion
½   cup water
2   sleeves Ritz® crackers,
     crushed
2   cups shredded Cheddar
     cheese

4   eggs, beaten
1½ cups milk
1   stick butter, divided
1   teaspoon salt
Black pepper to taste

Preheat oven to 400 degrees. Place squash and onion in a large skillet over medium heat. Add water. Cover and cook until squash is tender, about 5 to 10 minutes. Drain well and place in a large bowl; set aside. In a medium bowl, mix together cracker crumbs and cheese. Stir half of the cracker mixture into the cooked squash and onion. In a small bowl, mix together eggs and milk; add to the squash mixture. Stir in ½ stick of melted butter and season with salt and pepper. Spread into a 9x13-inch baking dish. Sprinkle with remaining cracker mixture and dot with remaining butter. Bake for 25 minutes or until lightly browned.

Makes 10 to 12 servings

LYNDA BUSH

VEGETABLE CASSEROLE

1   cup chopped celery
1   cup chopped onion
1   stick plus 2 tablespoons
     butter, divided
2   (16 ounce) packages frozen
     mixed vegetables

1   cup mayonnaise
1   cup shredded Mexican style
     four cheese
1   sleeve Ritz® crackers,
     crumbled

Preheat oven to 350 degrees. Sauté celery and onion in 2 tablespoons of butter until onion is translucent. Cook mixed vegetables according to package directions and drain. Pour mixed vegetables in a 9x13-inch baking dish. Spoon the celery and onion on top of the vegetables. Then spread the mayonnaise and cheese on top. Mix 1 stick melted butter with crumbled crackers and sprinkle on top of cheese. Bake for 30 minutes.

Makes 8 to 10 servings

VIANA DIAL

STEAMED BROCCOLI WITH SARRAH'S SAUCE

1 head of broccoli, cut into spears or florets	2 teaspoons lemon juice
½ cup sour cream	3 tablespoons mayonnaise
1 tablespoon fresh chopped chives	Salt and pepper to taste
	Paprika to taste

Steam broccoli until just tender. While broccoli is cooking, mix together sour cream, chives, lemon juice, mayonnaise, salt, pepper and paprika in a small saucepan. Heat over medium-low heat and serve over cooked broccoli.

Note: The sauce may also be served chilled.

Makes 4 servings

HELEN CVIK

BROCCOLI CASSEROLE

2 (16 ounce) bags frozen broccoli florets	½ cup mayonnaise
1 cup water	1 egg, beaten
1 (10.75 ounce) can cream of chicken soup	¼ teaspoon salt
2 cups shredded sharp Cheddar cheese	1 cup Panko bread crumbs or 1½ cups herb seasoned stuffing
½ cup milk	½ stick butter, melted

Preheat oven to 350 degrees. Place broccoli and water in a medium saucepan. Bring to a boil and simmer for 5 minutes or until tender. Drain and set aside. While broccoli is cooking, mix together cream of chicken soup, cheese, milk, mayonnaise, egg and salt. Add broccoli. Spoon mixture into a greased 9x13-inch baking dish. Mix together bread crumbs and melted butter and spread on top of casserole. Bake for 45 minutes.

Note: You can add 1½ cups of cooked and cubed chicken to this casserole to make a full meal.

Makes 10 to 12 servings

CAULIFLOWER AU GRATIN

1 cauliflower, separated into
   florets
⅓ cup all-purpose flour
5 eggs, slightly beaten
1 cup heavy cream

⅔ cup milk
3 slices bacon, cooked and
   crumbled
⅔ cup grated Gruyere cheese
Salt and pepper to taste

Preheat oven to 425 degrees. Cook cauliflower florets in boiling salted water for 10 minutes or until tender, but still crisp. Drain and rinse under cold water. Pat dry with paper towels. Arrange cauliflower in a single layer in a buttered 2½-quart baking dish. Place flour in a large bowl and gradually whisk in eggs, mixing until smooth. Add cream, milk, bacon, cheese, salt and pepper and mix well. Pour over cauliflower. Bake for 25 minutes or until golden brown and a knife inserted into the center comes out clean.

Makes 6 servings

Betty and Bill's three children, Shelah, Billy and Blair in 2008.

FRIED VEGETABLES

3   tablespoons oil
2   medium carrots, cut into matchstick thin strips
1   (10 ounce) package frozen broccoli
½   teaspoon sugar
1   (4 ounce) can sliced mushrooms

In a large skillet, heat oil; add carrot strips and broccoli. Stir quickly and frequently. Cook until tender, but still slightly crisp. Add sugar to can of mushrooms and stir. Add mushrooms with their liquid to the carrots and broccoli. Cover and cook until liquid has dissolved.

Note: Gives a wonderful flavor to the vegetables.

Makes 4 servings

DEBRA SWAIN

 # HOW TO MAKE GRAVY

Canned chicken or beef broth
Butter
Gravy flour
Salt and pepper to taste

In a small saucepan, pour a small amount of broth (approximately ¼ cup) into the pan. Over medium heat, swirl the broth around the pan until it almost evaporates. Add a little more broth and again, swirl it around the pan until it almost evaporates. Continue doing this a few times until there is a brown residue on the pan. Be careful not to burn the broth. Add butter and allow to melt, stirring in the broth residue. Slowly add gravy flour and whisk continually until blended and smooth. Cook for 5 minutes. Add additional broth to the flour mixture, stirring continually. Continue adding broth until the gravy coats a spoon or until it reaches desired consistency. Add salt and pepper to taste.

Note: Amounts are not given so that you can make the amount of gravy desired. This recipe makes great gravy when you do not have turkey, chicken or beef drippings to use. "Browning" the broth adds flavor to the gravy.

Tomato Pie

3 (14.5 ounce) cans tomatoes, stewed or whole
1½ cups sugar
4½ slices bread, broken into small pieces

2 teaspoons pure vanilla extract
Salt and pepper to taste
1 stick butter

Preheat oven to 400 degrees. Mix together tomatoes, sugar, bread, vanilla, salt and pepper. Pour into a greased 8x8-inch baking dish. Dot the top with butter. Bake for 35 to 40 minutes.

Makes 8 servings

ELAINE CALE

Garlic Mashed Potatoes

4 pounds all-purpose potatoes, peeled and cut into ½-inch pieces
Water
1½ sticks butter, divided
12 garlic cloves, minced

1 teaspoon sugar
1½ cups half-and-half
½ cup water
1 teaspoon salt, plus more to taste
Pepper to taste

Place cut potatoes in colander. Rinse under cold running water until water runs clear. Drain thoroughly. Melt 4 tablespoons of butter in a Dutch oven over medium heat. Cook garlic and sugar, stirring often, until sticky and straw colored, 3 to 4 minutes. Add rinsed potatoes, 1¼ cups half-and-half, water and 1 teaspoon salt to pot and stir to combine. Bring to boil; reduce heat to low and simmer, covered and stirring occasionally, until potatoes are tender and most of the liquid is absorbed, about 25 to 30 minutes. Remove from heat and add remaining butter to pot and mash with potato masher until smooth. Using rubber spatula, fold in remaining half-and-half until liquid is absorbed and potatoes are creamy. Season with salt and pepper.

Note: Cutting the potatoes into ½-inch pieces ensures that maximum surface area is exposed and soaks up the garlic.

Makes 8 to 10 servings

THE LUNCH BELL MASHED POTATOES

6	all-purpose potatoes, peeled and diced	2	teaspoons salt
Water		1	cup evaporated milk
		½	stick butter

Place diced potatoes in a medium saucepan; cover with water. Add salt; bring to a boil. Boil for 15 minutes or until potatoes are fork tender. Drain well, saving the water. Place potatoes in a mixing bowl. Add ½ cup of the potato water to the evaporated milk to thin. Add the butter to the potatoes; gradually add the milk. Whip potatoes with a hand mixer until light and fluffy.

Note: If you like thicker potatoes, do not add all of the milk and water mixture.

Makes 6 to 8 servings

STUFFED BAKED POTATO CASSEROLE

8	unpeeled medium baking potatoes	1½	teaspoon salt
1½	sticks butter, melted	1	teaspoon white pepper
4	cups shredded Cheddar cheese, plus more for garnish	½	cup chopped green onion, including tops
1½	cups sour cream	1	cup bacon bits
		Freshly chopped chives	

Preheat oven to 350 degrees. Bake potatoes for an hour or until a fork can easily pierce the potatoes. Cool slightly; do not peel. Slice potatoes in a 9x13-inch baking dish. In separate bowl, mix together butter, cheese, sour cream, salt, pepper, green onion and bacon bits. Pour cheese mixture over potatoes and stir well. Bake for 30 minutes or until golden brown. Garnish with shredded cheese and chives.

Makes 10 to 12 servings

BLAIR SWAIN SANCHEZ

QUICK AND EASY CHEESE POTATOES

6 unpeeled medium baking
   potatoes
1 stick butter
2 cups shredded Cheddar
   cheese
1 cup sour cream

1 teaspoon salt
½ teaspoon white pepper
½ cup chopped green onion,
   including tops
Paprika

Pierce potatoes with a fork. Do not peel. Place in microwave on a paper towel. Cook on high for 20 minutes or until potatoes are fork tender. Cool slightly; do not peel. Slice and set aside. Place butter in medium glass microwave-safe bowl; cook on high for approximately 1 minute to melt. Remove from oven and stir in cheese. When cheese melts, add sour cream, salt, pepper and green onion. Gently stir cheese mixture into potatoes; spoon into a microwave-safe 8x12-inch baking dish. Sprinkle paprika on top. Cook in microwave uncovered on high for 7 to 8 minutes.

Note: This recipe saves 1 hour of cooking time when compared to the conventional cooking method.

Makes 8 servings

BLAIR SWAIN SANCHEZ

*Blair is Betty's oldest daughter and currently manages **The Lunch Bell**. She has worked there for many years and shares Betty's love for the restaurant.*

SENATOR RUSSELL'S SWEET POTATOES

POTATOES

3 cups cooked and mashed
   sweet potatoes
1 cup sugar
2 eggs

½ cup whole milk
1 tablespoon pure vanilla
   extract
1 stick butter, melted

TOPPING

1 cup firmly packed light
   brown sugar
⅓ cup all-purpose flour

5⅓ tablespoons butter, melted
1 cup chopped pecans

Preheat oven to 325 degrees. Mix together sweet potatoes, sugar, eggs, milk, vanilla and butter. Put into a greased 9x13-inch baking dish. Combine brown sugar, flour, butter and pecans and crumble on top of potatoes. Bake for 35 minutes.

Makes 6 to 8 servings

LOUISE HALLETT

POTATO CASSEROLE

6	medium red potatoes, skins on	1	cup sour cream
Water		2	cups shredded Cheddar cheese
1	stick butter, melted		Salt and pepper

Place potatoes in a stockpot and cover with water; boil potatoes until fork tender. Drain and set aside to cool. Preheat oven to 350 degrees. Once cooled, grate potatoes with their skins on. Place potatoes in a 9x13-inch baking dish. Pour butter over potatoes. Stir in sour cream and cheese. Bake for 30 minutes.

Makes 4 servings

DEBRA SWAIN

RED POTATO CASSEROLE

2½	pounds red potatoes, peeled	⅛	teaspoon black pepper
6	cups cold water	1	egg, beaten
½	teaspoon salt	1	cup half-and-half
8	ounces ricotta cheese	2	tablespoons butter, softened
½	cup minced fresh parsley	1½	cups shredded Swiss cheese
¼	teaspoon salt		Paprika for garnish

Preheat oven to 350 degrees. Slice potatoes into very thin slices. Place potatoes in a medium saucepan. Cover with water; add salt and bring to a boil. When boiling, cook for 1 minute, remove and rinse in cold water. Drain well on paper towels. In a small bowl, combine ricotta, parsley, salt and pepper; set aside. Mix egg and half-and-half; set aside.

Grease a 9x13-inch baking dish with butter. Layer ⅓ of the potatoes in the bottom of the dish. Let edges of potatoes overlap slightly. Spoon half of the ricotta mixture on top of the potatoes. Top with ½ cup Swiss cheese. Add another ⅓ of the potatoes, the remaining ricotta mixture and another ½ cup Swiss cheese. Top with a third layer of potatoes; sprinkle remaining Swiss cheese on top. Pour egg mixture over top and sprinkle with paprika. Bake for 35 to 40 minutes or until potatoes are done and top of casserole is golden brown. Do not over bake.

Note: Can be made a day in advance. Do not pour egg mixture over potatoes until ready to bake.

Makes 6 to 8 servings

Favorite Sweet Potato Casserole

POTATOES

1½ sticks butter, softened

1 cup sugar

4 eggs

2½ teaspoons pure vanilla extract

Dash of ground cinnamon

Dash of allspice

⅔ cup heavy whipping cream

½ teaspoon salt

6 cups cooked and mashed sweet potatoes

TOPPING

1 stick and 2 tablespoons butter, melted

1 cup firmly packed brown sugar

½ cup and 2 tablespoons all-purpose flour

1 cup pecans

Preheat oven to 350 degrees. Cream together butter and sugar. Add eggs, vanilla, cinnamon, allspice, whipping cream, salt and sweet potatoes and mix well. In a separate bowl, combine butter, brown sugar, flour and pecans and mix well. Pour sweet potato mixture into a greased 9x13-inch baking dish and top with brown sugar mixture. Bake for 20 to 25 minutes.

Makes 10 to 12 servings

JUDYE HAFLING

 # Betty's Favorite Rice Casserole

1 cup uncooked rice (not quick-cooking rice)

1 stick butter, softened

2 tablespoons chopped onion

1 (10 ounce) can beef consommé

1 (10.75 ounce) can cream of chicken and mushroom soup

½ cup chopped pecans

Preheat oven to 350 degrees. Mix together rice, butter, onion, beef consommé, soup and pecans. Pour into an ungreased 6x10-inch glass baking dish. Bake uncovered for approximately 1 hour and 15 minutes or until the center is set. Do not overcook.

Note: Can be prepared early in the day and baked when ready to serve. Cream of chicken or cream of mushroom soup may be substituted for the cream of chicken and mushroom soup.

Makes 8 servings

WILD RICE AND CHEESE CASSEROLE

1 (6 ounce) box long grain and
   wild rice
1 stick butter
2 tablespoons flour

1 cup milk
8 ounces cream cheese
1 teaspoon salt
1 cup button mushrooms

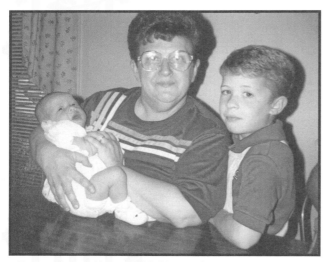

Betty with two of her grandchildren, Tyler and Annie, in 1994.

Cook rice according to package directions; set aside. Preheat oven to 325 degrees. In a skillet, melt butter; add flour and stir until thickened. Add milk slowly, stirring constantly. Add cream cheese and stir until melted and sauce is smooth. Add salt. Butter a 1½-quart baking dish. Alternate layers of rice, mushrooms and cream sauce. Repeat until dish is filled, being sure to put a generous amount of sauce on top. Bake for 20 to 30 minutes or until mixture is golden brown on top.

Makes 12 servings

FRESH BASIL PESTO LINGUINI

Pasta should be cooked "al dente" (to the tooth) or just until it offers slight resistance when you bite it. Drain pasta in a colander and serve immediately.

2 cups fresh basil leaves,
   washed and dried
2 garlic cloves, peeled
¼ cup pine nuts
⅔ cup olive oil

1 cup freshly grated Parmesan
   cheese, plus extra for
   topping
Salt and pepper to taste
1 pound linguini, cooked

In a food processor, chop basil, garlic and pine nuts. While processing, slowly add olive oil. Turn off processor. Add cheese and salt and pepper to taste. Briefly process, just until cheese is combined. Stir into cooked linguini. Top with freshly grated Parmesan cheese.

Note: Pesto freezes well. Double or triple the recipe and store in freezer bags.

Makes 4 to 6 servings

Baked Macaroni and Cheese

Casserole

6	cups salted water	1	bay leaf
2	cups uncooked elbow macaroni	½	teaspoon paprika
3	tablespoons butter	1	egg, beaten
3	tablespoons all-purpose flour	3	cups shredded sharp Cheddar cheese
1	tablespoon dry mustard	1	teaspoon salt
3	cups whole milk		Fresh black pepper
½	cup minced yellow onion		

Topping

3	tablespoons butter	1	cup Panko bread crumbs

Preheat oven to 350 degrees. On high heat, bring 6 cups of salted water to a boil. Add the macaroni and cook until al dente, about 7 minutes. Drain and set aside. In a large saucepan, melt the butter over medium heat. Add the flour and mustard and whisk for 5 minutes. Make sure it is free of lumps. Stir in the milk, onion, bay leaf and paprika. Simmer for 10 minutes; remove the bay leaf.

Slowly add in the egg, stirring constantly. Stir in 2 cups of the Cheddar cheese and stir until melted. Season with salt and pepper. Fold in the macaroni and pour into a 2-quart baking dish sprayed with cooking spray. Top with remaining cheese.

For the topping, melt the butter; toss in the bread crumbs. Stir until well coated. Top the macaroni with the bread crumbs. Bake for 30 minutes. Remove from the oven and let rest for 5 minutes before serving.

Makes 6 to 8 servings

To easily clean your baking dish after baking macaroni and cheese, fill your sink with boiling hot water. Place the dish upside down in the sink to steam it; soak for 12 to 15 minutes. Immediately scrub the dish and the food will easily come off the pan. Note: You must remove the dish from the hot water and clean it before it gets cold or the food will re-stick to the pan.

MACARONI AND CHEESE WITH TOMATO

½	stick butter, plus more for baking dish	2	teaspoons dry mustard
6	cups salted water	¼	teaspoon paprika
½	(16 ounce) box uncooked elbow macaroni	2	cups whole milk
2	tablespoons minced onion	3	cups shredded Cheddar cheese, divided
4	tablespoons all-purpose flour	2	ripe tomatoes, blanched, peeled and cut into ½-inch thick slices
1	teaspoon salt, plus more for seasoning		Freshly ground black pepper

Preheat the oven to 375 degrees. Lightly butter or spray a 9x13-inch baking dish. On high heat, bring 6 cups of salted water to a boil. Add the macaroni and cook until al dente, about 7 minutes. Drain; place in large bowl and set aside. In a large saucepan, melt ½ stick butter over medium heat. Add the onion and cook until tender, stirring constantly. Add the flour, salt, dry mustard and paprika and mix well. Cook for 3 to 4 minutes, stirring frequently. Stir in the milk and cook until thickened, about 5 minutes. Add 2 cups of the Cheddar cheese and stir until melted. Pour cheese mixture over the macaroni and stir. Place mixture into the baking dish. Cover the macaroni with the tomato slices and season with salt and pepper. Bake for 35 to 45 minutes. A few minutes before the macaroni is finished cooking, sprinkle the top with the remaining Cheddar cheese. Return to the oven until the cheese melts. Remove from the oven and let rest for 5 minutes before serving.

Makes 6 servings

SCALLOPED PINEAPPLE

1½	sticks butter, melted	6	slices bread broken into small pieces
2	cups sugar	1	(20 ounce) can crushed pineapple or 1 (20 ounce) can pineapple chunks, drained
3	eggs		
1	cup whole milk		

Preheat oven to 350 degrees. Mix together butter, sugar, eggs and milk. Add bread pieces and drained pineapple. Pour into a greased 9x13-inch baking dish and bake for 35 to 40 minutes.

Makes 6 servings

EXCELLENT MACARONI AND CHEESE

1	(16 ounce) box uncooked elbow macaroni	¾	stick butter
28	ounces sharp Cheddar cheese, shredded	1	cup evaporated milk
		3	cups whole milk
		4	eggs, beaten

Preheat oven to 350 degrees. Grease a large mixing bowl. In a saucepan, cook macaroni according to package directions; drain. In a deep baking dish, layer the macaroni, cheese and dots of butter. Continue layering until top of bowl, ending with cheese and butter. In a saucepan, scald evaporated and whole milk slowly (do not boil). In a separate medium bowl, beat the eggs and add milks slowly to the eggs, being careful not to cook the eggs. Pour milk mixture over macaroni. Bake for 50 minutes or until brown on top.

Note: Baking dish should be at least 5 inches deep and approximately 8¾ inches across top and 5 inches across bottom.

Makes 8 servings

LILLIAN BAKER

*Eleanor Mabry was a longtime customer of **The Lunch Bell**. One of her dying requests was to have **The Lunch Bell** cater her memorial service. She made it clear to everyone that she wanted lots of coconut cream pie, but NO vegetables!*

THE LUNCH BELL DRESSING

1	small onion, chopped	1	teaspoon salt
2	celery stalks, chopped	1	teaspoon black pepper
1	stick butter	1	teaspoon poultry seasoning (optional)
4	cups chicken broth or more if needed	1	pound rolls, cubed and dried
1	egg, beaten		

Preheat oven to 325 degrees. In a large skillet, sauté onion and celery in butter until onion is lightly browned. Add chicken broth, egg, salt, pepper and poultry seasoning; mix together and heat thoroughly. Add bread gradually to vegetable mixture, tossing lightly until mixed. Avoid over mixing, which causes dressing to be soggy and compact. Place mixture into a greased 9x13-inch baking dish. Bake for 1 hour and 15 minutes.

Note: The amount of liquid needed will depend on the dryness of the bread. Betty uses day old crusty rolls for her dressing. Any bread can be used and toast it to dry it out.

Makes 12 servings

CROCKPOT CORNBREAD STUFFING

2	(8.5 ounce) boxes corn muffin mix	1½	teaspoons sage
8	Grand's® biscuits	1	teaspoon poultry seasoning
3-4	cups dry herb seasoned stuffing	1	teaspoon dried thyme
2	sticks butter, melted	½	teaspoon salt
2	cups finely chopped onion	½	teaspoon black pepper
2	cups chopped celery	½	teaspoon marjoram
		3	cups chicken broth
		2	eggs, beaten

A day before serving stuffing, make cornbread and biscuits according to package directions; set aside. On the day the stuffing is to be served, crumble the cornbread and biscuits to about ½ to 1-inch cubes. Dry out the cornbread and biscuit cubes by toasting them in the oven on a sheet pan. In a large bowl, combine cornbread, biscuits and stuffing to make about 13 cups. Add more dried stuffing if needed.

Melt butter in a large roasting pan and sauté onion and celery until limp. Add sage, poultry seasoning, thyme, salt, pepper and marjoram and stir into the liquid. Next add bread/stuffing mixture and toss together well. Pour in chicken broth and stir well. Add beaten eggs and mix together. Pack lightly into a Crockpot that has been sprayed with cooking spray. Cover and cook on high for 45 minutes; reduce to low for 4 to 8 hours.

Note: You may use any old bread, hamburger buns or rolls to make up the 13 cups. You may also pulse the bread in a food processor until you get the desired size of cubes.

Makes 8 to 10 servings

BARBARA HOLLAND EBY

BETTY'S CRANBERRY SAUCE

1	cup sugar	1	(12 ounce) package fresh cranberries, rinsed and drained
1	cup water		

Combine sugar and water in a medium saucepan. Bring to a boil; add cranberries and return to boil. Reduce heat and simmer for 10 minutes, stirring occasionally. Cover and cool completely at room temperature. Refrigerate until serving time.

Makes 8 to 10 servings

Hot Pineapple Dish

1 (20 ounce) can pineapple chunks, drained, reserving juice
½ cup sugar
3 tablespoons all-purpose flour
½ stick butter, melted
1½ cups (6 ounces) shredded cheese, divided
⅔ cup (about 14) coarsely crushed saltines or Ritz's® crackers

Preheat oven to 350 degrees. Drain the pineapple, reserving the juice; set aside. In a medium bowl, combine sugar and flour. Add butter and 1 cup cheese; mix well. Gently stir in the pineapple. Pour into a greased 1½-quart baking dish. Sprinkle crushed crackers on top; drizzle with reserved pineapple juice. Bake uncovered for 30 to 35 minutes or until bubbly around edges. Remove from the oven and sprinkle with remaining cheese.

Makes 6 servings

ROSEMARY MURPHY

Apple-Cranberry Casserole

1½ cups sugar
3 cups chopped red apples (do not peel)
2 cups raw cranberries
1 stick butter, melted
1 cup oatmeal
½ cup all-purpose flour
½ cup firmly packed brown sugar
½ cup chopped pecans

Preheat oven to 350 degrees. Mix together sugar, apples and cranberries. Put into a buttered 8x8-inch baking dish. Mix together butter, oatmeal, flour and brown sugar until crumbly. Spread on top of apple mixture. Sprinkle with pecans. Bake for 1 hour.

Note: This dish is good served hot, warm or cold.

Makes 6 to 8 servings

MARGARET SWAIN

SWEET AND SOUR PICKLES

32	ounces whole dill pickles (not Kosher)	15	whole cloves
1½	cups sugar	1	teaspoon celery seed
		½	teaspoon dry mustard

Drain pickles, saving the jar and lid, but discarding the juice. Slice pickles crosswise in ¼-inch slices and place in large bowl. Add sugar, cloves, celery seed and dry mustard. Mix and let stand at room temperature for 8 hours, stirring occasionally. Pour pickles and juice back into the original pickle jar and refrigerate until ready to serve.

Note: Pickles will be crisp and tasty.

Makes about 3 cups of pickles

RUTH BREEGER

CURRIED FRUIT

1	(15.25 ounce) can sliced peaches	1	(6 ounce) jar maraschino cherries
1	(15 ounce) can pears	1	cup chopped pecans
1	(15 ounce) can apricots	½	stick butter
1	(20 ounce) can pineapple chunks	¾	cup firmly packed brown sugar
		2	teaspoons curry

Preheat oven to 325 degrees. Drain, slice and arrange fruit and pecans in a medium baking dish. Melt butter and add brown sugar and curry; mix well. Pour curry mixture over fruit. Bake for 1 hour.

Makes 8 servings

LIZ JOHNSON

CRANBERRY RELISH

1	(16 ounce) package fresh cranberries	4	large red apples, cored but not peeled
1	large orange, seeded but not peeled	2	cups sugar
		1	cup chopped pecans

In a food processor, coarsely chop the cranberries and place in a bowl. Coarsely chop the orange, with the rind; add to cranberries. Coarsely chop the apples; add to the cranberry mixture. Add sugar and pecans and mix well.

Makes 8 to 10 servings

MAIN DISHES

MAIN DISHES

**FEATURED RECIPE
ON FRONT:**

*Spinach, Feta and
Sun-Dried Tomato
Quiche, page 179*

Hot Chicken Salad

2 cups cooked and cubed chicken
2 cups chopped celery
½ cup cashews
1 tablespoon minced onion
⅛ teaspoon salt
1 tablespoon lemon juice
1 cup Duke's® mayonnaise, plus or minus a little
1 cup shredded Cheddar cheese
1 cup crushed potato chips
½ cup seasoned bread crumbs

Preheat the oven to 350 degrees. Mix together chicken, celery, cashews, onion, salt and lemon juice. Add mayonnaise until it is moist. Pour into an 8x8-inch baking dish. Sprinkle cheese over top of casserole. In a separate bowl, combine potato chips and bread crumbs. Sprinkle potato chip and bread crumb mixture on top, covering all of the cheese. Bake for 20 to 30 minutes until hot and brown. Serve immediately.

Makes 4 servings

*Hot Chicken Salad is one of the most popular dishes at **The Lunch Bell** and is served on Monday's and Thursday's!*

Chicken & Broccoli Casserole

1 (20 ounce) package frozen broccoli
2 (10.75 ounce) cans cream of chicken soup
¾ cup mayonnaise
¾ cup milk
2 teaspoons lemon juice
¼ teaspoon black pepper
¼ teaspoon paprika
4 large chicken breasts, cooked and cubed
2 cups shredded Cheddar cheese
1 (8 ounce) package herb seasoned stuffing mix (not cubed)
2 sticks butter, melted

Preheat oven to 350 degrees. Cook broccoli according to package directions; drain and set aside. In a medium bowl, combine cream of chicken soup, mayonnaise, milk, lemon juice, pepper and paprika and mix until smooth. In a greased 9x13-inch baking dish, spread broccoli on the bottom; top with cooked chicken. Spread soup mixture over the chicken. Sprinkle cheese on top. Combine stuffing mix with melted butter; spread on top of the cheese. Bake for 35 to 45 minutes.

Note: You can use fresh broccoli instead of frozen; just steam it lightly before putting it in the baking dish.

Makes 6 servings

BARBARA HOLLAND EBY

Barbara was pregnant with her first child during the creation of this cookbook. Her daughter, Brooke Olivia, was born on January 20, 2010.

Barbara Eby's daughter, Brooke Olivia Eby.

Luscious Chicken Casserole

1	cup sour cream	1	stick butter, melted
1	(10.75 ounce) can cream of chicken soup	12	ounces herb seasoned stuffing mix
1	(10.75 ounce) can cream of mushroom soup	4	chicken breasts, cooked and cubed
½	teaspoon salt	3	cups chicken broth
¼	teaspoon black pepper		

Preheat oven to 350 degrees. In a medium bowl, mix together sour cream, cream of chicken soup, cream of mushroom soup, salt and pepper. Pour melted butter in a 9x13-inch baking dish. Place a ⅓ of the stuffing in the bottom of the baking dish. Put half of the chicken on top of the stuffing. Spoon ½ of soup mixture over the chicken. Repeat layers; top with remaining stuffing. Poke holes in the casserole and pour chicken broth over top, letting it seep down into the casserole. Bake uncovered for 45 minutes.

Note: Add more stuffing mix if desired, adding additional broth to moisten the stuffing. Casserole may be made ahead of time and frozen, thawed and then cooked.

Makes 6 to 8 servings

MARILYN HOLLAND

 # Treasure Island Chicken

5⅓	tablespoons butter	1	teaspoon lemon juice
½	cup all-purpose flour	3	whole chicken breasts, cooked
1	teaspoon salt		
1	cup milk	2	(15 ounce) cans asparagus spears (or fresh asparagus)
2	cups chicken broth		
¼	teaspoon black pepper	½	cup bread crumbs
1	cup mayonnaise		

In a large skillet, melt butter, then add flour and salt. Combine milk with chicken broth and pepper and slowly add to butter mixture. Cook over low heat, stirring until thick and smooth. Remove from heat and add mayonnaise and lemon juice. Stir well. Layer chicken and asparagus in a buttered baking dish. Pour sauce over chicken. Cover with bread crumbs. Bake for 50 minutes.

Makes 3 servings

LIZ JOHNSON

CHICKEN AND WILD RICE CASSEROLE

1 (6 ounce) box long grain and wild rice
½ cup chopped onion
½ stick butter
¼ cup all-purpose flour
1 (4 ounce) can sliced mushrooms
1¼ cups chicken broth
1½ cups half-and-half

3 cups cooked and cubed chicken
¼ cup diced red bell pepper
½ cup diced water chestnuts, drained
1 tablespoon minced fresh parsley
½ teaspoon salt
⅛ teaspoon black pepper
½ cup sliced almonds

Cook rice according to package directions; set aside. Preheat oven to 350 degrees. In a large skillet, sauté onion in butter until softened. Stir in flour and cook, stirring constantly for 3 minutes over medium-low heat. Drain mushrooms, reserving liquid. Combine ¼ cup mushroom broth with chicken broth. Add broths to flour mixture and stir constantly. Add half-and-half and stir until thickened. Remove from heat. Add cooked rice, mushrooms, chicken, red pepper, water chestnuts, parsley, salt and pepper. Spoon into a 9x13-inch baking dish and top with almonds. Bake for 25 to 30 minutes or until heated through and almonds are golden brown.

Note: Can be made a day in advance. Cover, refrigerate and bake when ready to serve.

Makes 8 servings

CREAMED CHICKEN

6 tablespoons butter
6 tablespoons all-purpose flour
½ cup milk
½ cup half-and-half

3 cups chicken broth
1 cup cooked, cubed chicken
⅛ teaspoon black pepper
Cooked rice or toast

In a medium saucepan, melt butter; whisk in flour. Cook for 5 minutes, but do not brown. Gradually add milk, half-and-half and chicken broth; stirring constantly. Cook until thickened. Add chicken and pepper. Serve over rice or toast.

Makes 2 to 4 servings

CHICKEN SPECTACULAR

1	(6 ounce) box long grain and wild rice	1	medium onion, chopped
1	(10.75 ounce) can cream of celery soup	2	(14.5 ounce) cans French-style green beans, drained
½	cup mayonnaise	1	cup water chestnuts, drained and chopped
3	cups cooked and cubed chicken	1½	cups shredded Cheddar cheese
1	(4 ounce) jar diced pimento peppers, drained		Salt and pepper to taste

Cook rice according to directions on package; set aside. Preheat oven to 350 degrees. In a large bowl, mix the cream of celery soup and mayonnaise together. Add the cooked rice, chicken, pimentos, onion, green beans, water chestnuts, ½ cup cheese, salt and pepper and stir well. Transfer to a 9x13-inch baking dish. Top the casserole with remaining cheese. Bake for 25 to 30 minutes or until heated thoroughly.

Note: This dish freezes well.

Makes 10 servings

HELEN CVIK

CHICKEN AND RICE CASSEROLE

¾	cup chopped celery	½	teaspoon salt
1	small onion, chopped	2	cups cooked and cubed chicken
2	tablespoons butter	2	cups cooked rice
1	(10.75 ounce) can cream of celery soup	½	cup slivered almonds
1	(10.75 ounce) can cream of chicken soup	1	(8 ounce) can water chestnuts, chopped
⅓	cup mayonnaise		Shredded Cheddar cheese
½	tablespoon fresh lemon juice		

Preheat oven to 350 degrees. Sauté celery and onion in butter until onion is translucent. In a large bowl, mix together soups, mayonnaise, lemon juice and salt. Add chicken, rice, almonds, water chestnuts, celery and onion and mix well. Put into a greased 9x13-inch baking dish. Bake for 20 minutes. Put cheese on top and bake for another 15 minutes or until cheese is melted and bubbling.

Makes 8 servings

LYNDA BUSH

CHICKEN WITH DROP DUMPLINGS

1 (3 to 4 pound) rotisserie
   cooked chicken, cut up
2 stalks celery, diced
2 tablespoons chicken bouillon
   granules
1 bay leaf

8 cups water
12 frozen biscuits, uncooked
1 (10.75 ounce) can cream of
   chicken soup
1 can water
Salt and pepper to taste

Place the chicken, celery, bouillon granules and bay leaf in a large stockpot. Add the water and bring to a boil over medium-high heat. Reduce the heat and cook for 30 minutes or until the chicken is very tender. Remove the chicken and let it cool slightly. Pick the meat off of the bones, discarding the bones and skin. Set chicken aside.

Drop the biscuits into the boiling broth. Do not stir the dumplings, just gently shake the pot. Cover, reduce the heat and gently simmer the dumplings for 15 minutes without lifting the lid.

While the dumplings are cooking, heat the cream of chicken soup with can of water in a small saucepan. When the dumplings are cooked, gently drizzle the soup over the dumplings. Shake the pot gently. Return the chicken to the pot and shake again in a rotating motion. Season with salt and pepper.

Makes 6 servings

NELDA'S SPECIAL CHICKEN

1 (8 ounce) bottle French
   dressing
1 stick butter, melted
½ cup firmly packed brown
   sugar

Salt and pepper to taste
2 tablespoons vegetable oil
6 chicken breasts
All-purpose flour
Bacon bits (optional)

Preheat oven to 350 degrees. Mix together dressing, butter, brown sugar, salt and pepper; set aside. In a skillet, heat vegetable oil. Dredge chicken breasts in flour and brown in pan on both sides (do not cook through). Place chicken in a baking dish. Pour dressing mixture over chicken. Bake for 30 to 45 minutes or until thoroughly cooked. Sprinkle with bacon bits.

Makes 6 servings

NELDA MARTIN

THE LUNCH BELL CHICKEN POT PIE

Puff pastry, cut into desired
   shape
1   egg, beaten
½   cup chopped onion
½   stick butter
½   cup all-purpose flour
¼   teaspoon black pepper
2   stalks celery, sliced

3   carrots, sliced
5½ cups chicken stock, divided
Salt to taste
3   cups cooked and cubed
   chicken
½   (16 ounce) bag mixed
   vegetables

Preheat oven to 375 degrees. Bring puff pastry to room temperature. Place on an ungreased cookie sheet. Brush with beaten egg and let set for 30 minutes. Place in oven and brush with beaten egg every 5 minutes, for 20 minutes or until golden brown; set aside.

In a large skillet, sauté onion in butter over medium heat until translucent. Add flour and pepper to onion and stir until well blended. Cook about 10 minutes on low heat, stirring occasionally. While sauce is thickening, in a medium saucepan, sauté celery and carrots in ½ cup chicken broth until partially done, about 15 minutes. Drain; set aside. Slowly add remaining stock to flour mixture, stirring constantly with a wire whisk. Cook on medium heat until thickened, stirring often. Check for seasoning and add salt if necessary. Add cooked chicken, celery and carrots. Add uncooked mixed vegetables and stir gently. Cook until vegetables are heated.

Cut puff pastry in half, lengthwise. Place ½ of pastry in a ramekin. Put a large scoop of pot pie mixture on top of pastry; top with other half of pastry.

Makes 6 to 8 servings

EXCELLENT BARBEQUE CHICKEN

1	cup ketchup		2	teaspoons salt
1	cup cider vinegar		1	teaspoon cayenne pepper
1	cup water		¼	cup Worcestershire sauce
¼	cup firmly packed light brown sugar		6	tablespoons olive oil
½	cup prepared mustard		8-10	pounds chicken, cut into serving pieces
1	stick butter			

In a large saucepan, combine ketchup, vinegar, water, brown sugar, mustard, butter, salt, cayenne pepper and Worcestershire sauce. Cook for 30 minutes or until slightly thickened; set aside. Preheat oven to 350 degrees. Heat olive oil in a large skillet over medium high heat. Add the chicken pieces and sauté for 2 to 3 minutes per side, just to sear the meat. Transfer chicken to a 9x13-inch baking dish and cover each piece well with the barbeque sauce. Bake for 35 to 45 minutes, basting with the sauce every 15 minutes.

Makes 8 to 10 servings

ITALIAN OVEN-FRIED CHICKEN

¾	cup Italian seasoned bread crumbs		1	egg, beaten
½	cup freshly grated Parmesan cheese		½	cup milk
			1	tablespoon all-purpose flour
¼	cup chopped fresh parsley		1	(3 to 3½ pound) chicken, cut into serving pieces
¾	teaspoon dried oregano			

Preheat oven to 400 degrees. In a small bowl, combine bread crumbs, Parmesan cheese, parsley and oregano; stir well. In a separate bowl, combine egg, milk and flour; mix well. Dip each piece of chicken in egg mixture and then dredge in bread crumb mixture, coating well. Lightly spray a baking dish with cooking spray and arrange chicken in a single layer. Bake for 25 to 30 minutes or until chicken is done.

Makes 4 servings

Fireman's Chicken

1	pound chicken breasts and thighs with skin on	1½	teaspoons poultry seasoning
5	teaspoons salt	1	cup vinegar
¼	teaspoon black pepper	1	egg, beaten
		½	cup vegetable oil

Preheat oven to 350 degrees. Place chicken in a 9x13-inch baking dish. In a small bowl, whisk together salt, pepper, poultry seasoning, vinegar, egg and oil. Set ¼ cup of marinade aside to baste with later. Pour rest of marinade over chicken and marinate for at least 1 hour. Bake for 30 minutes or until thoroughly cooked or cook on grill. Baste halfway through cooking with marinade. Do not use marinade as a cold sauce.

Makes 4 servings

JALENE BREEGER

 ## King Ranch Chicken

4	boneless, skinless chicken breasts	2	(10 ounce) cans diced tomatoes with green chiles, undrained
¼	teaspoon salt	1	(10.75 ounce) can cream of chicken soup
¼	teaspoon black pepper		
2	tablespoons butter	12	(6-inch) corn tortillas cut into quarters
1	medium green bell pepper, chopped	2	cups shredded mixed Cheddar and mozzarella cheese
1	medium onion, chopped		

Preheat oven to 325 degrees. Sprinkle chicken with salt and pepper and place into a 9x13-inch baking dish. Bake for 20 minutes; let cool. Coarsely chop chicken; set aside. In a large skillet, melt butter over medium heat. Add pepper and onion and cook, stirring constantly, until vegetables are tender, but still crisp. Remove from heat and stir in chicken, tomatoes and soup. Place ⅓ of the tortilla quarters in the bottom of a lightly greased 9x13-inch baking dish. Top with ⅓ of the chicken mixture; sprinkle ⅔ cup of the cheese over the chicken. Repeat layers twice, reserving the last remaining ⅔ cup of cheese. Bake at 325 degrees for 35 minutes. Remove casserole from oven and sprinkle with remaining cheese. Return to oven and bake an additional 5 minutes. Let stand 5 minutes before serving.

Makes 6 servings

SHELAH SWAIN

"Where I grew up on the Eastern Shore of Maryland, the volunteer firemen would make this chicken and sell it by the side of the road every Saturday in the summer as a fundraiser. They would serve the chicken wrapped in a piece of foil with a potato roll. It's the best!"

Jalene Breeger

Chicken Rotel®

4 chicken breasts
2 quarts water
12 ounces vermicelli
1 stick butter
1 onion, chopped
1 medium green bell pepper, chopped

1 (4 ounce) can mushrooms, drained
2 (10 ounce) cans Rotel® tomatoes with chilies
1 pound Velveeta cheese, cut into 1-inch cubes
1 (8.5 ounce) can English peas, drained

Boil chicken in water until chicken is no longer pink in the middle. Reserve broth. Cut chicken into cubes; set aside. Preheat oven to 350 degrees. In a large stockpot, cook vermicelli in 1½ quarts of reserved chicken broth until liquid is almost completely absorbed. In a skillet, melt butter and sauté onion and pepper until onion is translucent. Add onion and green pepper to pasta. Add chicken, mushrooms, tomatoes with chiles, cheese and peas to pasta. Stir well. Pour into a 9x13-inch baking dish and bake for 30 minutes or until cheese is melted and bubbling.

Note: Can be made 1 day ahead of time and baked on day of serving. Freezes well.

Makes 10 to 12 servings

JOANN STOUT

Chicken Crescents

2 large boneless, skinless chicken breasts, cooked and cubed
2 tablespoons milk
3 ounces cream cheese, softened

2 tablespoons finely chopped onion
½ teaspoon salt
⅛ teaspoon black pepper
1 can Pillsbury® crescent rolls
2 tablespoons butter, melted

Preheat oven to 350 degrees. Mix together chicken, milk, cream cheese, onion, salt and pepper in a large bowl. Separate crescent rolls into 4 rectangles and close the seams between the triangles by patting them together. Put 1 large spoonful of chicken mixture in the center of each rectangle and close by bringing the 4 corners together. Brush the tops of the rolls with melted butter. Bake for 20 to 25 minutes.

Makes 4 servings

MARY ODER

CHICKEN WITH ARTICHOKES

6	boneless, skinless chicken breasts	3	tablespoons finely chopped green onion
½	teaspoon black pepper	1	tablespoon cornstarch
1	teaspoon paprika	1	teaspoon chicken bouillon granules
2	tablespoons olive oil, divided	⅔	cup water
1	(14 ounce) can artichoke hearts, drained	¼	cup dry sherry
1⅓	cups sliced fresh mushrooms	½	teaspoon dried rosemary, crushed

Season chicken with pepper and paprika. Heat 1 tablespoon olive oil in a large skillet and add chicken. Cook 5 minutes or until browned, turning once. Place chicken in a lightly greased 9x13-inch baking dish. Arrange artichoke hearts around chicken. Preheat oven to 375 degrees. In a skillet, sauté mushrooms and green onion in 1 tablespoon olive oil for 5 minutes or until tender. In a small bowl, combine cornstarch, chicken bouillon, water, sherry and rosemary; mix well. Add to mushrooms and green onion; bring to a boil. Boil for 1 minute, stirring constantly. Pour over chicken and artichokes. Cover and bake for 30 minutes or until chicken is done.

Makes 6 servings

ROSEMARY CHICKEN WITH MUSHROOMS

4 chicken breasts

5 tablespoons extra virgin olive oil

1 tablespoon chopped fresh rosemary

1 teaspoon ground pepper

1 pound shiitake mushrooms, stems discarded and caps thinly sliced

½ pound crimini mushrooms, stems discarded and caps thinly sliced

1 small onion, finely chopped

2 cloves minced garlic

1 teaspoon chopped fresh thyme

3 medium tomatoes, halved, seeded and diced

Salt and pepper to taste

Brush chicken with olive oil and rub with rosemary and season with pepper. Let set for 30 minutes. Heat remaining oil in large skillet. Add mushrooms and sauté over medium to high heat until brown, approximately 6 minutes. Add onion, garlic and thyme and cook for an additional 4 minutes. Add tomatoes; season with salt and pepper. Cook for 15 minutes. While tomatoes and mushrooms are cooking, heat grill to medium heat. Season chicken with salt and pepper and grill chicken until no longer pink in the center. Serve chicken topped with tomatoes and mushrooms.

Note: You can bake the chicken in the oven at 350 degrees for 30 minutes or until chicken is no longer pink.

Makes 4 servings

BARBARA HOLLAND EBY

Barbara and Scott Eby at home in their kitchen, where many recipes were tested.

FRIED CHICKEN

1-2 cut up frying chickens
Salt
Vegetable shortening

1 tablespoon butter, more if needed
1¼ cups all-purpose flour
¼ teaspoon black pepper

Separate thighs from drumsticks. Cover chicken with cold water and add 1 tablespoon salt. Let soak for 20 to 30 minutes. Drain. Wash under cold water, and pat dry with paper towels. In an electric fryer, melt enough shortening to come up ½-inch in the pan. Add butter. Bring temperature up to 380 degrees. Put flour, 1 teaspoon salt and pepper in a brown paper bag. Shake chicken pieces, a few at a time, in the flour. Shake off excess flour and put in hot grease, skin side up. Cover pan, close steam vent and cook until golden brown on one side, about 10 minutes. Turn and brown on other side about 8 minutes. Remove to a pan lined with paper towels to drain. Do not cover or chicken will not stay crisp. Each time you put more chicken in the grease, be sure the temperature is back up to 380 degrees and add an additional tablespoon of butter before each batch.

Makes 8 to 10 servings

GRAY BOWDITCH

Gray Bowditch has submitted recipes from his grandmother's cookbook entitled "From the Kitchen at Hornsby House." His grandmother's name was Marian Hornsby Bowditch.

NANNY'S MEATLOAF

2 pounds ground beef
2 eggs, beaten
2½ cups tomato juice, divided (or tomato soup)

1 cup quick oats
1 teaspoon salt
1 teaspoon Morton's® Nature Seasoned Salt (optional)

Preheat oven to 400 degrees. In a medium bowl, combine ground beef, eggs, 1½ cups tomato juice, oats and salt. Shape into a loaf and place in a greased 9x13-inch baking dish. Pour remaining cup of tomato juice on top. Bake for 15 minutes. Reduce heat to 300 degrees and bake for an additional hour. Do not open the oven while cooking.

Note: To make Mexican meatloaf, use 2 cups of salsa instead of tomato juice to raw meat. Then cover with Mexican 4 cheese blend after taking the meatloaf out of the oven.

Makes 6 to 8 servings

MALLORY MCKEE

Mallory McKee, Jennie Swain, Annie Swain, Tyler McKee and Grae Muth, five of Betty's grandchildren. Not pictured are Jay and Ashley Darcy.

GRIMBALL'S CHICKEN BOG

1 (3 pound) chicken, skinned
4 cups water, or more if needed
3 teaspoons salt
1 teaspoon black pepper
1 teaspoon poultry seasoning
1 teaspoon dried thyme
1 teaspoon dried rosemary
1½ teaspoons onion flakes (or ¼ cup of chopped raw onion)
1½ cups uncooked white rice
3 medium onions, chopped
2-3 celery stalks, chopped
1 pound Hillshire Farm® smoked sausage, sliced into ¼-inch rounds

In a 4-quart stockpot, cover the chicken with water and add salt, pepper, poultry seasoning, thyme, rosemary and onion flakes. Cover and simmer for 40 minutes or until chicken is thoroughly cooked. Remove the chicken, debone and cut into bite-sized chunks; set aside.

Add rice, onion and celery to the stockpot and cook for approximately 15 minutes or until rice is about halfway cooked. Add the sliced sausage and stir. Cook for 5 more minutes; stir in the chicken. Cook for an additional 10 minutes or until the rice and celery are tender.

Note: This recipe will leave the rice fairly moist. If too moist for your liking, adjust the quantity of water added.

Makes 6 large servings

CAROLYN GRIMBALL

"Carolyn is my aunt, who is an excellent cook. She has a large garden and cans and freezes a lot of vegetables every year."
Barbara Holland Eby

MOM'S MEATLOAF

2 eggs, beaten
¾-1 cup bread crumbs
⅓-½ cup Tabasco® Bloody Mary Mix
½ teaspoon salt
¼ heaping teaspoon black pepper
¼ heaping teaspoon oregano
1 garlic clove, minced
½ cup chopped onions
2 pounds ground sirloin

Preheat oven to 350 degrees. In a large bowl, combine eggs, bread crumbs, Bloody Mary Mix, salt, pepper, oregano, garlic and onion. Mix in ground sirloin by hand and form into loaf. Bake in an ungreased baking dish for 1 to 1¼ hours.

Makes 6 to 8 servings

PAULA MARIA ORPHANIDYS

 ## *The Lunch Bell* Meatloaf and Gravy

Meatloaf

6	pounds ground beef	½	medium green bell pepper, finely chopped (optional)
3½	cups fresh bread crumbs	2	cups crushed tomatoes
2	cups milk	¼	cup Worcestershire sauce
6	eggs, beaten	1	tablespoon salt
½	medium onion, finely chopped	½	tablespoon pepper

Gravy

16-32 ounces beef broth

Butter

All-purpose flour

Salt and pepper to taste

Preheat oven to 325 degrees. With hands, mix together all ingredients for meatloaf. Shape into a football and place in a large baking dish. Bake for 1 hour and 15 minutes or until internal temperature reaches 180 degrees. Allow to cool for 10 minutes prior to slicing.

To make gravy, remove meatloaf from pan and set aside. Based on how much gravy you desire, add beef broth to pan and scrape bottom and sides to remove meatloaf drippings. In a Dutch oven, melt butter over medium heat. Whisk in flour and let brown, stirring constantly. Slowly add broth to flour mixture, whisking constantly until smooth and thickened. Season with salt and pepper. Serve over meatloaf.

Note: Betty uses leftover rolls for the bread crumbs. The rolls are ground in a food processor to make the crumbs.

Makes 12 servings

MOIST AND SAUCY MEATLOAF

MEATLOAF
2	pounds ground sirloin	2	eggs, lightly beaten
1	onion, minced	¼	cup steak sauce
1	green bell pepper, diced	3	tablespoons ketchup
¾	cup firmly packed brown sugar	1	teaspoon salt
½	cup crushed saltines (about 20)	½	teaspoon garlic salt

MUSTARD SAUCE
½	cup firmly packed brown sugar	¼	cup prepared mustard

TOMATO SAUCE
1	cup canned crushed tomatoes	¼	teaspoon salt
1	(8 ounce) can tomato sauce	¼	teaspoon garlic salt
		¼	teaspoon black pepper

Preheat oven to 350 degrees. In a large bowl, combine ground sirloin, onion, bell pepper, brown sugar, saltines, eggs, steak sauce, ketchup, salt and garlic salt. Shape into a loaf and place in a greased 9x13-inch baking dish. In a small bowl, mix together brown sugar and mustard until smooth. In a separate bowl, stir together tomatoes, tomato sauce, salt, garlic salt and pepper. Brush top of meatloaf with Mustard Sauce. Bake for 45 minutes; pour Tomato Sauce over meatloaf and cook 15 minutes more or until loaf is no longer pink in the middle. Let stand 15 minutes before serving.

Makes 8 to 10 servings

DONNA LEVITT

SALISBURY STEAK

1	(10.75 ounce) can golden mushroom soup, divided	¼	cup minced and soaked onion
1½	pounds ground beef		Dash black pepper
½	cup dry bread crumbs	⅓	cup water
1	egg, beaten		

Preheat oven to 350 degrees. In a large bowl, combine ¼ cup of the soup with ground beef, bread crumbs, egg, onion and pepper. Mix thoroughly and shape into 6 patties. Place in a shallow baking dish. Mix remaining soup with water and pour over patties. Bake for 30 minutes.

Makes 6 servings

COUNTRY-STYLE STEAK

2-3 pounds round steak, cubed by butcher
All-purpose flour
¼ cup oil
½ stick butter
½ medium onion, chopped
3 tablespoons gravy flour
2 cups cold water
Salt and pepper to taste

Preheat oven to 350 degrees. Dredge the steak in flour. Heat oil and butter in large skillet until butter has melted. Brown steak on both sides. Remove steak from pan. Cook onion in pan drippings until onion is translucent. Add flour to pan and stir with a fork until flour is medium brown. Add water slowly, stirring constantly. Bring to a simmer; reduce heat to low and cook about 5 minutes. Add salt and pepper to taste. Return meat to pan and cover. Place pan in oven and bake for 1 hour.

Note: Serve with mashed potatoes and green beans.

Makes 4 to 6 servings

MINIATURE MEATLOAVES

1½ pounds ground chuck
1 cup fine dry bread crumbs
2 tablespoons finely chopped onion
½ teaspoon salt
¼ teaspoon black pepper
1 (5 ounce) can evaporated milk
¾ cup of your favorite barbeque sauce

Preheat oven to 450 degrees. Combine ground chuck, bread crumbs, onion, salt, pepper and evaporated milk, stirring until mixture is thoroughly blended. Shape mixture into 6 loaves; place loaves on rack of a greased broiler pan. Spoon barbeque sauce over loaves. Bake for 25 minutes.

Note: Freezes well.

Makes 6 servings

THE LUNCH BELL POT ROAST

ROAST
1   (3½ to 5 pound) chuck or
    shoulder roast

1   cup water for each pound of
    roast
2   envelopes onion soup mix

VEGETABLES
6   carrots, cut in chunks
6   stalks celery, cut in chunks

2   cups chicken broth
½   cup water

GRAVY
Liquid from roast

4-6 tablespoons gravy flour

Preheat oven to 350 degrees. Place roast in a roasting pan and add water to the bottom of the pan. Sprinkle onion soup mix over roast. Cover tightly with plastic wrap and then cover with aluminum foil. Bake for 1 hour. Reduce heat to 300 and cook an additional 3 hours; turn off the oven and let roast set overnight or at least 4 hours. Do not open oven.

About 1 hour prior to serving roast, place carrots and celery in a small skillet. Add chicken broth and water. Cook for 30 minutes or until tender.

To make gravy, put liquid from roast in a Dutch oven over medium heat. In a separate bowl, whisk together gravy flour and small amount of liquid until smooth. Slowly add flour mixture to the roast liquid and stir constantly until thickened.

About 30 minutes prior to serving, preheat oven to 300 degrees. Cut roast into 1-inch chunks. Pour gravy over roast, cover with plastic wrap and then cover with aluminum foil. Bake for 30 minutes or until warm. Serve with vegetables.

Note: Chuck roast is preferable to shoulder. Instead of cooking the roast overnight in the oven, you may cook the roast in a Crockpot on high for 8 hours.

Makes 12 servings

You can use plastic wrap in an oven up to 350 degrees, when covered with aluminum foil. The plastic wrap will keep the roast from sticking to the aluminum foil.

STANDING RIB ROAST

1	(5 pound) standing rib roast	¼	cup coarse black pepper
Olive oil		¼	cup garlic powder
1	cup Kosher salt		

Allow roast to stand at room temperature for at least 1 hour. Preheat oven to 375 degrees. Rub roast generously with olive oil. Mix together seasonings and rub over roast. Place roast on a rack in a cooking pan with the rib side down and the fatty side up. Roast for 1 hour. Turn off oven. Leave roast in oven but do not open door for 3 hours. About 30 to 40 minutes before serving, turn oven to 375 degrees and reheat the roast. Important note: Do not remove roast or open the oven door from the time the roast is put in until ready to serve.

Note: The seasonings can be mixed together ahead of time and stored in an airtight container for up to six months.

Makes 6 to 8 servings

JEAN BECKERDITE

EASY "JOHNNY MARZETTI'S"

1	pound ground beef	1	cup water
1	medium onion, chopped	Salt and pepper to taste	
2	cups chopped celery	2	cups shelled macaroni, uncooked
1	(10.75 ounce) can condensed tomato soup	2	cups shredded sharp Cheddar cheese
1	(8 ounce) cans tomato sauce		

Preheat oven to 350 degrees. In a large skillet, cook ground beef until no pink remains; add onion and celery and cook until they are softened. Drain fat. Add tomato soup, tomato sauce and water; stir well. Add salt and pepper to taste. Simmer for 15 minutes on low heat. While meat mixture is simmering, cook shelled macaroni according to package directions or until soft. Drain macaroni. In a greased 9x13-inch baking dish, put half of the macaroni in the dish, add half of the hamburger mixture and layer with half of the cheese. Repeat layers. Bake for 30 to 35 minutes or until the cheese is bubbly.

Makes 6 to 8 servings

RUBY BINDER

CROCKPOT SPAGHETTI SAUCE

1   pound ground beef
¼   cup olive oil
1   medium onion, chopped
½   medium green bell pepper, chopped
8   cloves garlic, minced
2   (28 ounce) cans crushed tomatoes
1   (12 ounce) can tomato paste
1   (8.5 ounce) jar sliced mushrooms, drained
⅓   cup sugar
1   tablespoon salt
1   teaspoon black pepper
¼   cup dried oregano
1   (2 ounce) can flat fillets of anchovies, chopped (optional)
Cooked pasta of your choice
Olive oil
Garlic salt

In a large skillet, lightly brown ground beef in olive oil. Add onion, green pepper and garlic and continue to cook until onion is translucent. Drain fat. Pour beef mixture into a preheated Crockpot. Add tomatoes, tomato paste, mushrooms, sugar, salt, black pepper and oregano. Add anchovies, if desired. Stir well. Cook on high for 3 hours, stirring occasionally. Reduce heat and simmer until sauce is desired consistency. Cook pasta according to package directions. Drain thoroughly; add enough olive oil to coat pasta. Sprinkle with garlic salt. Serve spaghetti sauce over pasta.

Note: To allow spaghetti sauce to thicken, place skewers across the top of the Crockpot at right angles to one another; cover with paper towels. This will allow the moisture to escape. Sauce is even better reheated the next day.

Makes 4 to 6 servings

ARNOLD WALKER

AUNT ETHIE'S SPAGHETTI SAUCE

1½ pounds ground beef, divided
1 egg
½ teaspoon salt
¼ teaspoon black pepper
½ teaspoon oregano
2 (½-inch thick) bone-in pork chops
1 medium onion, chopped
1 tablespoon vegetable shortening
2 (8 ounce) cans tomato sauce
1 (6 ounce) can tomato paste
1 (28 ounce) can whole tomatoes
2 cups water
Cooked pasta of your choice

Preheat oven to 350 degrees. In a medium bowl, mix together 1 pound of ground beef with egg, salt, pepper and oregano. Form into 1-inch meatballs and place onto a baking sheet that has been sprayed with cooking spray. Bake for 20 minutes or until browned; do not overcook. In a large saucepan on medium heat, brown remaining ground beef, pork chops and onion in vegetable shortening. Drain fat. Add meatballs, tomato sauce, tomato paste, whole tomatoes and water. Cook over low heat for 1½ hours. Serve over cooked pasta.

Makes 6 to 8 servings

ETHIE COFFEY

CRESCENT ROLL LASAGNA

1 pound ground beef
½ cup chopped onion
1 teaspoon basil
1 teaspoon oregano
1 teaspoon garlic powder
1 teaspoon salt
1 tablespoon dried parsley
1 cup ricotta cheese
½ cup freshly grated Parmesan cheese
1 cup shredded American cheese
2 cans crescent rolls
Sesame seeds

Preheat oven to 350 degrees. In a large skillet, brown ground beef with onion. Drain fat. Add basil, oregano, garlic powder, salt and parsley. In a small bowl, mix together ricotta cheese, Parmesan cheese and American cheese. Unroll 1 can of crescent rolls and place on a greased cookie sheet. Pinch perforations together to form 1 large rectangle. Spoon half of meat mixture onto dough. Spread half of cheese mixture on meat. Add remaining meat mixture and top with cheese mixture. Place second can of crescent rolls on top, sealing all perforations and sealing the sides. Sprinkle with sesame seeds. Bake for 25 to 30 minutes.

Makes 8 servings

ASHLEY DARCY

Betty spent many hours in the kitchen with her aunt Ethie. Betty is deeply grateful for all of the love and guidance given to her from aunt Ethie.

Ashley is Betty's granddaughter-in-law and is happy to submit some of her favorite recipes.

THREE CHEESE LASAGNA

MEAT SAUCE

1   large onion, chopped
1   garlic clove, minced
1-2 tablespoons chopped fresh
      parsley
¼   cup olive oil
2   (28 ounce) cans Italian
      tomatoes, undrained

2   (6 ounce) cans tomato paste
2   bay leaves
1½ teaspoons salt
¼   teaspoon black pepper
1½ teaspoons dried oregano
1   pound ground beef,
      browned and drained

CHEESE SAUCE

1   small onion, finely chopped
½   stick butter
3   tablespoons all-purpose flour

¾   cup freshly grated Parmesan
      cheese
2   cups milk
2   egg yolks, slightly beaten

OTHER INGREDIENTS

1   pound lasagna noodles,
      cooked al dente
8   ounces mozzarella cheese,
      sliced and torn into pieces

8   ounces provolone cheese,
      sliced and torn into pieces
Freshly grated Parmesan cheese

For meat sauce, sauté onion, garlic and parsley in olive oil in a large saucepan over medium heat until onion is translucent. Add tomatoes, tomato paste, bay leaves, salt, pepper and oregano. Stir in cooked ground beef and simmer for 1 hour over low heat, stirring occasionally. Remove bay leaves.

For cheese sauce, cook onion in butter in a small saucepan until onion is translucent. Add flour, stirring until smooth. Stir in Parmesan cheese. Gradually stir in milk and continue cooking over medium heat, stirring constantly, until sauce is the consistency of heavy cream. Whisk a small amount of hot cheese mixture into egg yolks; add egg yolk mixture into hot cheese mixture, stirring constantly. Cook over low heat for 10 minutes. Remove from heat and set aside.

Preheat oven to 350 degrees. In a greased lasagna pan, layer one-third of the cooked noodles, tomato sauce and cheese sauce. Top cheese sauce with one-third of the mozzarella cheese and one-third of the provolone cheese. Repeat procedure 2 times with remaining ingredients. Sprinkle top with Parmesan cheese. Bake for 30 minutes or until thoroughly heated. Let stand for 10 minutes before serving.

Makes 8 to 10 servings

JACKY'S PASTA

This recipe is from Jacky Robinson, a friend of the Swain family who lives in Richmond.

1	medium onion, chopped	½	cup red wine
2	celery stalks, chopped	1	(6 ounce) can tomato paste
2	carrots, peeled and chopped	1	(14 ounce) can beef broth
2	tablespoons butter	3	tablespoons Italian seasoning
2	tablespoons olive oil		¼-½ cup heavy whipping cream
1	pound pork sausage		Cooked pasta of your choice
1½	pounds ground beef		

In a large skillet, sauté onion, celery and carrots in butter and oil for 5 minutes. Add sausage and ground beef and cook until meat is brown. Drain fat. Reduce heat. Add wine and let simmer on low for 5 minutes, without stirring. Add tomato paste, broth and Italian seasoning and simmer for 2 hours. Add whipping cream and stir; keep warm until ready to serve. Serve over cooked pasta.

Makes 6 servings

JACKY ROBINSON

BEEF STROGANOFF

1¾	pounds beef, cut into strips	1	(8 ounce) can sliced mushrooms or 1 cup fresh mushrooms
3	large onions, sliced thin		Salt, pepper and Worcestershire sauce to taste
2	garlic cloves, minced		
2	tablespoons butter	2	cups sour cream
2	tablespoons vegetable oil		Cooked rice or noodles
2	tablespoons all-purpose flour		
1	(6 ounce) can tomato paste		
1	(10.5 ounce) can beef consommé		

In a large skillet, sauté meat, onion and garlic in butter and oil until meat is browned. Add flour, tomato paste, consommé, mushrooms, salt, pepper and Worcestershire sauce. Cover and simmer over low heat for 1 hour and 30 minutes. Just before serving, stir in sour cream. Serve over rice or noodles.

Makes 4 to 6 servings

MEATBALL SUB CASSEROLE

MEATBALLS

⅓ cup chopped green onion

¼ cup Italian bread crumbs

¼ cup freshly grated Parmesan cheese

1 pound ground beef

CASSEROLE

1 loaf Italian bread

8 ounces cream cheese, softened

½ cup mayonnaise

1 teaspoon Italian seasoning, more to taste

¼ teaspoon black pepper, more to taste

Garlic powder

2-3 cups mozzarella cheese, divided

1 (28 ounce) jar spaghetti sauce (Four Cheese is recommended)

1 cup water

2 garlic cloves, minced

Preheat oven to 400 degrees. In a medium bowl, combine onion, bread crumbs and Parmesan cheese. Add ground beef and mix well, using hands. Shape into 1-inch balls. Place in greased baking dish. Bake for 15 to 20 minutes.

Reduce oven to 350 degrees. Cut Italian bread into 1-inch cubes. Arrange bread in a single layer in a 9x13-inch baking dish. In a bowl, combine cream cheese, mayonnaise, Italian seasoning and pepper. Spread cheese mixture over bread. Sprinkle with garlic powder and Italian seasoning. Top with 1 cup of mozzarella cheese. In a separate bowl, combine spaghetti sauce, water and garlic. Add meatballs. Pour over cheese in baking dish. Top with remaining mozzarella cheese. Bake for 30 minutes, until hot and bubbly.

Makes 6 to 8 servings

ASHLEY DARCY

Ashley and Jay Darcy,
Betty's two oldest grandchildren,
live in Georgia.

Stroganoff "La Boheme" (Poor Man's Stroganoff)

1	pound lean ground beef	1	cup uncooked elbow macaroni
1	cup chopped onion	2	tablespoons sugar
2	cups stewed tomatoes	1	tablespoon chili powder
1½	cups sour cream	2	teaspoons salt

In a large skillet, sauté beef and onion until meat is browned. Drain off fat. Add tomatoes, sour cream, macaroni, sugar, chili powder and salt. Cover and simmer for 25 to 30 minutes. Turn off heat and steam for 5 more minutes.

Note: This meal is good served with tossed salad and hot French garlic bread.

Makes 6 to 8 servings

BENITA EDWARDS

If you burn the bottom of a pan, fill it halfway with water and bring to a boil. Add 2 Bounce® dryer sheets to the water and cover. Turn off the heat; let set until cooled. The burnt material will fall right off the pan.

Our Favorite Flank Steak

2	flank steaks	2	tablespoons soy sauce
2	teaspoons meat tenderizer	1	tablespoon honey
1	tablespoon sugar	1	teaspoon salt
2	tablespoons wine, any color		

Place flank steaks in a 9x13-inch baking dish. Puncture steaks with a fork. Mix meat tenderizer, sugar, wine, soy sauce, honey and salt. Pour mixture over steaks. Marinate at least 1 hour, longer if possible, turning the steak once. Broil in the oven or put on grill for 3 to 4 minutes on each side. Do not overcook. Let meat set for 10 minutes before slicing. Slice thinly across the grain of the meat.

Note: Our family has used this recipe since 1972 and we never tire of it. You can also marinate the steak in a plastic bag, being sure to turn the steak at least once.

Makes 8 to 10 servings

HELEN CVIK

BRISKET OF BEEF

5-6 pounds first cut (fresh beef) brisket	1 cup firmly packed dark brown sugar
1 package onion soup mix	¾ cup ketchup
	½ cup cider vinegar

Preheat oven to 350 degrees. Place brisket on sheet of heavy foil, large enough to wrap around brisket. Mix together soup mix, brown sugar, ketchup, and vinegar. Pour vinegar mixture over meat. Wrap foil around meat. Bake for 2½ to 3 hours.

Note: This brisket is good reheated, great for sandwiches and can be frozen.

Makes 10 to 12 servings

HELEN CVIK

"When we visited once a year in Chicago, my aunt and uncle always treated us to a delicious meal. We have thoroughly enjoyed this one."
Helen Cvik

PINEAPPLE HAM

1 (3 pound) shank portion ham or pit ham (do not use spiral ham)	1 tablespoon cornstarch
1 (20 ounce) can crushed pineapple, undrained	¼ teaspoon salt
	2 tablespoons lemon juice
1 cup firmly packed light brown sugar	1 tablespoon prepared yellow mustard

Trim fat off of ham; cut ham off bone into 3 inch pieces or chunks. Place ham in Crockpot. In medium saucepan, combine pineapple, brown sugar, cornstarch, salt, lemon juice and yellow mustard. Bring to light boil over medium heat, stirring constantly. Remove from heat as soon as it comes to light boil. Pour mixture over ham in Crockpot, making sure that it drizzles down and coats all of the ham. Cover and cook on low in Crockpot about 6 hours or until tender but not falling apart. You may start the ham on high for 1 hour if you have less cooking time; reduce temperature to low for the remaining hours of cooking. Do not overcook or the ham will break apart.

Note: This is a delicious recipe for the holidays or anytime! This recipe has been in our family for almost 30 years. We received it from a friend and fellow co-worker who is no longer with us.

Makes approximately 12 servings

TERRY ROBERTS AND MAE WENZEL

*"We have been eating at **The Lunch Bell** with Mae since our boys were babies, and they are now 24 and 19 years old! We plan all of our appointments around eating lunch there as often as possible. It's our family's favorite lunch place ever!"*
Terry Roberts

TANGERINE-GLAZED HAM WITH BABY CARROTS

1 (8 to 10-pound) smoked ham, bone-in, skin on	2 cups tangerine juice
Kosher salt and freshly ground black pepper	2 cups firmly packed light brown sugar
1 bunch fresh sage leaves	1 cup water
¼ cup extra-virgin olive oil	¼ teaspoon whole cloves
2 sticks unsalted butter, cut in chunks	2 cinnamon sticks
2 tangerines, sliced thin, seeds removed	1½ pounds baby carrots

Preheat oven to 300 degrees. Put the ham in a large roasting pan, fat-side up. Using a sharp knife, score the ham with cuts across the skin, about 2-inches apart and ½-inch deep. Cut diagonally down the slashes to form a diamond pattern; season the meat generously with salt and pepper. Chop about 8 of the sage leaves and place in a bowl; mix with the oil to make a paste. Rub the sage-oil mixture over the ham, being sure to get the flavor into all the slits. Bake the ham for 2 hours.

For the glaze, add butter, tangerines, tangerine juice, brown sugar, water, cloves and cinnamon to a saucepan. Slowly cook the liquid, over medium heat, for 30 to 40 minutes or until it is syrupy.

After the ham has been baking for a couple of hours, pour the tangerine glaze over it, with the pieces of fruit and all. Scatter the remaining sage leaves on top and put the ham back in the oven. Continue to cook for 1½ hours, basting with the juices every 30 minutes.

Scatter the carrots around the ham and coat in the tangerine glaze. Put the ham back in the oven and cook for a final 30 minutes, until the carrots are tender, and the ham is dark and crispy.

Note: Set the ham on a cutting board to rest before carving. Serve the carrots and tangerine glaze on the side.

Makes 10 to 12 servings

HAM AND MACARONI CASSEROLE

1   (8 ounce) box elbow
    macaroni
2   tablespoons butter
4   teaspoons minced onion
1   tablespoon all-purpose flour
¼   teaspoon dry mustard
½   teaspoon salt
Pepper to taste

2   cups milk
1½ cups cooked and chopped
    ham
2   cups shredded sharp
    Cheddar cheese
4   teaspoons melted butter
¾   cup bread crumbs

In a saucepan, cook macaroni according to package directions, drain. Preheat oven to 400 degrees. In another saucepan over medium heat, melt butter; add minced onion, flour, dry mustard, salt and pepper to taste. Slowly stir in milk and cook until smooth and slightly thickened. Add ham and 1½ cups cheese. Cook until cheese melts. Put cooked macaroni in a greased 2-quart baking dish. Pour cheese sauce over macaroni and toss lightly until coated. Sprinkle remaining ½ cup shredded cheese on top. Blend butter and bread crumbs together and sprinkle on top of cheese. Bake 20 to 25 minutes or until golden brown.

Makes 4 to 6 servings

BETTY WALLACE ARMSTRONG

LANCASTER COUNTY HAM LOAF

HAM LOAF

1   pound fresh ground turkey
1   pound fresh ground ham
    (or turkey ham)
1   cup bread crumbs

SAUCE

⅔   cup firmly packed brown
    sugar
1   teaspoon dry mustard

1   egg, beaten
1   teaspoon salt
⅛   teaspoon pepper
¾   cup milk

½   cup water
¼   cup vinegar

Preheat oven to 350 degrees. Grind meat (if necessary) and mix with bread crumbs, egg, salt, pepper and milk. Shape into a loaf and place in a 9x13-inch baking dish. Bake for 1 hour.

Mix together brown sugar, dry mustard, water and vinegar. Pour sauce over loaf and continue to bake for 1 more hour.

Makes 8 servings

BETTY LASSEN

"We are submitting this recipe with a great deal of love and fond memories of our mother, Betty Wallace Armstrong. During the 1990's, Betty Armstrong frequented **The Lunch Bell** *in its former location on Thimble Shoals Boulevard. Her children and good friends would go with her and her favorite dish was the Hot Chicken Salad. After Betty's death in March, 2000, her children made it an annual "date" to eat lunch at* **The Lunch Bell** *on her birthday, September 11. The first year on September 11, 2000, we met for lunch and guess what was on the menu? Hot Chicken Salad! It seems like for several years we met and Betty's favorite dish was the special of the day."*

Susan Tweedy,
Tricia Michael,
Rick Wallace and
Lynetta Wapner

CAROLINA STYLE BARBEQUE

2	(3 to 4 pound) pork Boston butt roasts	¼	cup sugar
1	cup white vinegar	1	tablespoon crushed red peppers
1	cup apple cider vinegar		Salt to taste

Place pork in a Crockpot on low heat. Mix together vinegars, sugar, red pepper and salt. Pour over pork and cook for approximately 6 to 8 hours or until pork is very tender.

Makes 10 to 12 servings

PATSY TAYLOR

CROCKPOT CAROLINA STYLE PORK

PORK ROAST

2	tablespoons paprika	1	teaspoon black pepper
3	tablespoons brown sugar	1	(5 to 6 pound) pork shoulder or Boston butt roast
1	teaspoon salt		

BARBEQUE SAUCE

8-10	ounces apple cider vinegar	½	teaspoon garlic salt
4	teaspoons Worcestershire sauce	½	teaspoon sugar
½	teaspoon dry mustard	½	teaspoon cayenne red pepper or more to taste

Mix together paprika, brown sugar, salt and pepper. Rub over entire pork roast. Place pork roast in Crockpot on low for 10 to 11 hours or until very tender. (May cook on high for 6 to 7 hours.)

In a jar, mix together vinegar, Worcestershire sauce, mustard, garlic salt, sugar and cayenne pepper. Cover and shake well. Set aside until roast is ready.

When pork is very tender, using a fork, remove roast from Crockpot. Chop roast into small pieces. Pour 1 to 2 tablespoons of sauce over the chopped roast. Serve with extra sauce, adding as much or as little as you like.

Note: Pork can also be placed on toasted hamburger buns for sandwiches.

Makes 10 to 12 servings

PORK BARBEQUE

1 (3 to 4 pound) pork Boston butt roast
Salt
2 tablespoons butter
3 tablespoons chopped onion
1 cup ketchup
¾ cup water
¼ cup vinegar
2 tablespoons Worcestershire sauce
1 teaspoon dry mustard
1 teaspoon garlic powder
¼ teaspoon cayenne pepper
2 tablespoons brown sugar

Place pork in a stockpot and cover with water. Add salt to taste and boil pork for 4 to 6 hours or until meat falls off the bone; set aside. Put butter and onion in a skillet and cook until translucent. Add remaining ingredients. Cook for 10 minutes or until slightly thickened. Cut up pork in small pieces. Mix together with sauce and serve. Freezes well.

Note: Add Tabasco® to the sauce to spice it up!

Makes 6 to 8 servings

PAULA MARIA ORPHANIDYS

PORK FRIED RICE

6-8 boneless pork chops, cut into bite-sized pieces
½ stick butter, divided or ½ cup olive oil
6-7 carrots, peeled and thinly sliced
1 large onion, chopped
1 large green bell pepper, chopped
5 stalks celery, chopped
4-5 medium potatoes, peeled and cut in small chunks
2 bags boil-in-the-bag rice, cooked (about 4 cups cooked)
Soy sauce to taste
Dash of salt
Dash of pepper
1 teaspoon Italian seasoning
1 teaspoon crushed oregano

Place pork chop pieces in small frying pan with half of butter or olive oil. Cook until tender and done; set aside. Grease a large wok or large deep skillet with the remaining butter or olive oil. Add carrots, onion, green pepper, celery and potatoes to pan and cook until almost tender, but do not overcook or they will become mushy. When veggies are done, add pork and rice to wok. Add enough soy sauce to coat all of mixture. Add salt, pepper, Italian seasoning and oregano and combine well.

Makes 8 to 10 servings

TERRY ROBERTS AND MAE WENZEL

BRINED PORK CHOPS
WITH SPICY CHUTNEY BARBEQUE SAUCE

PORK CHOPS

8   cups water, divided
½   cup coarse salt
½   cup firmly packed golden
    light brown sugar

¼   cup chili powder
8   (1½-inch-thick) bone-in pork
    rib chops
Olive oil

SPICY CHUTNEY BARBEQUE SAUCE

2   tablespoons butter
1   medium onion, finely
    chopped
2   garlic cloves, minced
1   (12 ounce) bottle chili sauce
1   (9 to 10 ounce) jar mango
    chutney

⅓   cup apple cider vinegar
2   tablespoons Worcestershire
    sauce
2   tablespoons Dijon mustard
1½ teaspoons hot pepper sauce
    (preferably habanero
    pepper)

Combine 2 cups water, salt, brown sugar and chili powder in large stockpot. Bring to boil, stirring to dissolve salt and brown sugar. Remove from heat. Add 6 cups cold water. Cool brine completely. Add pork chops, pressing to submerge. Cover pot; chill at least 6 hours and up to 24 hours.

Prior to grilling pork, melt butter in heavy saucepan over medium heat. Add onion; sauté until golden brown, about 5 minutes. Add garlic; stir 1 minute. Stir in chili sauce, chutney, vinegar, Worcestershire sauce, and mustard; bring to boil. Reduce heat to medium-low and simmer until mixture is reduced to 2 ¾ cups, stirring frequently, about 10 minutes. Stir in hot pepper sauce. Transfer sauce to bowl; cool to room temperature. Cover; chill. Bring to room temperature before serving.

Bring grill to medium-high heat. Drain pork; pat dry with paper towels. Brush pork on both sides with oil; sprinkle with pepper. Grill pork to desired doneness, about 10 minutes per side or until instant red thermometer registers 150 degrees for medium. Serve pork with Spicy Chutney Barbeque Sauce.

Note: Brining ensures a moist grilled chop. Mango chutney and habanero chili spike this fantastic sauce. The chutney can be made 3 days ahead of time.

Makes 8 servings

HELEN CVIK

HONEY GRILLED PORK CHOPS

6	(¾-inch-thick) pork loin chops	6	tablespoons dark brown sugar
1	cup soy sauce	6	tablespoons honey
2	teaspoons ground ginger	5	teaspoons dark sesame oil
5	garlic cloves, halved		

Place pork chops in a resealable plastic bag. In a small bowl, combine soy sauce, ginger and garlic and pour over pork chops. Seal and refrigerate at least 3 hours, turning occasionally. Prepare grill. In a saucepan, combine brown sugar, honey and sesame oil. Cook over low heat until sugar dissolves, stirring constantly.

When ready to grill, remove pork chops from marinade; discard marinade. Grill pork chops over medium heat for 10 minutes on each side or until done; baste with honey mixture.

Note: The honey mixture becomes very thick when cooled. Keep warm while grilling pork chops by placing the saucepan directly on the grill rack.

Makes 6 servings

It's a family affair at **The Lunch Bell**! Blair and Shelah have both worked at the restaurant over the years.

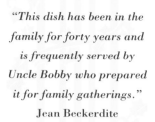

Uncle Bobby's Pork Tenderloin

1	(2 pound) pork tenderloin	½	teaspoon garlic powder
1	teaspoon Greek seasoning	3	tablespoons Worcestershire sauce
1	teaspoon sea salt		
1	teaspoon lemon pepper		

Bring the pork tenderloins to room temperature prior to applying the seasonings. Apply Greek seasoning, sea salt, lemon pepper, garlic powder and Worcestershire sauce and place in a 1 gallon resealable plastic bag to marinate. Allow to marinate 4 hours for mild flavor or overnight for robust flavor. Preheat grill to medium temperature. Remove pork from bag and discard marinade. Grill, turning frequently until internal temperature reaches 165 degrees. Remove from grill and allow to rest for 15 minutes before slicing. Slice and serve.

Note: This dish can be used to serve large groups and can be prepared in advance and heated. Simply slice and place in party-size rolls for appetizers or serve as a main dish. Cavender's® is a good Greek seasoning to use.

Makes 6 servings

JEAN BECKERDITE

"This dish has been in the family for forty years and is frequently served by Uncle Bobby who prepared it for family gatherings."
Jean Beckerdite

 # The Lunch Bell Crab Cakes

1	egg, beaten	1	teaspoon Dijon mustard
3	tablespoons mayonnaise	1	cup fresh bread crumbs
1	teaspoon salt	1	pound back fin crabmeat
1	teaspoon black pepper	2	tablespoon vegetable oil
1½	tablespoons Worcestershire sauce	2	tablespoons butter

Mix together egg, mayonnaise, salt, pepper, Worcestershire sauce, mustard and bread crumbs. Gently fold in the crabmeat to avoid breaking up the crab. Shape crab mixture into 6 balls, and gently pat them down into crab cakes. Sauté in vegetable oil and butter on medium-high heat until light brown on both sides, being sure to turn them only once.

Makes 6 crab cakes

To ensure removal of crab shells, place crab on a baking sheet and bake at 275 degrees for 6 to 8 minutes. Any shells will be easy to find, as they will turn white.

SEAFOOD CASSEROLE

WHITE SAUCE

2	tablespoons butter	1	cup shredded Cheddar cheese
2	tablespoons all-purpose flour		
½	cup milk		

CASSEROLE

1	cup mayonnaise	½	cup chopped onion
½	tablespoon Worcestershire sauce	½	cup chopped celery
1	tablespoon mustard	1½	cups shredded bread
¼	cup sherry	2	cups crabmeat
¼	teaspoon curry	2	pounds cooked and peeled shrimp
1	tablespoon chopped fresh parsley		Rice or pastry shells

Preheat oven to 350 degrees. Melt butter in a large saucepan; slowly whisk in flour to make a roux. Add milk and cheese and stir until smooth. Add each casserole ingredient (excluding rice or pastry shells) to the white sauce one at a time, mixing well after each. Transfer to a 9x13-inch baking dish and bake for 30 minutes. Serve over rice or in pastry shells.

Makes 6 servings

 # THE LUNCH BELL LOBSTER ROLL

2	pounds lobster meat, coarsely chopped	1	cup Duke's® mayonnaise
1	cup finely chopped celery	½	teaspoon salt
1	teaspoon finely minced onion	¼	teaspoon black pepper
		6	tablespoons butter, softened
		6	hot dog buns

Mix together lobster, celery, onion, mayonnaise, salt and pepper in a medium bowl. Chill for at least 30 minutes. Butter hot dog buns and grill or toast. Fill with lobster mixture.

Makes 6 servings

Shrimp and Scallop Casserole

⅔ cup dry white wine
4 tablespoons butter, divided
1 tablespoon fresh chopped parsley
1 teaspoon salt
1 medium onion, thinly sliced
½ cup sliced fresh mushrooms
3 tablespoons all-purpose flour
1 cup half-and-half
½ cup grated Swiss cheese

2 teaspoons fresh lemon juice
⅛ teaspoon black pepper
1 pound large shrimp, peeled and deveined
1 pound large sea scallops
1 cup soft bread crumbs
¼ cup freshly grated Parmesan cheese
Hot cooked rice
Paprika

In a saucepan, combine wine, 1 tablespoon butter, parsley, salt and onion. Cook for 5 minutes, stirring occasionally. In a separate saucepan, melt 3 tablespoons butter and sauté mushrooms until tender. Stir in flour and cook 1 minute, stirring constantly. Gradually add half-and-half, stirring until thickened. Stir in Swiss cheese. Gradually stir in wine mixture, lemon juice and pepper. Add shrimp and scallops. Spoon mixture into a lightly greased 7x11-inch baking dish. Cover and refrigerate overnight or for at least 8 hours.

Remove from refrigerator and let stand at room temperature for 30 minutes. Preheat oven to 350 degrees. Cover casserole with aluminum foil and bake for 20 to 30 minutes or until shrimp turn pink and scallops are opaque. In a small bowl, combine bread crumbs and Parmesan cheese and sprinkle over casserole. Bake for 5 more minutes. Serve over hot cooked rice and garnish with paprika.

Makes 8 servings

SHRIMP ÉTOUFFÉE

1 stick butter
2 medium onions, chopped
1 stalk celery, finely chopped
4 garlic cloves, minced
1½ teaspoons minced jalapeño pepper
2 tablespoons all-purpose flour
1 (14 ounce) can Italian chopped tomatoes, undrained
1 tablespoon paprika
1 teaspoon salt
1 teaspoon black pepper
Dash cayenne pepper
2 pounds shrimp, shelled and deveined
1 bunch green onion, chopped, including green tops
¼ cup chopped fresh parsley
Hot cooked rice

In a skillet, melt butter and add onion and celery. Cook until onion is translucent and tender. Add the garlic and jalapeño pepper and cook for 2 minutes. Add the flour, stirring constantly for 3 to 4 minutes.

Stir in the tomatoes, paprika, salt, black pepper and cayenne pepper. Bring to a simmer and cook for 5 to 10 minutes. Add the shrimp and cook on medium heat until they turn pink, about 3 to 5 minutes. Stir in the green onion and parsley and serve over cooked rice.

Makes 6 servings

CRAB CAKES FROM ACROSS THE RIVER

½ cup all-purpose flour
½ cup pancake mix
1 teaspoon prepared mustard
3 tablespoons mayonnaise
1 medium stalk celery, minced
Dash Tabasco® sauce, or more to taste
1 tablespoon Worcestershire sauce, or more to taste
Salt and pepper
1 pound fresh lump crabmeat
1 egg, beaten
½ cup vegetable oil, or more if needed

In a medium bowl, mix flour and pancake mix together; set aside. In a separate bowl, combine mustard, mayonnaise, celery, Tabasco® sauce, Worcestershire sauce, salt and pepper. Gently fold in the crabmeat to avoid breaking up the crab. Shape crab mixture into 6 balls, and gently pat them down into crab cakes. Dip crab cakes into beaten egg, then into flour mixture. Fry in vegetable oil in frying pan on medium-high heat until light brown on both sides, being sure to only turn them once.

Note: The pancake mix in this recipe lightens the coating.

Makes 6 crab cakes

SOUTHERN STYLE SHRIMP AND GRITS

SHRIMP SAUCE

3	tablespoons vegetable oil
1½	cups country ham, soaked to remove some of the saltiness, then sliced and cut into small bite-sized pieces
2	cups chopped onion
¾	cup chopped green bell pepper

¾	cup chopped red bell pepper
1	teaspoon garlic powder
¼	cup all-purpose flour
2½	cups chicken broth

Dash cayenne pepper, or more to taste

2	cups small shrimp, shelled and deveined

GRITS

3½	cups chicken broth
⅔	cup grits
2	ounces goat cheese

½	teaspoon salt
¼	teaspoon black pepper

In saucepan, heat vegetable oil; add country ham and cook until done, about 4 to 5 minutes. Add onion and pepper and cook on low until tender, stirring as it cooks. Add garlic powder and flour. Continue cooking and stirring for 4 to 5 minutes. Add chicken broth slowly and stir continuously. Bring to a low boil and continue cooking until it reaches the creamy consistency you desire. Add shrimp and continue to cook and stir until the shrimp are pink and tender (4 to 5 minutes). Add dash of cayenne pepper.

While making shrimp sauce, pour chicken broth into pot and bring to a boil. Add grits, salt, and pepper and return to a boil. Add goat cheese. Stir and cook on low until it reaches the consistency you like. Serve shrimp sauce on top of grits.

Makes 4 servings

LINDA CARSON

TARTAR SAUCE FOR CRAB CAKES

1	tablespoon capers
1	teaspoon chopped olives
1	teaspoon cucumber pickle
¼	teaspoon onion juice

1	tablespoon chopped fresh parsley
1	cup mayonnaise

In a medium bowl, mix together capers, olives, pickle, onion juice and parsley. Stir in mayonnaise.

Makes about 1 cup

SHRIMP AND FETA CHEESE OVER PASTA

1 pound medium shrimp, peeled and deveined

Pinch of crushed red pepper flakes

¼ cup olive oil, divided

4 ounces crumbled feta cheese

½ teaspoon crushed garlic

1 (14.5 ounce) can tomato wedges, undrained

¼ cup dry white wine (or white cooking wine)

¾ teaspoon dried basil

½ teaspoon dried oregano

¼ teaspoon salt

¼ teaspoon black pepper

8 ounces uncooked angel hair pasta

Preheat oven to 400 degrees. In a large skillet, sauté shrimp and red pepper flakes in 2 tablespoons olive oil for 2 to 3 minutes or until shrimp are slightly pink. Arrange shrimp in a medium baking dish and sprinkle with feta cheese; set aside. Add remaining oil to skillet; sauté garlic over low heat. Add tomatoes and juice and cook for 1 minute. Stir in wine, basil, oregano, salt and pepper and simmer, uncovered for 10 minutes. Spoon tomato mixture over shrimp. Bake uncovered for 10 minutes. Cook pasta according to package directions and serve shrimp over pasta.

Makes 3 to 4 servings

BERDA COLE

CRAB IMPERIAL

1 pound backfin or lump crabmeat

2 eggs, beaten

½ cup mayonnaise

¼ cup half-and-half

3 tablespoons butter, melted

1 teaspoon lemon juice

1½ teaspoons Worcestershire sauce

10 saltine crackers, crushed

¾ teaspoon dry mustard

2 tablespoons chopped green bell pepper

2 tablespoons chopped red bell pepper

1 teaspoon salt

1 teaspoon Old Bay® seasoning

Dash Tabasco® sauce

Paprika

Preheat oven to 400 degrees. Gently pick through crabmeat to remove all shells. Do not break up lumps of crab; set aside. Combine eggs, mayonnaise, half-and-half, butter, lemon juice and Worcestershire sauce. Mix well. Stir in crackers, dry mustard, green pepper, red pepper, salt, Old Bay® seasoning and Tabasco® sauce. Fold in crabmeat. Place into 8 individual baking shells or into a greased 8x8-inch baking dish. Sprinkle with paprika. Bake for 15 to 20 minutes until bubbly and lightly browned.

Makes 4 servings

CARTER'S CREEK CRAB CAKES
WITH TARTAR SAUCE

CRAB CAKES

2	cups mayonnaise
1	lemon, for juice
1	tablespoon white wine
1	tablespoon Old Bay® Seasoning
¼	teaspoon Tabasco® sauce
½	cup Worcestershire sauce
1	egg
1	cup white bread crumbs (instructions below)
1	pound lump crabmeat
1	tablespoon chopped fresh parsley

TARTAR SAUCE

½	cup dill pickle relish (not sweet)
¼	cup finely chopped yellow onion
4	cups mayonnaise
½	teaspoon Worcestershire sauce
¼	teaspoon Tabasco® sauce
	Dash salt
	Dash pepper
	Fresh lemon wedges for garnish

In a large bowl, combine mayonnaise, lemon juice, white wine, Old Bay® Seasoning, Tabasco® sauce, Worcestershire sauce and egg. To make bread crumbs, trim and discard crust from 8 to 10 pieces of white sandwich bread; grind in a food processor. Add crabmeat, bread crumbs and parsley to mayonnaise mixture and fold gently to avoid breaking up the crabmeat. Portion crabmeat mixture into 5 (4 ounce) or 7 (3 ounce) crab cakes that are approximately ¾-inch thick. Sauté in a minimal amount of hot vegetable oil on medium-high heat until light brown on both sides. Drain off any excess grease.

Press the pickles into a fine sieve or squeeze out in a piece of cheesecloth so that they don't make the sauce too thin. Combine pickles, onion, mayonnaise, Worcestershire sauce, Tabasco® sauce, salt and pepper in a stainless steel bowl and mix well. Serve crab cakes with tartar sauce and fresh lemon wedges.

Note: Crab cakes may also be broiled until golden.

Makes 5 to 7 crab cakes, depending on the size

CALVIN HEBBONS

HONEY GRILLED SALMON

6   tablespoons margarine
⅓   cup honey
⅓   cup firmly packed dark
      brown sugar
2   tablespoons fresh lemon
      juice
1   teaspoon liquid smoke
      flavoring
Dash of hot sauce
4   salmon steaks

In a saucepan, combine margarine, honey, brown sugar, lemon juice, liquid smoke flavoring and hot sauce. Cook over low heat, stirring frequently, for 5 minutes or until margarine melts and sugar dissolves. Cool marinade to room temperature. Place salmon steaks in a glass dish and pour marinade over fish. Cover and refrigerate for 30 minutes, turning once. Prepare grill. Drain salmon and grill over medium heat for 5 to 7 minutes. Turn and grill 5 more minutes or until done.

Makes 4 servings

TROUT/ROCKFISH MEUNIÈRE

6   trout or rockfish fillets
All-purpose flour
1-2 teaspoons salt
¼   teaspoon black pepper
6   tablespoons butter or more
2   tablespoons chopped fresh
      parsley or 1 teaspoon dried
      parsley
1   tablespoon chopped green
      onion tops (optional)
Dash of Worcestershire sauce
Dash of hot sauce or cayenne
      pepper
2   tablespoons lemon juice
Dash of garlic powder
½   cup small shrimp or can of
      crabmeat (optional)

Pat fillets dry and roll lightly in flour seasoned with 1 teaspoon salt and pepper. In a large skillet, sauté fillets in hot butter. Once fish is browned, about 5 minutes, turn and cook on the other side for 3 more minutes. Put cooked fillets in a warm serving dish. Sprinkle fish with parsley, green onion, salt and pepper. Add Worcestershire sauce, cayenne, lemon juice and garlic powder to the skillet. Cook until foamy, then add shrimp or crabmeat. Pour over the fish.

Makes 6 servings

PHIL LEATHERBURY

BROILED TILAPIA PARMESAN

½	cup freshly grated Parmesan cheese	¼	teaspoon ground black pepper
½	stick butter, softened	⅛	teaspoon onion powder
3	tablespoons mayonnaise	⅛	teaspoon celery salt
2	tablespoons fresh lemon juice	¼	cup bread crumbs
¼	teaspoon dried basil	2	pounds thawed tilapia fillets
			Old Bay® Seasoning

Preheat your oven's broiler. Grease a broiling pan or line pan with aluminum foil. In a small bowl, mix together the Parmesan cheese, butter, mayonnaise and lemon juice. Add dried basil, pepper, onion powder, celery salt and bread crumbs. Mix well and set aside.

Arrange fillets in a single layer on the prepared pan. Sprinkle both sides with Old Bay® Seasoning. Broil a few inches from the heat for 2 to 3 minutes. Flip the fillets over and broil for a couple more minutes. Remove the fillets from the oven and cover them with the Parmesan cheese mixture on the top side. Broil for 2 more minutes or until the topping is browned and fish flakes easily with a fork. Be careful not to overcook the fish.

Makes 8 servings
BARBARA HOLLAND EBY

 # VEGETABLE QUICHE

3	eggs	1	cup diced fresh vegetables (tomatoes, squash, zucchini, broccoli, green pepper and/or carrots)
3	tablespoons all-purpose flour		
½	cup whole milk		
1	cup Duke's® mayonnaise	1	(10-inch) deep dish frozen pie shell
1	cup shredded cheese (Cheddar, Swiss, feta, American, etc.)		

Preheat oven to 350 degrees. Beat eggs with a wire whisk. Add flour, milk and mayonnaise, stirring well. Fold in cheese and vegetables. Pour into pie shell and bake for 25 to 30 minutes or until golden brown.

Makes 8 servings

SPINACH, FETA AND SUN-DRIED TOMATO QUICHE

3	eggs	½	cup Swiss cheese
3	tablespoons all-purpose flour	1½	cups packed raw spinach
½	cup whole milk	¼	cup sun-dried tomatoes
1	cup Duke's® mayonnaise	1	(10-inch) deep dish frozen pie shell
½	cup feta cheese		

Preheat oven to 350 degrees. Beat eggs with a wire whisk. Add flour, milk and mayonnaise, stirring well. Fold in cheeses, spinach and sun-dried tomatoes. Pour into pie shell and bake for 25 to 30 minutes or until golden brown.

Makes 8 servings

CHICKEN CORDON BLUE QUICHE

3	eggs	½	cup smoked, cubed ham
3	tablespoons all-purpose flour	1	teaspoon chopped fresh parsley
½	cup whole milk	1	(10-inch) deep dish frozen pie shell
1	cup Duke's® mayonnaise		
1	cup shredded Swiss cheese		
1	(4 ounce) chicken breast, cooked and cubed		

Preheat oven to 350 degrees. Beat eggs with a wire whisk. Add flour, milk and mayonnaise, stirring well. Fold in cheese, chicken, ham and parsley. Pour into pie shell and bake for 25 to 30 minutes or until golden brown.

Makes 8 servings

 ## CHICKEN AND BROCCOLI QUICHE

3 eggs
3 tablespoons all-purpose flour
½ cup whole milk
1 cup Duke's® mayonnaise
1 cup shredded cheese (Cheddar, Swiss, feta or American)

2 (4 ounce) chicken breasts, cooked and cubed
1 cup fresh broccoli florets
1 (10-inch) deep dish frozen pie shell

Preheat oven to 350 degrees. Beat eggs with a wire whisk. Add flour, milk and mayonnaise, stirring well. Fold in cheese, chicken and broccoli. Pour into pie shell and bake for 25 to 30 minutes or until golden brown.

Makes 8 servings

 ## HAM, BACON AND TOMATO QUICHE

3 eggs
3 tablespoons all-purpose flour
½ cup whole milk
1 cup Duke's® mayonnaise
1 cup shredded Cheddar cheese

½ cup smoked, cubed ham
½ pound bacon, fried crisp and crumbled
½ cup diced tomatoes
1 (10-inch) deep dish frozen pie shell

Preheat oven to 350 degrees. Beat eggs with a wire whisk. Add flour, milk and mayonnaise, stirring well. Fold in cheese, ham, bacon and tomatoes. Pour into pie shell and bake for 25 to 30 minutes or until golden brown.

Makes 8 servings

 ## CRAB QUICHE

3 eggs
3 tablespoons all-purpose flour
½ cup whole milk
1 cup Duke's® mayonnaise
1 cup Swiss cheese

½ pound lump crabmeat
1 tablespoon chopped fresh parsley
1 (10-inch) deep dish frozen pie shell

Preheat oven to 350 degrees. Beat eggs with a wire whisk. Add flour, milk and mayonnaise, stirring well. Fold in cheese, crabmeat and parsley. Pour into pie shell and bake for 25 to 30 minutes or until golden brown.

Makes 8 servings

SAUSAGE, APPLE & CHEDDAR QUICHE

½ pound pork breakfast sausage

3 eggs

3 tablespoons all-purpose flour

½ cup whole milk

1 cup Duke's® mayonnaise

1 cup shredded Cheddar cheese

½ cup diced fresh sweet apples

1 (10-inch) deep dish frozen pie shell

Preheat oven to 350 degrees. Brown the sausage in a frying pan until thoroughly cooked. Drain the fat and place sausage on paper towels; set aside. Beat eggs with a wire whisk. Add flour, milk and mayonnaise, stirring well. Fold in cheese, sausage and apples. Pour into pie shell and bake for 25 to 30 minutes or until golden brown.

Makes 8 servings

SPINACH AND MUSHROOM QUICHE

1 cup frozen, chopped spinach, thawed

2 tablespoons butter

½ small onion, chopped

1 cup sliced fresh mushrooms

1 (10-inch) deep dish frozen pie shell

8 ounces cream cheese, cut into small pieces

½ cup shredded Swiss cheese

½ cup shredded Monterey Jack cheese

8 eggs

1 cup half-and-half

1 teaspoon nutmeg

Preheat oven to 425 degrees. Squeeze thawed spinach between paper towels to remove water. In a medium saucepan, melt butter over medium-high heat and sauté onion until translucent. Add mushrooms and sauté until browned. Cover the bottom of the pie shell with cream cheese pieces. Add onion, mushrooms and spinach. Top with shredded Swiss and Monterey Jack cheeses. In a medium bowl, combine eggs, half-and-half and nutmeg. Pour egg mixture over ingredients in pie shell. Bake for 15 minutes. Reduce temperature to 350 degrees and bake for an additional 30 to 40 minutes or until golden brown.

Makes 8 servings

ASPARAGUS QUICHE

Always allow quiche to cool slightly before cutting and serving.

1   pound fresh asparagus,
    trimmed and cut into
    ½-inch pieces
10 slices bacon
2   (8-inch) unbaked pie shells
1   egg white, lightly beaten

4   eggs
1½ cups half-and-half
¼   teaspoon ground nutmeg
Salt and pepper to taste
2   cups shredded Swiss cheese

Preheat oven to 400 degrees. Place asparagus in a steamer over 1 inch of boiling water; cover. Cook until tender but still firm, about 2 to 6 minutes. Drain and cool. Place bacon in a large, deep skillet. Cook over medium high heat until evenly brown. Drain, crumble and set aside. Brush pie shells with beaten egg white. Sprinkle crumbled bacon and chopped asparagus into pie shells. In a bowl, beat together eggs, half-and-half, nutmeg, salt and pepper. Sprinkle Swiss cheese over bacon and asparagus. Pour egg mixture on top of cheese. Bake uncovered for 35 to 40 minutes or until golden brown.

Makes 2 quiches, 6 servings each

PUDDINGS AND PIES

PUDDINGS AND PIES

**FEATURED RECIPE
ON FRONT:**

*Lemon Meringue Pie,
page 200*

CINNAMON BANANA PUDDING

1   (14 ounce) box cinnamon
    graham crackers
8   medium bananas
7   cups whole milk

2   (5.1 ounce) boxes vanilla
    instant pudding
1   (16 ounce) container frozen
    whipped topping, thawed

In a 10x14-inch baking dish, break up entire box of graham crackers, leaving the crackers in large pieces. Slice bananas over crackers. In large mixing bowl or pitcher, combine milk and vanilla pudding. Mix with a whisk quickly, removing all lumps. Immediately pour into the center of the crackers and bananas. Once set, spread whipped topping over top of pudding. Refrigerate and serve.

Note: Pudding mixture must be liquid when poured over crackers and bananas in order to soak into crackers.

Makes 24 servings

MOTHER'S FUNERAL BANANA PUDDING

2   (5.1 ounce) boxes vanilla
    instant pudding mix
½   gallon milk for pudding
2   (20 ounce) cans crushed
    pineapple, drained

2   (16 ounce) containers frozen
    whipped topping, thawed,
    divided
2   (12 ounce) boxes vanilla
    wafers
5   pounds bananas, sliced
Pineapple chunks for garnish

Mix together the vanilla pudding mix and milk according to the box instructions. Fold well-drained crushed pineapple and half a container of whipped topping into the pudding. Layer the bottom of a large serving bowl with vanilla wafers. Add a layer of sliced bananas. Pour some of the pudding mixture over bananas to just cover. Repeat layers of vanilla wafers, bananas and pudding to fill bowl. Top with remaining whipped topping and garnish with pineapple chunks and crushed vanilla wafers. Chill 2 hours prior to serving.

Makes 30 or more servings
JEAN BECKERDITE

*"This dish serves a crowd
and is expected at our
family gatherings or
bereavement occasions."*
Jean Beckerdite

THE LUNCH BELL BREAD PUDDING

3	cups sugar		Bread, rolls, donuts and/or cake, cubed
6	tablespoons cornstarch	1	(20 ounce) can crushed pineapple, undrained
6	eggs, beaten		
2	cups whole milk	3	sticks butter, melted
1	quart half-and-half		

Preheat oven to 350 degrees. In a large bowl, mix together sugar, cornstarch, eggs, milk and half-and-half with a whisk. Fill a large baking dish with an assortment of bite-size pieces of bread, rolls, donuts and cake. Spread pineapple over bread, then pour milk mixture over entire pan. Pour melted butter on top. Put baking dish in a large roasting pan. Add enough hot water to roasting pan to reach halfway up side of baking dish. Bake for 45 to 60 minutes or until set.

Makes 16 to 18 servings

BREAD PUDDING

5⅓	tablespoons butter, melted	1½	cups sugar
24	slices white bread, cut into ½-inch cubes	3	cups milk
		1	teaspoon ground cinnamon
¾	cups seedless raisins	1	teaspoon ground nutmeg
3	eggs, lightly beaten	1	teaspoon pure vanilla extract

The behind-the-scenes staff: Gayle Britton, Lewis, Will Reaves and LaTria Hebbons.

Preheat oven to 250 degrees. Pour the butter into a 9x13-inch baking dish. Add the bread cubes and sprinkle with raisins; set aside. Beat together the eggs and sugar. Stir in the milk, cinnamon, nutmeg and vanilla. Pour over the bread mixture, being sure to coat all of the bread pieces. Bake for 45 minutes or until golden. Cool completely.

Makes 12 to 15 servings

CALVIN HEBBONS

Oreo® Pudding

1	large package Oreo® cookies	3½	cups milk
½	stick butter	2	(3.4 ounce) boxes instant French vanilla pudding
8	ounces cream cheese, softened	1	(12 ounce) container frozen whipped topping, thawed
1	cup confectioners' sugar		

Crush 1 whole package of Oreo® cookies (may use a hand chopper to chop cookies); set aside. Cream together butter, cream cheese and confectioners' sugar. In separate bowl, mix together milk and pudding mix; add to creamed mixture. Fold in whipped topping.

In a 9x13-inch baking dish, layer cookies and pudding mix. End with cookies. Refrigerate.

Makes 12 to 15 servings

DENISE CREWS

Pudding Ice Cream Delight

50	Ritz® crackers, crushed	¾	half-gallon vanilla ice cream
1	stick butter, melted	1	(9 ounce) container frozen whipped topping, thawed
3	(3.4 ounce) boxes instant vanilla pudding		
3	cups whole milk		

Combine crackers and butter. Set aside ¾ cup of cracker mixture. Put remaining cracker mixture into a 9x13-inch baking dish. With an electric mixer, mix together pudding and milk. Add ice cream and beat until smooth. Spread over crackers. Top with frozen whipped topping; sprinkle with remaining crackers. Refrigerate overnight before serving.

Makes 12 to 15 servings

SHELAH SWAIN

ICE CREAM DELIGHT

24 ice cream sandwiches
1 (16 ounce) container frozen whipped topping, thawed

1 (5 ounce) container Whoppers®

Unwrap half of the ice cream sandwiches and place in 9x13-inch glass baking dish. Spread half of the whipped topping over the ice cream sandwiches. Crunch half of the Whoppers® and sprinkle them on top. Repeat.

Makes 12 to 15 servings

NANCY MILLER BOUTEILLER

GOOD LEMON CURD

5 egg yolks
4 lemons, juiced to make ⅓ cup (add water if needed)

1 cup sugar
Lemon zest (optional)
1 stick butter

Strain the egg to remove the membrane. Whisk together lemon juice and sugar; add eggs yolks and lemon zest. Place mixture in a bowl over a pan of boiling water or use a double boiler. Whisk about 8 minutes or until mixture coats a spoon. Remove bowl from boiling water. Add butter, one pat at a time, mixing well after each addition. Cover with plastic wrap to prevent a hard film from forming. Refrigerate up to 2 weeks.

Makes about 2 cups

JUDYE HAFLING

PECAN TURTLE TRIFLE

8 ounces mascarpone cheese or cream cheese
1½ cups whipping cream
1½ teaspoons toffee flavoring or pure vanilla extract

1 (2 pound) frozen pecan pie (Edwards®), thawed and cut into large bite-sized pieces
⅓ cup fudge topping
⅓ cup caramel topping
½ cup toasted pecan pieces

Beat mascarpone or cream cheese, whipping cream and flavoring. Place ½ of pecan pie pieces in trifle dish. Spread half of cream cheese mixture over pie pieces. Drizzle half of fudge, caramel and toasted pecans over mixture. Repeat layers. Cover and chill for 5 to 8 hours for best results.

Makes 10 to 12 servings

JUDYE HAFLING

CONNIE'S ENGLISH TRIFLE

CUSTARD SAUCE

3 tablespoons cornstarch
4 cups light cream, divided
8 egg yolks, beaten

1 cup sugar
2 teaspoons pure vanilla
 extract

CAKE LAYERS

1 pound cake, sliced into
 ¼-inch slices
3 tablespoons cream sherry
1 (12 ounce) jar seedless
 raspberry jam

24 coconut macaroons,
 crumbled
4 cups crushed pineapple,
 raspberries, bananas,
 blueberries and/or
 strawberries

TOPPING

2 cups heavy whipping cream
2 tablespoons confectioners'
 sugar

½ cup slivered almonds,
 toasted

In a large mixing bowl, dissolve cornstarch in ¼ cup light cream. Combine egg yolks with cornstarch mixture. Add remaining light cream and sugar. Mix thoroughly. Pour into a saucepan and cook on medium heat, stirring until sauce thickens, approximately 5 to 10 minutes. Do not boil mixture. Remove from heat; stir in vanilla. Transfer to a bowl and cover with plastic wrap. Cool in the refrigerator.

To assemble dessert, place slices of the pound cake on the bottom of a trifle or other decorative dish, covering the bottom of the entire dish. Sprinkle with cream sherry and spread the raspberry jam on the slices. Cover with a thin layer of macaroons. Top with layers of different fruits, as many or few as you wish. Cover the layered fruit with the prepared custard. Repeat layering by starting with the slices of pound cake, then macaroons and fruit as before, covering with remaining custard. Repeat until you fill the dish, cover and chill for 1 to 2 hours.

While trifle is chilling, whip cream with an electric mixer until stiff peaks form. Add confectioners' sugar and whip. Just before serving, top the trifle with the whipped cream and sprinkle with almonds.

Makes 10 to 12 servings

Betty makes her own vanilla extract. To make your own vanilla, buy about 10 fresh vanilla beans. Slice the side of each vanilla bean and place them in a half-gallon jar. Add 3 ounces of bourbon; fill the jar with vodka. Let the beans soak for at least 2 weeks prior to using. As you use the vanilla, keep adding more beans, vodka and a little bourbon.

BETTY'S FRENCH APPLE PIE

2	Pillsbury® refrigerated pie crusts	¼	cup firmly packed brown sugar
2	(12 ounce) packages Stouffer's® frozen harvest apples	2	tablespoons ground cinnamon
1	cup golden raisins	1	tablespoon cornstarch
Water		1	cup confectioners' sugar
1	teaspoon pure vanilla extract	2	tablespoons milk or water

Bring pie crusts to room temperature. If possible, leave pie crusts out overnight to soften. Place 1 pie crust in a 9.5-inch pie plate. Thaw apples at room temperature. Preheat oven to 400 degrees. Place raisins in microwave-safe bowl and cover with water. Microwave raisins on high for 3 minutes. Drain raisins and add vanilla. In a large bowl mix together apples, raisins, brown sugar, cinnamon and cornstarch. Pour apple mixture into crust. Top with second pie crust and flute the edges as desired. Do not cut top of pie crust to vent. Bake for 45 minutes or until golden brown.

Mix together confectioners' sugar and milk to make a thick frosting. Once pie has cooled, pour confectioners' sugar mixture over the pie.

Makes 8 servings

BLUEBERRY BANANA CREAM PIE

3	bananas	1½	cups sugar
2	(9-inch) graham cracker crusts	1	(8 ounce) container frozen whipped topping, thawed
8	ounces cream cheese, softened	1	(21 ounce) can blueberry pie filling, chilled

Slice bananas and spread over the bottom of each pie shell. Combine softened cream cheese with sugar and mix until well blended. Fold in whipped topping and spread mixture over bananas. Spoon blueberry pie filling over top of pie. Refrigerate.

Makes 2 pies, 8 to 10 servings each

NANCY CARR TISON

THE LUNCH BELL CHERRY PIE

2	Pillsbury® refrigerated pie crusts	1	tablespoon almond extract
2	(21 ounce) cans cherry pie filling	½	(6 ounce) box cherry gelatin
1	tablespoon cornstarch	1	cup confectioners' sugar
		1-2	tablespoons milk

Bring pie crusts to room temperature. If possible, leave pie crusts out overnight to soften. Place 1 pie crust in a 9.5-inch pie plate and flute the edges as desired. Preheat oven to 375 degrees. Mix together cherry pie filling, cornstarch and almond extract. Add cherry gelatin and mix well. Pour cherry mixture into crust. Top with second pie crust and flute the edges as desired. Do not cut top of pie crust to vent. Bake for 40 to 45 minutes or until golden brown.

Mix together confectioners' sugar and milk to make a thick frosting. Once pie has cooled, pour confectioners' sugar mixture over the pie.

Makes 8 servings

COCONUT CUSTARD PIE

2	Pillsbury® refrigerated pie crusts	6	eggs, beaten
3	cups sugar	2	tablespoons coconut extract
6	tablespoons cornstarch	1	tablespoon pure vanilla extract
4	cups half-and-half	3	sticks butter, melted
1	cup whole milk	3	cups angel flake coconut

Bring pie crusts to room temperature. If possible, leave pie crusts out overnight to soften. Place each pie crust in a 9.5-inch pie plate and flute the edges as desired. Preheat oven to 350 degrees. Mix together sugar, cornstarch, half-and-half, milk and eggs. Stir thoroughly. Add coconut and vanilla extract; mix well. Stir in butter and coconut. Pour half of coconut mixture into each pie. Bake for 45 to 50 minutes or until set and browned.

Makes 2 pies, 8 to 10 servings each

CHOCOLATE CREAM PIE

Vanilla sugar can be found in the baking aisle at most grocery stores.

PIE CRUST AND FILLING

2   Pillsbury® refrigerated pie crusts
2   cups sugar
7   level tablespoons cornstarch
10 tablespoons Hershey's® cocoa

1   cup whole milk
2   sticks butter, melted
4   cups half-and-half
2   tablespoons pure vanilla extract

WHIPPED CREAM

2   cups heavy whipping cream
1   (.32 ounce) pouch Dr. Oetker® natural vanilla sugar

1   cup sugar

Bring pie crusts to room temperature. If possible, leave pie crusts out overnight to soften. Preheat oven to 375 degrees. Place each pie crust in a 9.5-inch pie plate and flute the edges as desired. Thoroughly prick pie crusts with fork to ensure that no bubbles appear when baked. Bake for 12 minutes or until golden brown.

Whisk together sugar, cornstarch and cocoa in a 2-quart glass measuring pitcher. Stir in the milk. Add butter and stir until smooth. Add half-and-half and stir well. Cook mixture in microwave on high for 12 minutes, stirring every 4 minutes. Add vanilla and mix well. Pour half of chocolate mixture into each pie crust and let cool at room temperature.

With an electric mixer, whip cream until it starts to thicken. Add vanilla sugar. Once mixture is fairly thick, slowly drizzle the sugar into the cream and continue mixing until light peaks form. After pies have cooled, spread half of whipped cream on top of each pie. Refrigerate.

Makes 2 pies, 8 to 10 servings each

Mallory Joyce is a loyal customer of **The Lunch Bell**.

COCONUT CREAM PIE

PIE CRUST AND FILLING

2	Pillsbury® refrigerated pie crusts		4	cups half-and-half
2	cups sugar		1	tablespoon pure vanilla extract
8	level tablespoons cornstarch		2	tablespoons coconut extract
1	cup whole milk		2½	cups angel flake coconut
8	egg yolks			

WHIPPED CREAM

2 cups heavy whipping cream
1 (.32 ounce) pouch Dr. Oetker® natural vanilla sugar

1 cup sugar

Betty's Aunt Carrie used to make chocolate cream pie, coconut cream pie and lemon cream pie and those recipes were the inspiration for Betty's cream pies.

Bring pie crusts to room temperature. If possible, leave pie crusts out overnight to soften. Preheat oven to 375 degrees. Place each pie crust in a 9.5-inch pie plate and flute the edges as desired. Thoroughly prick pie crusts with fork to ensure that no bubbles appear when baked. Bake for 12 minutes or until golden brown.

Whisk together sugar, cornstarch, milk and egg yolks in a 2-quart glass measuring pitcher. Add half-and-half and mix well. Cook mixture in microwave on high for 12 minutes, stirring every 4 minutes. Add vanilla, coconut extract and flake coconut and mix well. Pour half of coconut mixture into each pie crust and let cool at room temperature.

With an electric mixer, whip cream until it starts to thicken. Add vanilla sugar. Once mixture is fairly thick, slowly drizzle the sugar into the cream and continue mixing until light peaks form. After pies have cooled, spread half of whipped cream on top of each pie. Refrigerate.

Note: If using a hand mixer to make whipped cream, beat at high speed.

Makes 2 pies, 8 to 10 servings each

BUTTERSCOTCH CREAM PIE

PIE CRUST AND FILLING

1 Pillsbury® refrigerated pie crust
1 cup firmly packed brown sugar
4 level tablespoons cornstarch
½ cup whole milk
1 stick butter, melted
4 egg yolks

2 cups half-and-half
1 teaspoon pure vanilla extract
1 teaspoon butter flavoring
1 teaspoon imitation maple flavoring
½ cup milk chocolate toffee bits

WHIPPED CREAM

1 cup heavy whipping cream
1 (.32 ounce) pouch Dr. Oetker® natural vanilla sugar

½ cup sugar

Bring pie crust to room temperature. If possible, leave pie crust out overnight to soften. Preheat oven to 375 degrees. Place pie crust in a 9.5-inch pie plate and flute the edges as desired. Thoroughly prick pie crust with fork to ensure that no bubbles appear when baked. Bake for 12 minutes or until golden brown.

Whisk together brown sugar, cornstarch, milk and butter in a 1-quart glass measuring bowl. Add eggs and half-and-half and stir well. Cook mixture on high in microwave for 7 to 8 minutes, stirring after 4 minutes. Add vanilla, butter and maple flavorings and stir well. Pour mixture into pie crust and let cool at room temperature.

With an electric mixer, whip cream until it starts to thicken. Add vanilla sugar. Once mixture is fairly thick, slowly drizzle the sugar into the cream and continue mixing until light peaks form. After pie has cooled, spread whipped cream on top. Refrigerate. When ready to serve, sprinkle with milk chocolate toffee bits.

Makes 8 to 10 servings

PEANUT BUTTER PIE

PIE CRUST AND FILLING

1   Pillsbury® refrigerated pie
       crusts
⅓   cup plus 2 tablespoons
       peanut butter, divided
¾   cup confectioners' sugar
1   cup sugar

4   level tablespoons cornstarch
½   cup whole milk
4   egg yolks
2   cups half-and-half
½   tablespoon pure vanilla
       extract

WHIPPED CREAM

1   cup heavy whipping cream
1   (.32 ounce) pouch
       Dr. Oetker® natural
       vanilla sugar

½   cup sugar

Bring pie crusts to room temperature. If possible, leave pie crust out overnight to soften. Preheat oven to 375 degrees. Place pie crust in a 9.5-inch pie plate and flute the edges as desired. Thoroughly prick pie crust with fork to ensure that no bubbles appear when baked. Bake for 12 minutes or until golden brown.

Mix together ⅓ cup peanut butter and confectioners' sugar until crumbly; set aside. Whisk together sugar, cornstarch, milk and egg yolks in a 2-quart glass measuring pitcher. Add half-and-half and mix well. Cook mixture in microwave on high for 12 minutes, stirring every 4 minutes. Add vanilla and mix well. Using ⅔ of crumbled peanut butter mixture, spread into bottom of pie crust; pour hot pie filling into pie. Swirl 2 tablespoons of peanut butter through pie. Let cool.

With an electric mixer, whip cream until it starts to thicken. Add vanilla sugar. Once mixture is fairly thick, slowly drizzle the sugar into the cream and continue mixing until light peaks form. After pie has cooled, spread whipped cream on top; sprinkle with remaining peanut butter mixture. Refrigerate.

Note: If using a hand mixer to make whipped cream, beat at high speed.

Makes 8 to 10 servings

CREAM CHEESE PIE

PIE

8	ounces cream cheese, softened	½	teaspoon butter extract
½	cup sugar	½	teaspoon almond extract
½	teaspoon pure vanilla extract	2	eggs
		1	(9-inch) graham cracker crust

TOPPING

2	cups sour cream	¼	teaspoon almond extract
5	tablespoons sugar	1	(20 ounce) can fruit topping (optional)
½	teaspoon pure vanilla extract		

Preheat oven to 350 degrees. Cream together cream cheese, sugar, vanilla, butter extract and almond extract. Mix thoroughly. Add eggs and mix until smooth. Pour into pie shell. Bake for 20 minutes.

While pie is baking, mix together sour cream, sugar, vanilla and almond extract until smooth. Once you remove the pie from the oven, immediately pour sour cream mixture evenly over top. Bake for an additional 5 minutes. Cool, refrigerate and then top with any fruit topping or just enjoy as is.

Note: You may make these two at a time. Extend cooking time from 20 to 25 minutes for pie and an additional 5 to 8 minutes after you add the sour cream topping.

Makes 8 to 10 servings

TAMMY LAWSON

BUTTERMILK PIE

1	stick butter	1	cup buttermilk
1¾	cups sugar	1	teaspoon pure vanilla extract
3	eggs	1	unbaked deep-dish pie shell
¼	cup all-purpose flour		

Preheat oven to 325 degrees. Cream together butter and sugar. Add eggs and flour. Beat until fluffy, about 2 minutes. Fold in buttermilk and vanilla. Pour into pastry shell. Bake for 50 minutes. Cool thoroughly before cutting.

Note: To keep the crust from getting soggy, sprinkle 1 tablespoon of flour on the bottom of the pie shell and rub it around before pouring in the filling.

Makes 8 to 10 servings

SYLVIA WEINSTEIN

This pie was served at the delightful Tearoom located in the Smith & Welton department store in Norfolk, Virginia.

PEACH CUSTARD PIE

1	Pillsbury® refrigerated pie crust	2	eggs, beaten
1½	cups sugar	1	cup half-and-half
4	tablespoons flour	1	teaspoon pure vanilla extract
1	stick butter, softened	1	(29 ounce) can peach halves, drained
Pinch of salt		Sprinkle of ground nutmeg	

Bring pie crust to room temperature. If possible, leave pie crust out overnight to soften. Place pie crust in a 9.5-inch pie plate and flute the edges as desired. Preheat oven to 350 degrees. With an electric mixer, mix together sugar, flour, butter and salt. Add well beaten eggs; mix well. Add half-and-half and vanilla. Pat peach halves dry with paper towels. Place peach halves cut side down in circles around the pie crust. Pour custard mixture over peaches. Sprinkle peaches with ground nutmeg. Bake for 30 to 40 minutes or until firm.

Makes 8 to 10 servings

HAWAIIAN PIE

2	Pillsbury® refrigerated pie crusts	1	(21 ounce) can cherry pie filling
1	(20 ounce) can crushed pineapple, drained	1	cup chopped pecans
1	cup sugar	1	cup angel flake coconut
1	(5.1 ounce) box orange gelatin	3	medium bananas, chopped
			Whipped cream for garnish

Bring pie crusts to room temperature. If possible, leave pie crusts out overnight to soften. Preheat oven to 375 degrees. Place each pie crust in a 9.5-inch pie plate and flute the edges as desired. Thoroughly prick pie crusts with fork to ensure that no bubbles appear when baked. Bake for 12 minutes or until golden brown.

Put drained pineapple and sugar in a saucepan and bring to boil. Turn off heat. Add gelatin, stirring until dissolved. Add cherry pie filling, pecans, coconut and bananas and stir well. Pour into pie shells and chill. Top with whipped cream before serving.

Makes 2 pies, 8 to 10 servings each

MARGARET SWAIN

Harry and Margaret Swain, who introduced Betty to Bill in 1956.

MILLION DOLLAR PIE

1	(14 ounce) can sweetened condensed milk	1	cup chopped pecans
¼	cup lemon juice	1	(16 ounce) container frozen whipped topping, thawed
1	(20 ounce) can crushed pineapple, undrained	2	(6 ounce) graham cracker pie crusts
1	(21 ounce) can cherry pie filling		

Mix together milk, lemon juice, pineapple, cherry pie filling and pecans. Fold in whipped topping. Pour into pie crusts. Serve chilled or frozen.

Makes 2 pies, 8 to 10 servings each

MARGARET SWAIN

HEAVENLY PINEAPPLE PIE

1   (9 ounce) graham cracker pie
    crust
1   egg white, beaten
8   ounces cream cheese,
    softened
1   (14 ounce) can sweetened
    condensed milk
⅓   cup lemon juice
1   teaspoon pure vanilla extract
1   (20 ounce) can crushed
    pineapple, drained
6   ounces frozen whipped
    topping, thawed
¼   cup chopped pecans
    (optional)

Preheat oven to 325 degrees. Brush graham cracker crust with egg whites. Bake crust for 5 minutes; set aside. In a large bowl with an electric mixer, blend cream cheese, milk, lemon juice and vanilla until smooth. Stir in pineapple. Fold in whipped topping. Pour into graham cracker crust. Sprinkle with pecans.

Note: You must use the large (9 ounce) graham cracker pie crust, not the smaller (6 ounce) size, as there will be too much filling. For a lighter pie, fold in additional whipped topping.

Makes 8 to 10 servings

MARILYN HOLLAND

LEMON CHESS PIE

2   cups sugar
1   tablespoon all-purpose flour
1   tablespoon cornmeal
4   eggs, unbeaten
½   stick butter, melted
¼   cup milk
Juice of 2 lemons
    (about 4 tablespoons)
Grated rind of 2 lemons
1   (9-inch) unbaked pie shell

Preheat oven to 350 degrees. Combine sugar, flour and cornmeal; mix lightly with a fork. Add eggs, butter, milk, lemon juice and lemon rind and beat until smooth. Pour into unbaked pie shell. Bake for 35 to 40 minutes or until top is golden brown. Serve warm.

Makes 8 to 10 servings

KITTY SMITH

The Daily Press wrote an article in November of 1999 regarding Andy Griffith trying **The Lunch Bell's** *lemon meringue pie. Griffith sent his pilot to pick up lunch, including 2 slices of lemon meringue pie. The pilot then flew the food to Manteo, NC, where Griffith and his wife lived. "He said the food was real good and the pie was awesome," said Betty Swain. The message was relayed through Griffith's secretary.*

PIE CRUST AND FILLING

1	Pillsbury® refrigerated pie crust
1⅔	cups sugar
7	level tablespoons cornstarch
¾	cup bottled lemon juice

1¼	cups water
7	beaten egg yolks
2	tablespoons butter
1	teaspoon lemon extract
1	teaspoon orange extract

MERINGUE TOPPING

6	egg whites
1	level teaspoon baking powder

1	teaspoon lemon extract
1	cup sugar
2	tablespoons light corn syrup

Bring pie crust to room temperature. If possible, leave pie crust out overnight to soften. Preheat oven to 375 degrees. Place pie crust in a 9.5-inch pie plate and flute the edges as desired. Thoroughly prick pie crust with fork to ensure that no bubbles appear when baked. Bake for 12 minutes or until golden brown.

Stir together sugar and cornstarch in a 1-quart glass measuring pitcher. In separate 2-cup glass measuring pitcher, combine lemon juice and water. Microwave lemon juice mixture on high for 3 minutes. Add hot liquid to sugar mixture and whisk thoroughly. Temper the egg yolks by adding ¼ cup of lemon mixture to the eggs and mix well. Then add the egg to the lemon mixture and whisk. Microwave mixture on high until thickened, approximately 2 to 3 minutes. Stir. Add 1 additional minute of cooking time if mixture is not completely thick. Add butter, lemon extract and orange extract and stir well. Pour lemon mixture into baked pie shell.

With an electric mixer, beat egg whites on high until they are frothy. Beat in baking powder and lemon extract. Slowly drizzle sugar into egg mixture while beating. Add corn syrup. Continue beating mixture until it is stiff and glossy. Do not under beat. Top lemon mixture with meringue, being sure to cover completely. Brown pie in oven for 15 minutes. Do not refrigerate.

Note: The lemon mixture should be glossy and bright yellow after microwaving. Instead of meringue, you can use the cream topping from the chocolate cream pie to make a lemon cream pie. Just cut the recipe in half.

Makes 8 to 10 servings

Lemon Pie

Pie

1 Pillsbury® refrigerated pie crust
1 (14 ounce) can sweetened condensed milk
3 egg yolks
½ cup bottled and/or fresh lemon juice
1 teaspoon grated lemon rind

Meringue

3 egg whites
½ teaspoon cream of tartar
½ cup sugar

Bring pie crust to room temperature. If possible, leave pie crust out overnight to soften. Preheat oven to 375 degrees. Place pie crust in a 9-inch pie plate and flute the edges as desired. Thoroughly prick pie crust with fork to ensure that no bubbles appear when baked. Bake for 12 minutes or until golden brown.

Using a hand mixer, beat milk and egg yolks thoroughly. Add lemon juice and rind and mix well. Pour into cooked pie crust.

Beat egg whites with cream of tartar on high until they are frothy. Slowly drizzle sugar into egg mixture while beating. Continue beating mixture until it is stiff and glossy. Do not under beat. Top lemon mixture with meringue, being sure to cover completely. Brown pie in oven at 350 degrees for 12 to 15 minutes. Cool. Chill thoroughly.

Makes 8 to 10 servings

DEMMIE LAYNE

To neatly cut a meringue pie, dip your knife in very hot water before every cut. This will prevent the meringue from sticking to the knife.

KEY LIME PIE

1¾ cups graham cracker crumbs
¼ cup firmly packed light
    brown sugar
5⅓ tablespoons butter, melted
2 (14 ounce) cans sweetened
    condensed milk

1 cup fresh Key lime juice
2 egg whites
¼ teaspoon cream of tartar
2 tablespoons sugar
Lime slices for garnish

Preheat oven to 350 degrees. Combine graham cracker crumbs, brown sugar and butter. Press into 9-inch glass pie plate, pressing into bottom of dish and up the sides to form crust. Bake for 10 minutes; cool. Stir together milk and lime juice until blended. Pour into crust. Beat egg whites and cream of tartar at high speed with an electric mixer just until foamy. Add sugar, 1 tablespoon at a time, beating until soft peaks form and sugar dissolves (2 to 4 minutes). Spread meringue over filling. Bake at 325 degrees for 25 to 28 minutes. Chill 8 hours. Garnish with lime slices, if desired.

Note: If fresh key limes aren't available in your area, you can opt for bottled Key lime juice. Nellie & Joe's® Key lime juice is a popular brand that does not contain the preservative sulfur dioxide, which some believe gives the pie a sulfur-like aftertaste.

Makes 8 to 10 servings

BEVERLY MOODY

LIME PIE

1 (12 ounce) can evaporated
    milk
1 (3 ounce) package lime
    gelatin
½ cup sugar

½ cup boiling water
⅓ cup lemon juice
1 teaspoon lemon rind
2 (6 ounce) graham cracker pie
    crusts

Put milk into an ice tray (not cubes) and place in freezer until ice forms around the sides. Put lime gelatin and sugar in boiling water and stir until dissolved. Cool. Add lemon juice and rind. Remove milk from tray and place in a medium bowl; beat until it almost peaks. Add gelatin mixture slowly while beating to a peak. Pour into 2 graham cracker pie crusts. Refrigerate until ready to serve.

Makes 2 pies, 8 to 10 servings each

FRANCES HOGGE

THE LUNCH BELL PUMPKIN PIE

PIE

2	Pillsbury® refrigerated pie crusts
1½	cups sugar
1	teaspoon salt
2	teaspoons ground cinnamon
1	teaspoon ground ginger

½	teaspoon ground cloves
4	eggs
1	(29 ounce) can pure pumpkin
2	(12 ounce) cans evaporated milk

WHIPPED CREAM

2	cups heavy whipping cream
1	(.32 ounce) pouch Dr. Oetker® natural vanilla sugar

1	cup sugar

Bring pie crusts to room temperature. If possible, leave pie crusts out overnight to soften. Place each pie crust in a 9-inch pie plate and flute the edges as desired. Preheat oven to 425 degrees. In a small bowl, mix sugar, salt, cinnamon, ginger and cloves. Beat eggs in large bowl. Stir in pumpkin and sugar-spice mixture. Gradually stir in evaporated milk. Pour mixture into pie shells. Bake for 15 minutes. Reduce temperature to 350 degrees; bake 40 to 50 minutes or until knife inserted near the center of the pie comes out clean. Cool on wire rack for 2 hours.

With an electric mixer, whip cream until it starts to thicken. Add pouch of vanilla sugar. Once mixture is fairly thick, slowly drizzle the sugar into the cream and continue mixing until light peaks form. After pie has cooled, spread whipped cream on top. Refrigerate.

Makes 2 pies, 8 to 10 servings each

No Crust Pumpkin Pie

1	(29 ounce) can pumpkin	1	teaspoon ground cinnamon
1	egg	½	teaspoon ground ginger
2	egg whites	¼	teaspoon ground cloves
¾	cup sugar	¼-½	teaspoon salt
½	cup Bisquick® baking mix	1	(12 ounce) can evaporated milk
1	teaspoon pure vanilla extract		Whipped topping

Preheat oven to 350 degrees. In a large bowl, combine pumpkin, egg, egg whites, sugar, Bisquick®, vanilla, cinnamon, ginger, cloves and salt. Beat with electric mixer until smooth. Slowly stir in evaporated milk. Pour into a greased 9-inch pie plate. Do not overfill. Bake for 35 to 40 minutes or until set. Serve with whipped topping.

Makes 8 to 10 servings

BARBARA WOOD

 # Down Home Sweet Potato Pie

1	Pillsbury® refrigerated pie crust	¾	cup evaporated milk
3	eggs	¼	cup whole milk
1	cup sugar	½	stick butter, melted
1	cup cooked, mashed sweet potato	2	teaspoons pure vanilla extract
			Whipped cream for garnish

Bring pie crust to room temperature. If possible, leave pie crust out overnight to soften. Place pie crust in a 9.5-inch pie plate and flute the edges as desired. Preheat oven to 400 degrees. With an electric mixer, beat together eggs, sugar and sweet potatoes. Add milk, butter and vanilla. Pour mixture into pie crust and bake for 10 minutes; reduce heat to 325 degrees and bake for 30 minutes more or until a knife inserted near the center of the pie comes out clean. Serve with a dollop of whipped cream.

Makes 8 to 10 servings

FRESH RHUBARB PIE

2   Pillsbury® refrigerated pie
    crusts
2   eggs, beaten
1½ cups sugar

4   tablespoons all-purpose flour
½   teaspoon salt
3   cups rhubarb cut into 1-inch
    cubes

Bring pie crusts to room temperature. If possible, leave pie crusts out overnight to soften. Place 1 pie crust in a 9-inch pie plate and flute the edges as desired. Preheat oven to 350 degrees. Blend together eggs, sugar, flour and salt. Stir in rhubarb. Pour rhubarb mixture into pie crust. Top with second pie crust and flute the edges as desired. Do not cut top of pie crust to vent. Bake for 45 minutes or until golden brown.

Makes 8 to 10 servings

SHARON BAKER

STRAWBERRY PIE

1   Pillsbury® refrigerated pie
    crust
Fresh strawberries, enough to fill
    pie
1   cup sugar

3   tablespoons cornstarch
1½ cups water
1   (3 ounce) box strawberry
    gelatin
Frozen whipped topping

Bring pie crust to room temperature. If possible, leave pie crust out overnight to soften. Preheat oven to 375 degrees. Place pie crust in a 9.5-inch pie plate and flute the edges as desired. Thoroughly prick pie crust with fork to ensure that no bubbles appear when baked. Bake for 12 minutes or until golden brown. Let cool.

Remove tops and cut strawberries in half. Place strawberries cut side down in the pie crust, filling the pie crust. Combine sugar, cornstarch and water in saucepan. Cook until thickened. Add strawberry gelatin and stir until dissolved. Cool. Pour mixture over strawberries. Refrigerate until serving time. Serve with whipped topping.

Makes 8 to 10 servings

GOURMET SWEET POTATO PIE

1	Pillsbury® refrigerated pie crust	¼	cup half-and-half
4	ounces cream cheese, softened	½	stick butter, melted
2	cups cooked, mashed sweet potatoes	2	eggs, beaten
		½	teaspoon ground cinnamon
1¼	cups sugar	1	teaspoon pure vanilla extract
			Whipped cream for garnish

Bring pie crusts to room temperature. If possible, leave pie crust out overnight to soften. Place pie crust in a 9.5-inch pie plate and flute the edges as desired. Preheat oven to 350 degrees. With an electric mixer, beat cream cheese and sweet potatoes together. Add sugar and half-and-half and continue to beat until mixture is fluffy. Add butter and eggs and mix well. Stir in cinnamon and vanilla. Pour sweet potato mixture into pie crust. Bake for 50 to 60 minutes or until a knife inserted near the center of the pie comes out clean. Serve with a dollop of whipped cream.

Makes 8 to 10 servings

SOUTHERN-STYLE PECAN PIE

1	Pillsbury® refrigerated pie crust	¼	teaspoon salt
¾	cup light corn syrup	2	tablespoons butter, softened
¾	cup sugar	2	teaspoons pure vanilla extract
3	eggs	1	cup halved pecans

Bring pie crust to room temperature. If possible, leave pie crust out overnight to soften. Place pie crust in a 9-inch pie plate and flute the edges as desired. Preheat oven to 350 degrees. In a saucepan, combine corn syrup and sugar and bring to a boil. In a separate bowl, beat eggs; slowly add sugar mixture, stirring constantly with a whisk. Add salt, butter and vanilla and mix well; fold in pecans. Pour pecan mixture into pie crust and bake for 25 to 30 minutes or until set.

Makes 8 to 10 servings

BERNICE JONES

SUSAN'S PARTY PIE

CRUST

1¼ cups crushed graham cracker crumbs

¼ cup sugar

½ stick butter, melted

FILLING

1 (5 ounce) box chocolate pudding and pie filling (not instant, cook and serve)

1 (5 ounce) box vanilla pudding and pie filling (not instant, cook and serve)

1 (2.6 ounce) package Dream Whip® whipped topping mix (makes 2 cups)

6½ cups cold milk, divided

1 tablespoon cocoa

1 plain chocolate candy bar

For crust, combine graham cracker crumbs and sugar. Add melted butter. Mix well with fork. Press into 9-inch glass pie plate, pressing into bottom of dish and up the sides to form crust. Refrigerate.

For the filling, prepare chocolate pudding according to package directions, using 3 cups of milk. Pour into crust. Refrigerate again. Next, prepare vanilla pudding according to package directions for pie filling, using 3 cups of milk. After chocolate layer is slightly set, pour vanilla pudding on top. Refrigerate again. Let chill until fairly firm. While pie layers are chilling, prepare whipped topping mix according to package directions, using ½ cup cold milk. Add cocoa to whipped topping, whipping in thoroughly. Spread whipped topping over vanilla layer of pie. Grate chocolate bar into small curls and sprinkle over whipped topping layer of pie for garnish. Keep pie refrigerated until serving time.

Makes 8 to 10 servings

TERRY ROBERTS AND MAE WENZEL

"OLD HOMESTEAD" PECAN PIE

3 eggs, slightly beaten

¾ cup sugar

1 stick butter, softened

1 cup dark corn syrup

2 cups coarsely chopped pecans

1 deep dish prepared pie crust

Preheat oven to 400 degrees. Mix together eggs and sugar. Add butter and cream together. Add corn syrup and pecans. Pour into pie crust. Bake for 10 minutes. Reduce oven temperature to 300 degrees. Continue baking for 45 minutes or until set.

Makes 8 servings

MARY WALLS

TOLLHOUSE PIE

1	Pillsbury® refrigerated pie crust	2	eggs
¾	cup firmly packed brown sugar	2	tablespoons bourbon
¾	cup sugar	2	sticks butter, melted
¾	cup all-purpose flour	1	cup chopped pecans
		1	cup semisweet chocolate chips

Bring pie crust to room temperature. If possible, leave pie crust out overnight to soften. Place pie crust in a 9.5-inch pie plate and flute the edges as desired. Preheat oven to 350 degrees. In a medium bowl, stir together brown sugar, sugar, flour, eggs and bourbon. Add butter and mix well. Stir in pecans and chocolate chips. Pour mixture into pie crust. Bake for 25 to 30 minutes or until set.

Makes 8 to 10 servings

BOURBON-CHOCOLATE PECAN PIE

1	refrigerated pie crust	1	tablespoon all-purpose flour
4	eggs	1	tablespoon pure vanilla extract
1	cup light corn syrup	1	cup coarsely chopped pecans
6	tablespoons butter, melted	1	cup (6 ounces) semisweet chocolate morsels, melted
½	cup sugar		
¼	cup firmly packed light brown sugar		
3	tablespoons bourbon (optional)		

Bring pie crust to room temperature. If possible, leave pie crusts out overnight to soften. Place pie crust in a 9-inch pie plate and flute the edges as desired. Preheat oven to 350 degrees. Whisk together eggs and next 7 ingredients until blended; stir in pecans and melted chocolate. Pour filling into pie crust. Bake on lowest oven rack for 1 hour or until set, shielding pie with aluminum foil after 20 minutes. Cool completely on a wire rack.

Note: This decadent chocolate pecan pie is every bit as sinful if you choose to leave out the bourbon. The pie is so rich, it doesn't need a garnish. But, if you're one who likes a topping on every dessert, then top the pie with whipped cream and chocolate shavings; drizzle with fudge sauce.

Makes 8 to 10 servings

TOMMIE FAULKNER

Brownie Ice Cream Pie

1   Pillsbury® refrigerated pie
    crust
1   box Duncan Hines® chewy
    fudge brownie mix
2   eggs
½   cup vegetable oil
¼   cup water

¾   cup semisweet chocolate
    chips
1   (10 ounce) package
    frozen sweetened sliced
    strawberries
Vanilla ice cream

Bring pie crusts to room temperature. If possible, leave pie crust out overnight to soften. Place pie crust in a 9.5-inch pie plate and flute the edges as desired. Preheat oven to 350 degrees. Combine brownie mix, eggs, oil and water in a large bowl. Stir with spoon until well blended. Stir in chocolate chips. Pour brownie mixture into pie crust. Bake for 40 to 45 minutes or until set. Cool completely. Purée strawberries in a food processor. Serve brownie pie with vanilla ice cream and puréed strawberries.

Makes 8 to 10 servings

PATSY TAYLOR

Ice Box Chocolate Pie

1½ cups sugar
2   sticks butter, softened
2   (1 ounce) squares semisweet
    chocolate, melted
4   eggs

2   teaspoons pure vanilla
    extract
1   (9-inch) baked pie shell
Whipped cream for topping

With an electric mixer, cream together sugar and butter; add chocolate. Add one egg at a time and beat 5 minutes per egg. Add vanilla and mix well; pour into baked pie shell and cool overnight. Add whipped cream when served, if desired.

Makes 8 to 10 servings

TOMMIE FAULKNER

Raspberry Cream Torte

1	(1-pound) pound cake	1	teaspoon pure vanilla extract
1	cup heavy whipping cream	½	cup fresh raspberries
¼	cup sugar		

Cut pound cake in half crosswise. Scoop out center of bottom half of cake, leaving ½-inch rim. Whip together whipping cream with sugar and vanilla, beating until smooth and creamy. Set aside 1 cup of cream mixture for frosting. Add ½ cup of raspberries to remaining cream mixture. Spread layer of cream mixture (without raspberries) on cut side of bottom cake half. Fill center with raspberry-cream mixture. Replace top; frost with remaining cream mixture (without raspberries) Sprinkle with fresh raspberries.

Makes 10 to 12 servings

DOROTHY SPARROW

"Growing up in Baltimore, I remember every wonderful August, picking and eating raspberries from our raspberry patches. Our mother, Margaret Willis Sparrow, would always make jams, jellies and sorbet from her beautiful garden."

Dorothy Sparrow

Fudge Pie

1¼	sticks butter	1	teaspoon pure vanilla extract
5-6	tablespoons cocoa		
6	tablespoons all-purpose flour	½-¾	cup chopped pecans (optional)
1½	cups sugar	1	(9-inch) unbaked deep dish pie shell
4	eggs		

Preheat oven to 350 degrees. Melt butter in a 1-quart glass bowl for 1 minute in the microwave. Using a spoon, stir in cocoa and flour; mix well. Add sugar and mix thoroughly by hand (do not use an electric mixer). Add eggs, one at a time, mixing thoroughly by hand after each egg. Add vanilla and nuts and stir well. Pour into unbaked deep dish pie shell and bake for 30 to 40 minutes or until set.

Note: Best served warm with a large dab of whipped topping. Can be frozen and used later.

Makes 8 to 10 servings

PEGGY ALLEN

TEN DOLLAR COBBLER

1   cup all-purpose flour
1   cup sugar, plus extra for fruit
2   teaspoons baking powder
1   cup whole milk

4   cups desired fresh fruit –
     blueberries, blackberries,
     peaches, etc.
1   stick butter, melted

Preheat oven to 350 degrees. Mix together flour, 1 cup sugar and baking powder. Add milk and mix well. In separate bowl, add sugar to fruit until desired sweetness. Pour butter into a 9x13-inch baking dish. Add fruit; cover with batter. Bake for 30 to 35 minutes or until golden brown.

Makes 8 servings

SHELAH HARRIS

Shelah is Betty's mother and Betty got her love of cooking from her mother and aunts. Betty spent many hours in the kitchen with them, observing, cooking and talking!

BLACKBERRY COBBLER

1   (16 ounce) bag frozen
     blackberries (or blueberries)
1½ cups sugar, divided
1   cup all-purpose flour

1   teaspoon baking powder
1   stick unsalted butter, melted
¾   cup milk
Vanilla ice cream

Preheat the oven to 350 degrees. In a large bowl, combine the frozen blackberries and ½ cup sugar. Toss to combine and set aside. In a medium bowl, combine the remaining 1 cup sugar, flour and baking powder. In a large bowl, beat the butter and milk until smooth. Gradually beat in the flour mixture and mix until smooth. Pour the batter into a 9x13-inch baking dish greased with cooking spray. Scatter the blackberries over the batter, letting them sink in, without mixing. Bake for 35 to 45 minutes or until the top is golden brown. Let cool slightly before serving. Spoon the cobbler into bowls and top with ice cream.

Makes 8 to 10 servings

Old-Fashioned Peach Crisp

Peaches

6	cups peaches, peeled and sliced	1	teaspoon lemon juice
⅓	cup light corn syrup	1	teaspoon ground cinnamon
		¼	teaspoon ground nutmeg

Topping

½	cup firmly packed brown sugar	⅛	teaspoon ground nutmeg
¼	cup all-purpose flour	⅛	teaspoon salt
½	cup old-fashioned oats	½	stick butter
¼	teaspoon ground cinnamon		Vanilla ice cream

Preheat oven to 375 degrees. Combine half of the peaches with the corn syrup. Combine the other half of the peaches with the lemon juice, cinnamon and nutmeg. In a greased 9-inch glass baking dish, place the peaches with the corn syrup; top with the peaches with the lemon juice mixture. In a separate bowl, combine brown sugar, flour, oats, cinnamon, nutmeg and salt. Cut in butter until crumbly; press firmly over peaches. Bake for 45 to 50 minutes. Do not overcook. Top with a scoop of ice cream.

Note: You may use 3 (16 ounce) cans of sliced peaches instead of fresh peaches. Rinse them and pat them dry with a paper towel before adding to recipe.

Makes 8 to 10 servings

TART RED-FRUIT CRISP

FRUIT MIXTURE

1 (14.5 ounce) can tart red cherries, drained, reserving juice
⅔ cup sugar
¼ cup cornstarch
½ teaspoon ground cinnamon
2 cups fresh or frozen raspberries
1 cup fresh cranberries

TOPPING

½ cup all-purpose flour
½ cup old-fashioned oats
½ cup firmly packed brown sugar
¼ teaspoon ground cinnamon
½ stick butter, cut into pieces
Vanilla ice cream or whipped topping

Preheat oven to 375 degrees. In a large saucepan, combine cherry juice, sugar, cornstarch and cinnamon. Cook over medium heat, stirring constantly, until mixture is bubbly and thickened. Gently stir in cherries, raspberries and cranberries. Spoon into greased 8x8-inch glass baking dish.

In medium bowl, combine flour, oats, brown sugar and cinnamon. Cut in butter and mix until crumbly. Sprinkle over fruit mixture. Bake for 30 to 35 minutes or until topping is golden brown and fruit mixture is bubbly. Cool for a few minutes; serve with ice cream or whipped topping.

Makes 8 servings

Crisps and cobblers are best served the same day they are made. The topping can be made a day in advance; just store it in the refrigerator until ready to use.

EXTRA FLAKY PIE CRUST

1¾ cups all-purpose flour   ⅔ cup vegetable shortening
1   teaspoon salt   ⅓ cup ice water

Preheat oven to 450 degrees. Sift flour and salt in a medium mixing bowl. Add shortening. Mix with a pastry blender until the mixture is in even bits about the size of peas. Sprinkle ice water over mixture, stirring with a fork until you can pat the dough into a ball. Divide into 2 balls. Do not knead. Work fast with mixture. Roll out on a well-floured surface. Press into 2 (9-inch) pie plates and flute as desired. Bake for 10 to 12 minutes or until golden brown.

Note: Crusts may be placed in storage bags once cooled and frozen for later use.

Makes 2 (9-inch) pie crusts
FRANCES BROWN

"I have used this pie crust recipe for nearly 40 years. It came from a cookbook that was published by the Abingdon Junior Woman's Club in Gloucester in 1968. The original recipe was from Martha Borden, one of Gloucester's more prominent citizens. She was a local math teacher and was wife of Carter Borden, one of Gloucester's Board of Supervisors."

Frances Brown

Bea Hoal, Shirley Phillips and Terry Barnes work hard to make
The Lunch Bell a delightful place to eat!

Cookies, Cakes
and Other Confections

Cookies, Cakes and Other Confections

FEATURED RECIPE
ON FRONT:

Chocolate Cream Cake,
page 254

CHOCOLATE KISS PEANUT BUTTER COOKIES

2⅔ cups sifted all-purpose flour
2　teaspoons baking soda
2　sticks butter, softened
⅔　cup room temperature creamy peanut butter
1　cup sugar plus extra for rolling

1　cup firmly packed brown sugar
2　eggs
2　teaspoons pure vanilla extract
5　dozen milk chocolate kisses, unwrapped

Preheat oven to 375 degrees. Sift flour with baking soda; set aside. With an electric mixer, cream together butter and peanut butter until well blended. Add sugar and brown sugar and beat until light and fluffy. Add eggs and vanilla and beat until smooth. Stir in flour mixture until well combined.

Using level tablespoons, shape into 5 dozen balls. Roll in granulated sugar and place 2 inches apart on ungreased cookie sheet. Bake for 8 minutes. Remove from oven and press a chocolate kiss on top of each. Bake for 2 minutes longer. Remove cookies and let cool before removing from pan.

Makes about 5 dozen cookies

NANCY MARTIN

CHRISTMAS THUMBKINS

2　sticks butter, softened
½　cup sugar
½　cup dark corn syrup
2　separated eggs

2½ cups all-purpose flour
2　cups finely chopped walnuts
Grape or strawberry jelly

In large bowl with an electric mixer, cream together butter and sugar. Beat in corn syrup and egg yolks until well mixed. Stir in flour. Chill 30 minutes or until firm enough to handle.

Preheat oven to 325 degrees. Roll dough into 1-inch balls. Dip into slightly beaten egg whites. Roll in nuts. Place 2 inches apart on greased baking sheet. With thumb make indentation in center of each cookie. Bake for 20 minutes or until golden brown. Remove from oven. While still warm, fill with a small amount of jelly.

Makes about 4 dozen cookies

STEPHANIE BAKER

At family gatherings, Betty's mother would always try to cook something for everyone because she wanted to make sure everyone got something they liked! This would create a feast of food, very similar to Betty's Thanksgiving dinner that she serves at her restaurant.

 # MEXICAN WEDDING COOKIES

2	sticks butter, softened	2	cups all-purpose flour
½	cup confectioners' sugar plus extra for rolling	½	teaspoon pure vanilla extract
		½	cup finely chopped walnuts

Preheat oven to 350 degrees. In a large bowl, cream together butter and sugar. Add flour and vanilla and mix well. Fold in walnuts. Roll into 1-inch balls and place about 2 inches apart on ungreased cookie sheet. Bake for 20 minutes. While still warm, roll cookies in confectioners' sugar.

Makes about 2 dozen cookies

SHELAH HARRIS

 # GIANT WHITE CHOCOLATE CHIP, CRANBERRY, PECAN COOKIES

½	cup vegetable shortening	½	teaspoon orange extract
2	sticks butter, softened	3¾	cups all-purpose flour
½	cup sugar	2	teaspoons baking soda
1¾	cups firmly packed brown sugar	½	teaspoon salt
3	eggs	2½	cups white chocolate chips
½	teaspoon pure vanilla extract	1½	cups chopped pecans
½	teaspoon lemon extract	1¾	cups dried cranberries

Preheat oven to 350 degrees. Cream together shortening, butter, sugars, eggs, vanilla, lemon and orange extract thoroughly. In a separate bowl, mix together flour, baking soda and salt. Stir dry ingredients into creamed mixture until moistened. Add chocolate chips, pecans and cranberries and mix well. Spoon cookies onto an ungreased cookie sheet using a 4-ounce food scoop or a very heaping spoon. Bake for 12 minutes (no longer).

Makes about 3 dozen large cookies

SHELAH SWAIN

Giant Triple Chocolate Chip Cookies

½   cup vegetable shortening
2   sticks butter, softened
½   cup sugar
1¾ cups firmly packed brown sugar
3   eggs
1   teaspoon pure vanilla extract
3¾ cups all-purpose flour
2   teaspoons baking soda
½   teaspoon salt
2   cups semisweet chocolate chips
1   cup milk chocolate chips
1   cup bittersweet chocolate chips (60% cocoa)
1   cup heath toffee bits

Preheat oven to 350 degrees. Cream together shortening, butter, sugars, eggs and vanilla thoroughly. In a separate bowl, mix together flour, baking soda and salt. Stir dry ingredients into creamed mixture until moistened. Add chocolate chips and toffee bits and mix well. Spoon cookies onto an ungreased cookie sheet using a 4-ounce food scoop or a very heaping small cookie scoop. Bake for 12 minutes (no longer).

Makes about 3 dozen large cookies

SHELAH SWAIN

Snickerdoodles

2   sticks butter, softened
1½ cups plus 3 tablespoons sugar
2   eggs
2¾ cups all-purpose flour
2   teaspoons cream of tartar
1   teaspoon baking soda
½   teaspoon salt
3   teaspoons ground cinnamon

Preheat oven to 400 degrees. Cream together butter, 1½ cups sugar and eggs thoroughly. In a separate bowl, mix together flour, cream of tartar, baking soda and salt. Stir dry ingredients into creamed mixture until moistened. Roll into 1-inch balls. In a small bowl, mix together 3 tablespoons sugar and cinnamon. Roll balls in cinnamon mixture and place about 2 inches apart on ungreased cookie sheet. Bake for 8 to 10 minutes or until lightly browned, but still soft.

Makes 2 to 3 dozen cookies

ALMOND SANDWICH COOKIES

COOKIES

1   (16.5 ounce) roll Pillsbury®
    refrigerated sugar cookies
½   cup all-purpose flour

½   teaspoon almond extract
1   tablespoon sugar

FILLING

2   cups confectioners' sugar
¼   cup butter, softened
4   teaspoons milk

¼   teaspoon almond extract
1   drop red food coloring

Preheat oven to 350 degrees. In a large bowl, break up cookie dough. Stir or knead in flour and almond extract until well blended. Shape dough into ½-inch balls. Place balls 1 inch apart on ungreased cookie sheet. Press bottom of glass dipped in sugar on each ball until ¼-inch thick; prick top of each cookie with a fork. Bake for 8 to 10 minutes until set but not brown. Cool 1 minute; remove from cookie sheet to cooling rack. Cool completely, about 15 minutes.

While cookies are baking, combine confectioners' sugar, butter, milk, almond extract and red food coloring. Beat with an electric mixer on low speed until smooth and creamy. Spread about 1 teaspoon of filling on bottom half of the cooled cookies. Top each with another cookie, bottom side down; press gently. Store in the refrigerator.

Makes 6 to 7 dozen small cookies

Bill Swain makes these beautiful
fruit displays for many catering events.

MONSTER COOKIES

1½	cups creamy peanut butter	2½	cups all-purpose flour
1	stick butter, softened	2	teaspoons baking soda
2	cups brown sugar	8	ounces plain M & M's®
1	cup sugar	¾	cup semisweet chocolate chips
3	eggs		
1	teaspoon pure vanilla extract	2	cups oatmeal

Preheat oven to 350 degrees. With a wooden spoon, cream together peanut butter and butter in a large bowl. Add brown sugar, sugar, eggs and vanilla and stir well. Sift together flour and baking soda; stir into peanut butter mixture. Fold in M & M's®, chocolate chips and oatmeal. Spoon cookies onto ungreased cookie sheet using a small cookie dipper. Bake 10 minutes. Take out of the oven before they are completely done, as the heat will stay in the pan and they will continue to cook a little longer. Allow to cool slightly before placing them on cookie racks.

Makes about 4 to 5 dozen cookies

MARGIE STALLINGS

"You can substitute Reese's® peanut butter chips and Reese's® pieces for a TOTAL peanut butter taste!!"
Margie Stallings

GIANT DATE-PECAN COOKIES

½	cup vegetable shortening	¼	teaspoon orange extract
2	sticks butter, softened	3¾	cups all-purpose flour
½	cup sugar	2	teaspoons baking soda
1¾	cups firmly packed brown sugar	½	teaspoon salt
3	eggs		Pinch to ¼ teaspoon ground nutmeg
2	teaspoons pure vanilla extract	3	teaspoon ground cinnamon
¼	teaspoon lemon extract	3	cups chopped dates
		2	cups chopped pecans

Preheat oven to 350 degrees. Cream together shortening, butter, sugars, eggs, vanilla, lemon and orange extract thoroughly. In a separate bowl, mix together flour, baking soda, salt, nutmeg and cinnamon. Stir dry ingredients into creamed mixture until moistened. Add dates and pecans and mix well. Spoon cookies onto an ungreased cookie sheet using a 4-ounce food scoop or a very heaping spoon. Bake for 12 minutes (no longer).

Makes about 3 dozen large cookies

SHELAH SWAIN

 # No Bake Chocolate Oatmeal Cookies

2 sticks butter	Dash salt
½ cup milk	½ cup peanut butter
2 cups sugar	1 teaspoon pure vanilla extract
½ cup cocoa powder	3 cups oatmeal

In a medium saucepan, combine butter, milk, sugar, cocoa and salt. Bring to a boil over medium heat and simmer for 5 minutes. Remove from heat. Add peanut butter and vanilla; stir well. Mix in oatmeal and let stand in pan for 5 to 10 minutes. Drop by rounded spoonful onto waxed paper.

Makes about 3 dozen cookies

SHELAH SWAIN

 # Million-Dollar Bars

BARS

4 cups rolled oats	¼ cup light corn syrup
1½ sticks butter	¼ cup peanut butter
1 cup firmly packed brown sugar	1 teaspoon pure vanilla extract

TOPPING

1 (11 ounce) package butterscotch chips	⅓ cup peanut butter
1 (12 ounce) package semisweet chocolate chips	1 cup salted, dry roasted peanuts

Preheat oven to 350 degrees. Pour oats into a large mixing bowl; set aside. Melt together the butter, brown sugar, corn syrup, peanut butter and vanilla in a saucepan over low heat. Pour over oatmeal and mix together. Press into a greased 9x13-inch baking dish and bake for 10 minutes or until lightly brown. Cool for 30 minutes.

Using the same saucepan, melt butterscotch chips, chocolate chips and peanut butter over low heat. Stir in peanuts and spread evenly over base. Cool to room temperature. Refrigerate 1 hour until firm enough to cut neatly into squares.

Makes about 2 to 3 dozen bars

PUMPKIN BARS

BARS

2½	cups pumpkin	2	teaspoons baking powder
2	cups sugar	1	teaspoon baking soda
1	cup vegetable oil	1	teaspoon salt
4	eggs	3-4	teaspoons ground cinnamon, depending on your taste
½	stick butter, softened	1	large pinch ground nutmeg
2	cups all-purpose flour		

CREAM CHEESE FROSTING

2	cups confectioners' sugar	1	teaspoon pure vanilla extract
1	stick butter, softened	¾	teaspoon maple syrup
3	ounces cream cheese, softened		

Preheat oven to 350 degrees. Beat together pumpkin, sugar, oil, eggs and butter. In a separate bowl, stir together flour, baking powder, baking soda, salt, cinnamon and nutmeg. Slowly add dry ingredients to pumpkin mixture and blend thoroughly. Pour batter into a greased and lightly sugared 9x13-inch metal pan (do not use glass). Bake for 25 to 30 minutes or until set. Cool completely.

For frosting, beat together confectioners' sugar, butter, cream cheese, vanilla and maple syrup. If the mixture is too thick, add a little milk. Once pumpkin bars have cooled, spread frosting over the top. Cut into bars.

Makes about 2 dozen bars

SHELAH SWAIN

RASPBERRY BARS

2	sticks butter, softened	2	cups all-purpose flour
1	cup sugar	½	cup seedless raspberry jam
2	egg yolks		

Preheat oven to 350 degrees. With an electric mixer, cream together butter and sugar. Beat in egg yolks. Gradually add flour. Press half of mixture into greased 8-inch square baking pan. Spread with jam and crumble remaining mixture over jam. Bake for 35 to 40 minutes or until lightly browned. Cool.

Makes 16 bars

JEANNIE DIODATO

PECAN TOFFEE BARS

CRUST
1½ cups sifted all-purpose flour

¾ cup firmly packed brown sugar

1½ sticks butter, softened

FILLING
2 eggs, beaten

1½ cups firmly packed brown sugar

1½ teaspoons pure vanilla extract

3 tablespoons all-purpose flour

1½ teaspoons baking powder

½ teaspoon salt

1⅓ cups coconut flakes

1½ cups chopped pecans

Preheat oven to 350 degrees. To prepare crust, combine flour and brown sugar in a bowl. Cut in butter until mixture is crumbly. Press into a greased 9x13-inch baking dish and bake for 15 minutes.

For filling, combine eggs, brown sugar and vanilla in a medium bowl. Stir in flour, baking powder and salt. Stir in coconut and pecans; mix well. Spread mixture over cooled crust. Bake for 30 minutes or until browned. Cool in pan and cut into bars.

Makes 2 dozen bars

BUTTERSCOTCH CHOCOLATE BARS

1 stick butter, melted

2 (14 ounce) cans sweetened condensed milk

2 teaspoons pure vanilla extract

1 (13½ ounce) box graham cracker crumbs

6 ounces semisweet chocolate chips

6 ounces butterscotch chips

1 cup chopped pecans

Preheat oven to 350 degrees. In a large bowl, combine butter, condensed milk, vanilla and graham cracker crumbs. Beat with an electric mixer until blended. Stir in chocolate chips, butterscotch chips and pecans. Pour into a greased 9x13-inch baking dish. Bake for 30 minutes or until golden brown. Cool in dish several hours or overnight; cut into bars.

Makes 2 dozen bars

SUGAR CREAM BARS

1 box Duncan Hines® yellow cake mix
3 eggs, divided
1 stick butter, softened

8 ounces cream cheese, softened
1 (1 pound) box confectioners' sugar

Preheat oven to 350 degrees. By hand, mix together cake mix, 1 egg and butter. Batter will be very thick. Spread onto a greased 9x13-inch cookie sheet. With an electric mixer, beat together cream cheese, 2 eggs and confectioners' sugar. Spread mixture on top of cake mixture. Bake for 30 minutes.

Makes about 2 dozen bars

SHELAH SWAIN

TEXAS BROWNIES

BROWNIES

5 eggs
1 (16 ounce) can chocolate syrup
1 can sugar

1 can all-purpose flour
¾ can vegetable oil
¼ teaspoon baking powder

FROSTING

1 stick butter
4 tablespoons cocoa
6 tablespoons milk
1 (1 pound) box confectioners' sugar

1 teaspoon pure vanilla extract
1 cup chopped pecans (optional)

Preheat oven to 350 degrees. With an electric mixer, beat the eggs until foamy. Add the chocolate syrup and then use the can for a measuring cup. Add the sugar, flour, oil and baking powder and mix well. Pour mixture into a greased 11¼x17¼-inch jelly roll pan and bake for 30 to 35 minutes.

When brownies are almost done baking, in a medium saucepan heat butter, cocoa and milk. Cook about 5 minutes or until butter has melted. Remove from heat and mix in confectioners' sugar and vanilla with a spoon. Stir until smooth. Fold in nuts. Spread frosting over hot brownies.

Makes 4 to 5 dozen brownies

ANN EDGAR

 # FROSTED CREAM CHEESE BROWNIES

BROWNIES

6   ounces cream cheese, softened
5   tablespoons butter, softened
⅓   cup sugar
5   eggs, divided
2   tablespoons all-purpose flour

¾   teaspoon pure vanilla extract
1   (21 ounce) box Duncan Hines® chewy fudge brownie mix
2   tablespoons water

FROSTING

2   tablespoons cocoa powder
3   tablespoons butter, melted
1½ cups confectioners' sugar

2   tablespoons milk or more if needed
1   teaspoon pure vanilla extract

Preheat oven to 350 degrees. With an electric mixer, cream together cream cheese and butter. Add the sugar, 2 eggs, flour and vanilla. Beat until smooth; set aside. In a separate bowl, mix together brownie mix, chocolate flavor pouch, water and 3 eggs. Mix by hand, about 50 strokes. Pour half of the brownie mixture into a greased 9x13-inch baking dish. Spread the cream cheese mixture over the brownie layer. Spoon small dollops of the brownie mixture over the cream cheese mixture, allowing some brownie batter to show through. Pull a knife through the batter in wide curves to create a swirled appearance. Bake for 35 to 40 minutes. Cool.

For frosting, add cocoa to melted butter; stir until dissolved. Add confectioners' sugar, milk and vanilla; stir until smooth. Add more milk if necessary. Frost brownies after they have cooled.

Makes 2 to 3 dozen brownies

CREAM CHEESE BROWNIES

BROWNIES

4	(1 ounce) squares unsweetened baking chocolate
1	stick butter
1	cup sugar
1	cup firmly packed light brown sugar
3	eggs, beaten

2	teaspoons pure vanilla extract
1½	cups all-purpose flour
½	teaspoon salt
1	cup chopped pecans, divided
1	cup semisweet chocolate chips

FILLING

8	ounces cream cheese, softened

1	egg, beaten
⅛	cup sugar

Preheat oven to 325 degrees. Place chocolate squares and butter in a 2-quart glass measuring pitcher. Heat in microwave on high for 2 minutes. Remove and stir until melted. Add both sugars and stir well. Mix in eggs and vanilla. Add flour and salt. Stir in ¾ cup pecans and chocolate chips.

For filling, blend together cream cheese, egg and sugar; set aside. In a greased 7x10-inch baking dish, spread ⅔ of brownie mixture in the bottom of the dish. Spread the cream cheese mixture on top. Spoon small dollops of the brownie mixture over the cream cheese mixture, allowing some brownie batter to show through. Pull a knife through the batter in wide curves to create a swirled appearance. Sprinkle with ¼ cup pecans. Bake for 30 to 35 minutes.

Makes 15 to 18 brownies

FIVE FLAVOR POUND CAKE

CAKE

2	sticks butter, softened	1	cup whole milk
½	cup vegetable shortening	1	teaspoon coconut extract
3	cups sugar	1	teaspoon rum extract
5	eggs	1	teaspoon butter flavoring
3	cups all-purpose flour	1	teaspoon lemon extract
½	teaspoon baking powder	1	teaspoon pure vanilla extract
¼	teaspoon salt		

GLAZE

1	cup sugar	1	teaspoon butter flavoring
½	cup water	1	teaspoon lemon extract
1	teaspoon coconut extract	1	teaspoon pure vanilla extract
1	teaspoon rum extract		

Instead of greasing and flouring cake pans, Betty always uses Baker's Joy®. She sprays a thin coat over the entire pan which takes the place of greasing and flouring.

Preheat oven to 325 degrees. With an electric mixer, cream together butter, shortening and sugar. Beat eggs until lemon colored; add to butter mixture. Stir together flour, baking powder and salt in separate bowl; sift. Combine milk and all flavorings in small bowl. Alternately, add dry ingredients, then wet ingredients to creamed mixture and mix until smooth. Very gently push batter into a greased and floured 10-inch tube pan. Bake for 1 hour and 15 minutes or until a toothpick inserted into the center of the cake comes out clean.

For glaze, combine sugar, water and all flavorings in saucepan. Heat to boiling, stirring until dissolved. Boil 1 minute. Pour over hot cake. Let cake set in pan until cool. Turn out onto cake plate and cover to store.

Makes 12 to 16 servings

PATSY TAYLOR

Patsy Taylor, while working at the second **Lunch Bell**.

BLACK WALNUT COCONUT POUND CAKE

CAKE

2	cups sugar	1	cup buttermilk
1	cup vegetable oil	1	cup chopped black walnuts
4	eggs, beaten	1	cup angel flake coconut
3	cups all-purpose flour	1	teaspoon black walnut extract
½	teaspoon baking powder	2	teaspoons coconut extract
½	teaspoon baking soda		
½	teaspoon salt		

HOT COCONUT SYRUP

½	cup water	1	teaspoon coconut extract
2	tablespoons butter	1	cup sugar

When making a cake and alternately adding wet and dry ingredients, always begin with dry ingredients and end with dry ingredients. This will help bind the batter.

Preheat oven to 325 degrees. With an electric mixer, cream together sugar, vegetable oil and eggs. Combine flour, baking powder, baking soda and salt in separate bowl; sift. Alternately add dry ingredients, then buttermilk to sugar mixture and mix well after each addition. Blend in walnuts, coconut, black walnut extract and coconut extract. Pour batter into a greased and floured 10-inch tube pan. Bake for 1 hour and 15 minutes or until a toothpick inserted into the center of the cake comes out clean.

Combine water, butter, coconut extract and sugar in a saucepan. Heat to boiling, stirring until dissolved. Boil 5 minutes. Pour over hot cake and leave cake in pan 3 hours to absorb syrup well. Let cake set in pan until cool. Turn out onto cake plate and cover to store.

Note: This is a very delicious moist cake that freezes exceptionally well.

Makes 12 to 16 servings

BEST YET POUND CAKE

3 sticks butter, softened
8 ounces cream cheese,
   softened
3 cups sugar

6 eggs, at room temperature
3 cups cake flour
1 tablespoon imitation vanilla
   butter and nut flavoring

With an electric mixer, cream together butter, cream cheese and sugar; add eggs, one at a time, mixing well after each addition. Add flour and flavoring and mix well. Pour batter into a greased and floured tube pan. Place into a cold oven. Bake at 300 degrees for 1 hour and 45 minutes or until a toothpick inserted into the center of the cake comes out clean. Let cake set in pan until cool. Turn out onto cake plate and cover to store.

Makes 12 to 16 servings

WILMA BINDER MORRIS

GLAZE FOR CAKES

½ cup sugar
¼ cup water
2 tablespoons butter

2 tablespoons pure vanilla
   extract or any other flavor

Combine sugar, water and butter in a small saucepan. Bring to a boil. Reduce heat to medium and gently boil for 4 to 5 minutes, stirring occasionally, until sugar dissolves. Remove from heat and cool for 15 minutes. Stir in vanilla (or other flavoring).

When cake has cooled, punch holes in top of cake with a wooden pick. Slowly spoon glaze on top of cake allowing glaze to absorb into cake.

Note: This glaze can be used on almost any cake to add flavor and moistness. The added flavor will spread throughout the cake, once the glaze soaks in. You may still frost the cake after adding this glaze.

Makes enough glaze for 1 cake,
either a tube cake,
pound cake or 9x13-inch cake

VIRGINIA'S BEST POUND CAKE

2 sticks butter, softened
½ cup vegetable oil
3 cups sugar
½ teaspoon salt
½ teaspoon baking powder
1 cup buttermilk

2 teaspoons vanilla
1 teaspoon lemon extract
6 eggs, beaten
3 cups all-purpose flour
Confectioners' sugar

Preheat oven to 325 degrees. With an electric mixer, beat together butter, oil, sugar, salt and baking powder until fluffy (it will look very light yellow). Add buttermilk, vanilla and lemon extract; add beaten eggs. Beat on medium speed for 3 minutes. Fold in the flour on low speed until well combined. Pour batter into a greased and floured tube pan. Bake for 1 hour and 20 minutes or until a toothpick inserted into the center of the cake comes out clean. Cool in pan. Turn onto serving plate once cooled. Dust with confectioners' sugar.

Makes 12 to 16 servings

If your cake doesn't rise like it should, then it might be the baking powder. Check the expiration date on the bottom of the can and discard if it is past expiration.

POLLY'S POUND CAKE

2 sticks butter, softened
¼ cup vegetable shortening
3 cups sugar
5 eggs
½ teaspoon pure vanilla extract

1 tablespoon lemon or almond extract
3½ cups all-purpose flour
½ teaspoon baking powder
Dash of salt
1 cup milk

Preheat oven to 350 degrees. With an electric mixer, cream together butter, shortening and sugar. Add eggs and beat 2 minutes at medium speed. Add vanilla and lemon extract. Sift together flour, baking powder and salt. Add milk and sifted dry ingredients, alternately to creamed mixture, and blend until dry ingredients are mixed in. Do not over mix. Pour batter into a greased and floured tube pan and bake for 1 hour and 20 minutes. Let cool in pan for 10 minutes; turn out onto a baking rack to finish cooling.

Makes 12 to 16 servings

POLLY BAILEY

Rowena's, a local business that creates and produces gourmet foods, recommends freezing pound cakes so that they retain their freshness. Freezing pound cakes improves the moisture, texture and taste of pound cakes.

BUTTER PECAN POUND CAKE

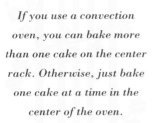

1	box butter pecan cake mix	3	tablespoons confectioners' sugar
4	eggs	¾	cup chopped pecans, divided
¼	cup vegetable oil		
1	cup water or milk		
1	(14.5 ounce) can coconut pecan frosting		

Preheat oven to 350 degrees. With an electric mixer, beat cake mix with eggs, oil and water (or milk). Fold in frosting and ½ cup pecans. Grease tube pan and sprinkle with confectioners' sugar and ¼ cup pecans. Pour batter into tube pan and bake for 40 minutes or until a toothpick inserted into the center of the cake comes out clean. Let cake set in pan until cool; turn out onto cake plate and cover to store.

Makes 12 to 16 servings

WILMA BINDER MORRIS

GRANDMA JONES' POUND CAKE

"Bernice Jones is my grandmother and she taught me a love of cooking. She would always have a large assortment of pies and cakes at Thanksgiving and Christmas."
Barbara Holland Eby

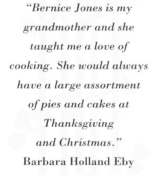

2	sticks butter, softened	1	cup whole milk or half-and-half
1	cup vegetable shortening	1	teaspoon pure vanilla extract
3	cups sugar	1	teaspoon lemon or almond extract
5	eggs	½	teaspoon baking powder
3	cups cake flour		

With an electric mixer, cream together butter and shortening. Add sugar and continue to cream for 10 minutes or until perfectly smooth. Add eggs one at a time, beating until well blended. Add cake flour a little at a time. Slowly add milk, vanilla and lemon (or almond) extracts. Lastly, add baking powder and mix well. Pour batter in a greased and floured tube pan and place in cold oven. Bake at 325 degrees for 1 hour and 15 minutes or until a toothpick inserted into the center of the cake comes out clean. Cool slightly; turn onto cake plate.

Makes 12 to 16 servings

BERNICE JONES

FRESH APPLE POUND CAKE

CAKE
2½ cups sugar
3½ cups self-rising flour
3 teaspoons ground cinnamon
1½ cups oil
4 eggs

2 teaspoons pure vanilla extract
3½ cups fresh diced apples
½ cup chopped walnuts

GLAZE
½ cup sugar
½ cup sour cream

¼ teaspoon baking soda
¼ cup chopped walnuts

Preheat oven to 325 degrees. Mix together sugar, flour and cinnamon in a large bowl with a spoon. Add oil, eggs, vanilla and mix well with spoon. Add apples and walnuts and stir. Pour batter into a greased and floured tube pan and cook for 1 hour or until a toothpick inserted into the center of the cake comes out clean. Turn onto cake plate.

While cake is baking, combine sugar, sour cream, and baking soda in a saucepan. Stir over medium heat until mixture is foamy. Make sure sugar is dissolved. Add walnuts and stir. Slowly pour glaze over cake as soon as it is removed from oven. Refrigerate after cake cools.

Makes 12 to 16 servings

WILMA BINDER MORRIS

When a recipe calls for eggs, Betty recommends using large or extra large eggs.

PAT'S ONE BOWL POUND CAKE

2 sticks butter, softened
½ cup vegetable shortening
3 cups sugar
3 cups all-purpose flour
5 eggs

1 cup milk
1 tablespoon pure vanilla extract
Pinch salt

Preheat oven to 325 degrees. Combine all ingredients and mix well. Pour batter into a greased and floured tube pan. Bake for 1 hour; increase heat to 350 degrees and bake for an additional 30 minutes or until a toothpick inserted into the center of the cake comes out clean. Let cake set in pan until cool; turn out onto cake plate and cover to store.

Makes 12 to 16 servings

PAT MACIEJEWSKI

Betty and Pat have been friends for over 45 years!

APPLE-PECAN POUND CAKE

CAKE

3	cups all-purpose flour
1	teaspoon baking soda
1	teaspoon salt
1	teaspoon ground cinnamon
½	teaspoon ground nutmeg
2	cups sugar
1½	cups vegetable oil
4	eggs

1	tablespoons pure vanilla extract
2	cups finely chopped, pared cooking apples (Golden Delicious, Rome or Granny Smith are recommended)
1	cup chopped pecans
½	cup raisins (optional)

TOPPING

½	cup applejack or Calvados (French apple brandy)
½	cup apple juice or apple cider

¼	cup firmly packed brown sugar
2	tablespoons butter

Preheat oven to 325 degrees. In a large bowl, mix together flour, baking soda, salt, cinnamon and nutmeg; set aside. With an electric mixer, beat the sugar, oil, eggs and vanilla until thoroughly combined. Gradually beat in the flour mixture until smooth. Fold in the apples, pecans and raisins. Pour batter into a greased and floured 10-inch tube pan. Bake for 1 hour and 15 minutes or until a toothpick inserted into the center of the cake comes out clean.

While cake is baking, combine applejack, apple juice, brown sugar and butter in a medium saucepan. Bring to a boil, stirring until sugar is completely dissolved. Cook for 4 minutes; cool slightly. When the cake is taken out of the oven, poke holes all over the cake with a toothpick. Spoon the topping over it, covering entire cake. Let cool in pan.

Note: The topping may be spooned over the cake at the time of serving.

Makes 12 to 16 servings

When cooling a pound cake, you should elevate the cooling rack on four cups in order to allow the cake to cool faster and evenly. The longer you leave a pound cake in the pan, the firmer the crust will be.

PINEAPPLE POUND CAKE

CAKE

2   sticks butter, softened
½   cup vegetable shortening
2¾ cups sugar
6   eggs
¼   cup milk
1   teaspoon pure vanilla extract

¾   cup crushed pineapple, undrained
3   cups all-purpose flour
1   teaspoon baking powder
Pinch salt

GLAZE

½   stick butter, softened
1½ cups confectioners' sugar

1   cup crushed pineapple, drained

With an electric mixer, cream together butter, shortening and sugar until light and fluffy. Add eggs, one at a time, beating well after each addition. Combine milk, vanilla, and crushed pineapple in a small bowl. Sift together flour, baking powder and salt in a separate bowl. Add dry ingredients to batter, alternately with milk mixture, beginning and ending with dry ingredients. Mix well. Pour batter into a greased and floured 10-inch tube pan and place in a cold oven. Set temperature at 325 degrees and bake for 1 hour and 15 minutes. Cool 10 to 15 minutes. Turn onto serving plate.

In a microwave-safe dish, combine butter, sugar and pineapple. Cook on high for 3 minutes; stir well. Cook for an additional 2 minutes; stir again. Drizzle top and sides of cake with glaze.

Note: This cake can be made a couple of days ahead, but must be refrigerated. It should not be frozen as it is made with pineapple.

Makes 12 to 16 servings

MARY JOYNER

"The cake is a favorite of my family and friends. When our pastor would announce that we were going to have a covered dish supper at church, he would say "and Mary Joyner is going to bring a Pineapple Pound Cake." It was always the first cake to be finished."

Mary Joyner

*Pound cake freezes
for up to a month when
double wrapped with
plastic wrap.*

CHOCOLATE POUND CAKE

2	sticks butter, softened	1	cup milk
½	cup vegetable shortening	2	cups sifted all-purpose flour
3	cups sugar	½	teaspoon baking powder
6	eggs	½	teaspoon salt
2	teaspoons pure vanilla extract	½	cup cocoa

Preheat oven to 325 degrees. With an electric mixer, cream together butter and shortening. Gradually add the sugar, beating until very smooth. Add eggs, one at a time, beating well after each addition. Add vanilla to milk; set aside. Sift together flour, baking powder, salt and cocoa. Add dry ingredients to batter, alternately with milk, beginning and ending with dry ingredients. Pour batter into a greased and floured tube pan and bake for 1 hour and 30 minutes or until a toothpick inserted into the center of the cake comes out clean. Cool in pan.

Makes 12 to 16 servings

EASY COCONUT CAKE

2	cups sour cream	1	tablespoon grated orange zest (optional)
1-2	cups sugar	1	box yellow cake mix
2	(12 to 16 ounce) packages grated coconut		

Combine sour cream, sugar (to taste), coconut and orange zest. Cover and place in the refrigerator overnight. The next day, make cake mix according to package directions. Pour batter evenly into 3 or 4 greased and floured 9-inch cake pans. Bake according to package directions. Allow to cool. Frost the cake with the coconut mixture, icing between layers and on top. Place the cake in an airtight container and store in the refrigerator for up to 4 days. Serve cool.

Makes 10 to 12 servings

HOPE NEWSOME

Fresh Coconut Cake

Cake

2	sticks butter, softened		½	teaspoon salt
2	cups sugar		1	cup milk
4	eggs		1	teaspoon pure vanilla extract
3	cups cake flour, sifted		½	teaspoon almond extract
3	teaspoons baking powder			

Frosting

1½	cups sugar		½	teaspoon cream of tartar
½	cup water		1	teaspoon pure vanilla extract
4	egg whites		2	cups shredded coconut

Preheat oven to 350 degrees. With an electric mixer, cream butter and gradually add sugar. Beat until light and fluffy. Add eggs one at a time, beating well after each addition. In another bowl sift flour with baking powder and salt. Combine milk and vanilla and almond extract. Add flour mixture alternately with milk mixture to creamed mixture, beating after each addition until smooth. Pour batter evenly into 3 greased and floured 9-inch cake pans. Bake for 25 to 30 minutes or until a toothpick inserted into the center of the cake comes out clean. Cool in pans for 10 minutes. Remove from pans and finish cooling on racks.

Boil sugar and water for 2 minutes. With an electric mixer, beat egg whites and cream of tartar until eggs stand up in stiff peaks, but are not dry. Pour boiling syrup into egg whites, beating at highest speed on mixer. When icing becomes stiff enough to spread (approximately 2 to 4 minutes), add vanilla. Spread between layers, on top and sides of cake. Sprinkle with coconut.

Makes 10 to 12 servings

MOM'S COCONUT CAKE

CAKE

2	sticks butter, softened	1	teaspoon salt
2	cups sugar	3	teaspoons baking powder
4	eggs, separated	1	cup milk
3	cups all-purpose flour	1	teaspoon vanilla

FROSTING

2	cups sugar	1	(14 ounce) bag coconut flakes
Water			
2	egg whites		

Preheat oven to 350 degrees. In a large bowl, cream together butter and sugar until light and creamy. Add well-beaten egg yolks; mix well. In a separate bowl, sift flour twice with salt and baking powder. Add milk and dry ingredients alternately to creamed mixture, mixing after each addition. Add vanilla; mix well. Fold in beaten egg whites. Pour batter evenly into 3 greased and floured 8-inch round cake pans. Bake for 30 minutes or until a toothpick inserted into the center of the cake comes out clean. Cool on racks.

For frosting, put sugar in a small saucepan and cover with water (about ¼ cup). Cook until syrupy. In a separate bowl, beat 2 egg whites until almost stiff; pour hot syrup over egg whites. Fold in coconut.

After cake has cooled, place first layer of cake top down on cake plate; then frost the top and sides. Repeat for second layer. Place the third layer top side up and frost the top and sides.

Note: This cake is best served the following day.

Makes 10 to 12 servings

PAULA MARIA ORPHANIDYS

So Good Coconut Cake

1   box white cake mix
1   (14 ounce) bag coconut
    flakes, divided
2   cups sour cream, divided

1   cup sugar
1   (12 ounce) container frozen
    whipped topping, thawed

Make cake according to directions on box. Pour batter evenly into 2 greased and floured 9-inch round cake pans and bake as directed. Cool completely. Cut cooled cake layers in half. Mix together ½ bag coconut flakes, 1 cup sour cream and sugar. Spread between cake layers. In a separate bowl, combine ½ bag coconut flakes, 1 cup sour cream and frozen whipped topping. Frost the top and sides of the cake with this icing.

Note: Refrigerated cake becomes moist and lasts for several days.

Makes 10 to 12 servings

JUDYE HAFLING

If a recipe for baking calls for butter, always use unsalted butter so that you can have more control over the flavor of the product.

Aunt Della's Pineapple Cake

CAKE

1   box Duncan Hines® yellow
    cake mix
1   cup sour cream
⅓   cup vegetable oil

5   eggs
¼   cup sugar
¼   cup milk
1   stick butter, softened

FILLING

2½ tablespoons cornstarch
1½ cups sugar
1   (20 ounce) can crushed
    pineapple, undrained

1   tablespoon lemon juice
Maraschino cherries for garnish

Preheat oven to 350 degrees. With an electric mixer, mix together cake mix, sour cream, oil, eggs, sugar, milk and butter. Beat on medium speed for 5 minutes. Pour batter evenly into 4 greased and floured 9-inch cake pans. Bake for 20 to 25 minutes or until a toothpick inserted into the center of the cake comes out clean.

About 10 minutes before cake is done, mix together cornstarch, sugar, pineapple and lemon juice in a 2-quart glass measuring pitcher. Microwave on high for 5 to 6 minutes or until thickened. Upon removing the cakes from oven, immediately spread filling between layers and on top of cake. Garnish with maraschino cherries. Serve while warm or after cooled.

Makes 10 to 12 servings

DELLA LEWIS

If desired, frost the sides of the Pineapple Cake with a cream cheese frosting.

Banana Cake

Cake

2	sticks butter, softened	4	eggs
½	cup canola oil	3	cups baking mix
2	cups sugar	2	cups mashed bananas

Frosting

8	ounces cream cheese, softened	1	tablespoon milk or more
1	stick butter, softened	1	(8 ounce) container frozen whipped topping, thawed
1	teaspoon pure vanilla extract	½	cup chopped walnuts or pecans
3	cups confectioners' sugar		

Preheat oven to 350 degrees. With an electric mixer, cream together butter, oil and sugar on medium speed. Add eggs one at a time and mix well. Add baking mix and mix well. Fold in the bananas. Pour batter evenly into 2 greased and floured 9-inch cake pans. Bake for 30 to 35 minutes or until a toothpick inserted into the center of the bread comes out clean. Cool cake in pan on wire rack for 10 minutes; remove and cool completely on wire rack.

Combine cream cheese, butter, vanilla, confectioners' sugar and milk and mix until smooth. If necessary, add a little extra milk. When cake is cool, spread whipped topping between layers. Frost the top and sides of cake with cream cheese frosting. Sprinkle cake with nuts.

Makes 10 to 12 servings

CARROT GOLD CAKE

CAKE

2 cups sugar
1½ cups vegetable oil
4 eggs, well beaten
2 cups all-purpose flour
2 teaspoons baking powder
1½ teaspoons baking soda

1 teaspoon salt
2 teaspoons ground cinnamon
1 cup crushed pineapple, drained
2 cups finely grated raw carrots

FROSTING

8 ounces cream cheese, softened
1 stick butter, softened
1 teaspoon pure vanilla extract
3 cups confectioners' sugar

1 tablespoon milk or more
1 (8 ounce) container frozen whipped topping, thawed
½ cup chopped walnuts or pecans

Betty does not put nuts in the cake, since many people cannot eat them or do not like them. The nuts are sprinkled on top and can be removed prior to eating if necessary.

Preheat oven to 350 degrees. With an electric mixer, cream together sugar and vegetable oil. Add eggs, beating until fluffy. In separate bowl, stir together flour, baking powder, baking soda, salt and cinnamon; sift. Add dry ingredients to egg mixture and blend. Fold in drained pineapple and carrots. Pour batter evenly into 3 greased and floured 9-inch cake pans and bake for 25 to 30 minutes or until a toothpick inserted into center of the cake comes out clean. Cool in pans on wire racks for 10 minutes. Remove from pans and cool completely on wire racks.

Combine cream cheese, butter, vanilla, confectioners' sugar and milk and mix until smooth. If necessary, add a little extra milk. When cake is cool, spread whipped topping between layers. Frost the top and sides of cake with cream cheese frosting. Sprinkle cake with nuts.

Note: If using a 9x13-inch baking dish, bake for 40 to 45 minutes. Only use half recipe of frosting for sheet cake.

Makes 10 to 12 servings

HUMMINGBIRD CAKE

CAKE

3   cups all-purpose flour
2   cups sugar
1   teaspoon salt
1   teaspoon baking soda
1   teaspoon ground cinnamon
3   eggs, beaten
1½ cups vegetable oil

1½ teaspoons pure vanilla extract
1   (8 ounce) can crushed pineapple, drained
2   cups chopped pecans or walnuts
2   cups chopped bananas

FROSTING

16 ounces cream cheese
2   sticks butter, softened

2   (1 pound) boxes confectioners' sugar
2   teaspoons vanilla

Preheat oven to 350 degrees. Combine flour, sugar, salt, baking soda and cinnamon in a large bowl. Add eggs and oil and STIR until dry ingredients are moistened (do not beat with a mixer). Stir in vanilla, pineapple, nuts and bananas. Pour batter evenly into 3 greased and floured 9-inch cake pans. Bake for 25 to 30 minutes or until a toothpick inserted into the center of the cake comes out clean. Cool in pans for 10 minutes. Remove from pans and finish cooling on racks.

For frosting, beat cream cheese and butter until smooth. Add sugar and mix well. Add vanilla and beat until smooth. Spread between layers and on top and sides of cake.

Makes 10 to 12 servings

SANDY SAMMONS

STRAWBERRY ICING CAKE

CAKE

2 eggs
1 cup sugar
1 teaspoon pure vanilla extract
1 cup light whipping cream

2 cups all-purpose flour
2½ teaspoons baking powder
¼ teaspoon salt

FROSTING

2 tablespoons butter, softened
3 cups sifted confectioners' sugar

½ cup crushed strawberries

Preheat oven to 350 degrees. In medium bowl, beat eggs until light and very thick. Add sugar and beat again. Add vanilla and cream. Sift flour with baking powder and salt and gradually add to egg mixture. Stir well. Pour batter evenly into 2 greased and floured 9-inch cake pans. Bake for 25 minutes or until a toothpick inserted into center of the cake comes out clean. Cool in pans for 5 minutes. Remove from pans and finish cooling on racks.

For frosting, mix together butter and sugar. Stir in strawberries and mix well. If too thin, add more sugar; if too thick, thin with cream. After cake has cooled, spread between layers and on top and sides of cake.

Makes 10 to 12 servings

MARGARET SWAIN

Margaret is Betty's sister-in-law and introduced Betty to her husband, Bill.

Fresh Apple Cake

2	cups sugar	1	teaspoon salt
3	eggs at room temperature	1½	teaspoons baking soda
1½	cups vegetable oil	5	Granny Smith apples, diced in ¼-inch cubes
3	cups all-purpose flour	1	cup chopped pecans, toasted and cooled
1	teaspoon ground cinnamon		
1	teaspoon ground nutmeg		
½	teaspoon ground cloves		

Preheat oven to 325 degrees. With an electric mixer, cream together sugar, eggs and oil until well blended. In a separate bowl, sift together the flour, cinnamon, nutmeg, cloves, salt and baking soda. Add the dry ingredients to the wet ingredients in 3 batches and STIR using a spoon until thoroughly moistened. Fold in the diced apples and pecan pieces. Pour batter into a buttered tube or Bundt pan. Bake for 1 hour and 30 minutes or until a toothpick inserted into the center of the cake comes out clean.

Makes 10 to 12 servings

CANDICE HILLIARD

Aunt Agnes' Strawberry Cake

Cake

1	box white cake mix	4	eggs, beaten
1	(3 ounce) box strawberry gelatin	3	tablespoons all-purpose flour
1	cup vegetable oil	1	cup frozen strawberries, thawed and drained, reserving juice for glaze

Glaze

Juice from frozen strawberries		1	cup confectioners' sugar

Preheat oven to 325 degrees. In a large bowl, combine cake mix, gelatin, oil, eggs, flour and strawberries. Beat well. Pour batter into a greased and floured tube or loaf pan. Bake for 1 hour or until a toothpick inserted into the center of the cake comes out clean.

Begin making the glaze about 10 minutes before the cake is done. Combine strawberry juice and confectioners' sugar. Spread over the cake while the cake is still warm.

Makes 10 to 12 servings

AGNES SMOAK HART

TENNESSEE JAM CAKE

CAKE

2   sticks butter, softened
1½ cups sugar
1   cup seedless blackberry jam
4   eggs
2½ cups all-purpose flour
1   teaspoon baking soda

1   teaspoon ground nutmeg
1   teaspoon ground cinnamon
1   teaspoon ground cloves
¼   teaspoon salt
1   cup buttermilk
1½ cups chopped pecans

TOPPING

1   stick butter
1   cup sugar
1   tablespoon light corn syrup

½   teaspoon baking soda
½   cup buttermilk

Preheat oven to 350 degrees. With an electric mixer, cream together butter and sugar in a large bowl. Add jam and eggs and mix well. In a separate bowl, stir together flour, baking soda, nutmeg, cinnamon, cloves and salt. Add dry ingredients alternately with buttermilk to creamed mixture, mixing well after each addition. Fold in nuts. Pour batter into a greased and floured 9x13-inch baking dish. Bake for 30 to 35 minutes or until a toothpick inserted into the center of the cake comes out clean.

In a medium saucepan, mix together butter, sugar, corn syrup, baking soda and milk. Boil for 3 to 4 minutes. When the cake is taken out of the oven, poke holes all over the cake with a toothpick. Spoon the topping over it, covering entire cake.

Makes 10 to 12 servings

LYNN GRIMSLEY

LEMON POPPY SEED CAKE

CAKE

2	tablespoons poppy seeds	1	teaspoon almond extract
½	cup cold water	6	eggs, separated
3	cups sugar	3	cups all-purpose flour
1	cup vegetable shortening	¼	teaspoon baking soda
1	teaspoon pure vanilla extract	¼	teaspoon salt
1	teaspoon butter flavoring	1	cup buttermilk

GLAZE

½	cup lemon juice	1	teaspoon butter flavoring
1	teaspoon pure vanilla extract	1½	cups confectioners' sugar

Soak poppy seeds in water overnight. Preheat oven to 350 degrees. With an electric mixer, cream together sugar, shortening, vanilla, butter flavoring, almond extract and egg yolks until smooth. In a separate bowl, mix together the flour, baking soda and salt. Add the dry ingredients to the creamed mixture, a little at a time, alternating with the buttermilk. Add poppy seeds with water and mix well. Beat egg whites until stiff. Fold egg whites into cake batter until mixed well. Pour batter into a greased and floured tube or Bundt pan. Since this cake rises considerably, the Bundt pan should be no more than ⅔ full when it goes into the oven or you risk the cake overflowing. Place in the center of the oven and bake for 1 hour to 1 hour and 30 minutes. Top of cake should split, and a tooth pick inserted into the center of the cake should come out clean.

About 15 minutes before cake is done, mix together lemon juice, vanilla, butter flavoring and confectioners' sugar until smooth. Remove cake from oven and immediately spread on glaze, while cake is still in pan, using a basting brush. Reserve ¼ of glaze. Flip cake over onto serving platter while still warm. Brush remaining glaze over cake. Allow to fully cool before serving.

Note: Poppy seeds can cause a false positive on a drug test, but this cake is good enough to take the risk!

Makes 10 to 12 servings

TAMMY LAWSON

FRUITLESS FRUITCAKE

2 sticks butter, melted
2 cups firmly packed brown sugar (light or dark)
2 cups applesauce, heated
3 eggs
4 cups all-purpose flour, sifted
2 teaspoons baking soda
½ teaspoon salt
2 teaspoons ground cinnamon
1 teaspoon allspice
1 teaspoon ground cloves
1 cup golden raisins

1 cup dark raisins
½ cup currants
1 (8 ounce) package chopped dates
1 cup chopped walnuts
1 cup chopped pecans
1 can pitted sour cherries, drained
1 (8 ounce) can crushed pineapple, drained
½ cup rum

Preheat oven to 350 degrees. Melt butter and beat in brown sugar. Add hot applesauce. Add eggs, one at a time, beating well after each addition. In a separate bowl, stir together flour, baking soda, salt, cinnamon, allspice and cloves; set aside. Dust the raisins, currants and dates in a small amount of flour. In a small bowl, combine raisins, currants, dates and nuts, being sure fruits are separated. Add flour and fruit mixtures in small batches to butter mixture. Mix well; add cherries and pineapple. At this point, beat the mixture, which is very thick, with a metal spoon for 20 minutes. If you use an electric stand mixer, beat for approximately 7 minutes.

Pour batter into a buttered and floured 10-inch Bundt pan or tube pan or 4 or 5 individual loaf pans. Bake for 1 hour and 15 minutes or until a toothpick inserted into the middle of the cake comes out clean. Let cool slightly in pan. Remove from pan, and while slightly warm, sprinkle with ½ cup rum. When completely cool, wrap in heavy-duty aluminum foil.

Note: Store in refrigerator if keeping longer than 1 month. Freezes well. You can sprinkle with rum weekly to help it stay moist.

Makes 10 to 12 servings

CATHERINE MORRIS

Catherine Morris is a long-time customer of **The Lunch Bell**.

"We call this "Fruitless Fruit Cake" because it doesn't have any candied fruit. I found this recipe in the Washington Post back in the 1980's when I was looking for a replacement to my Grandmother's turn-of-the-century recipe. That year, I baked two different cakes for the family, and this was the winner. We are still enjoying this cake today."

Catherine Morris

*Catherine Morris has been eating at **The Lunch Bell** for many years. She originally worked as a night clerk and was very unsatisfied in her career. A few years later, her sister offered to pay for her to go to college. Catherine jumped at the chance and enrolled at Christopher Newport University. She participated in the co-op program with NASA and after graduation she was hired on full-time. "She is truly a success story that warms my heart."*

Betty Swain

Oatmeal Spice Cake with Broiled Topping

*Betty's daughter,
Shelah, is married to
David Swain, so
Shelah is now "Shelah
Swain Swain!" Ann is
David's mother.*

*6 Things Betty
Must Have to Bake:
Electric Stand Mixer,
2-Quart Glass Measuring
Pitcher, Large Metal
Whisk, Baker's Joy®,
Duncan Hines® Cake
Mixes and Pillsbury®
Refrigerated Pie Crusts*

CAKE

1½	cups water	2	eggs, beaten
1	cup quick-cooking oatmeal	1⅓	cups all-purpose flour
1	stick butter	½	teaspoon salt
1	cup firmly packed brown sugar	1	teaspoon baking soda
		1	teaspoon ground cinnamon
1	cup sugar	½	teaspoon ground nutmeg

TOPPING

6	tablespoons butter, softened	1	teaspoon pure vanilla extract
½	cup sugar	1	cup coconut flakes
¼	cup milk	1	cup chopped pecans

Preheat oven to 350 degrees. In a 3-quart saucepan bring water to a boil. Add oatmeal, butter and brown sugar. Combine, cover and set aside for at least 10 minutes. Add sugar and eggs to oatmeal mixture. In a separate bowl, sift together flour, salt, baking soda, cinnamon and nutmeg. Add dry ingredients to oatmeal mixture and stir well. Pour batter into a greased and floured 9x13-inch baking dish. Bake for 25 to 30 minutes or until a toothpick inserted into the center of the cake comes out clean.

Begin making the topping about 10 minutes before the cake is done. Combine butter, sugar, milk, vanilla, coconut and pecans. Immediately after removing cake from oven, spread topping over cake. Broil until bubbly, watching it closely.

Note: This cake keeps well. It is good for any "bake and take" occasion since you can serve it right from the pan.

Makes 10 to 12 servings

ANN SWAIN

Gerry Seevers, David Swain and Shelah Swain
celebrate Thanksgiving together at **The Lunch Bell**.

 # FRANKLIN NUT CAKE

4	sticks butter, softened	¼	teaspoon salt
2	cups sugar	4	cups coarsely chopped nuts
6	eggs, beaten	½	pound red cherries
4	cups all-purpose flour, divided	½	pound green pineapple
		1	teaspoon pure vanilla extract
1	teaspoon baking powder	1	teaspoon lemon extract

Preheat oven to 250 degrees. With an electric mixer, cream together butter and sugar. Add eggs; mix well. Combine 3 cups sifted flour, baking powder and salt; add to creamed mixture. Mix remaining flour with nuts, cherries and pineapple; stir into batter. Add vanilla and lemon extract. Pour batter into a greased and floured 10-inch tube pan or 2 greased and floured 9x5x3-inch loaf pans. Place a pan of water on rack below cake. Bake tube cake for 2 hours and 40 minutes or until a toothpick inserted into the center of the cake comes out clean. Bake loaves for 2 hours or until a toothpick inserted into the center of the cake comes out clean. Let cool in pan.

Makes 10 to 12 servings

SHELAH SWAIN

 # AUNT DELLA'S YELLOW CAKE

1	stick butter	¼	teaspoon salt
½	cup vegetable shortening	3	teaspoons baking powder
2	cups sugar	1	cup milk
4	eggs, separated	1	teaspoon pure vanilla extract
3	cups sifted cake flour		Frosting of your choice

Preheat oven to 350 degrees. Cream together butter, shortening and sugar until fluffy. Add egg yolks, one at a time, beating thoroughly after each addition. Sift together cake flour, salt and baking powder 3 times. Add dry ingredients alternately with milk and vanilla to creamed mixture, beating after each addition. Beat until smooth. Fold in stiffly beaten egg whites. Pour evenly into 3 greased and floured cake pans. Bake for 25 minutes or until a toothpick inserted into the center of the cake comes out clean. Cool in pans for 10 minutes. Remove from pans and finish cooling on racks. Frost with your choice of frostings.

Makes 10 to 12 servings

DELLA LEWIS

Growing up, Bill Swain spent summers with his aunt Della. Betty received a few recipes from her after Bill commented that her cakes were good, "but not as good as Aunt Della's Pineapple Cake."

ORANGE-PINEAPPLE CAKE

CAKE

1 box Duncan Hines® butter recipe golden cake mix

½ cup vegetable oil

4 eggs

1 (11 ounce) can Mandarin oranges, undrained

FROSTING

1 (16 ounce) container frozen whipped topping, thawed

1 (20 ounce) can crushed pineapple, undrained

1 (3.4 ounce) box instant vanilla pudding

Preheat oven to 350 degrees. Pour cake mix into medium bowl and add oil. Mix in eggs one at a time, beating well after each. Add oranges with juice and stir well. Pour batter evenly into 2 greased and floured 9-inch cake pans. Bake for 30 to 35 minutes or until a toothpick inserted into the center of the cake comes out clean.

For frosting, mix together, whipped topping, pineapple and vanilla pudding. Once cake cools, spread frosting between layers and on top and sides of cake. Keep refrigerated.

Makes 10 to 12 servings

BETTY AND BERNIE GERVAIS

ITALIAN CREAM CAKE

CAKE

1	stick butter, softened	1	cup buttermilk
½	cup vegetable shortening	1	teaspoon pure vanilla extract
2	cups sugar	1	small can angel flake coconut
5	eggs yolks	1	cup chopped pecans
2	cups all-purpose flour	5	egg whites, stiffly beaten
1	teaspoon baking soda		

FROSTING

8	ounces cream cheese, softened	1	(1 pound) box confectioners' sugar
½	stick butter, softened	1	teaspoon pure vanilla extract
			Chopped pecans

Preheat oven to 350 degrees. With an electric mixer, cream together butter and shortening. Add sugar and beat until mixture is smooth. Add egg yolks and beat well. In a separate bowl, combine flour and baking soda and add to creamed mixture alternately with buttermilk. Stir in vanilla. Add coconut and nuts. Fold in egg whites. Pour batter evenly into 3 greased and floured 8-inch cake pans. Bake for 25 minutes or until a toothpick inserted into the center of the cake comes out clean. Cool.

For frosting, beat cream cheese and butter until smooth. Add sugar and mix well. Add vanilla and beat until smooth. Spread between layers and on top and sides of cake. Sprinkle top with pecans.

Note: You can also put pecans in the frosting.

Makes 10 to 12 servings

TOMMIE FAULKNER

"The Italian Cream Cake is very special to me because it was my daughter's favorite and we lost her to cancer in 1993 when she was only 29 years old. I make the cake in memory and honor of her, as she was so special. She always asked me to make this cake when she came home. She just loved it, and so does everyone else that has ever tasted it."

Tommie Faulkner

"Good" Cake

The name of this cake came from people asking for "that good cake" that Betty makes.

Cake

1	box Duncan Hines® butter recipe golden cake mix
1	cup sour cream
5	eggs

⅓	cup vegetable oil
1	stick butter, softened
¼	cup sugar
¼	cup whole milk

Topping

1½	sticks butter
1¼	cups sugar
1	(12 ounce) can evaporated milk

2	teaspoons pure vanilla extract
1	(20 ounce) can crushed pineapple, undrained

Frosting

8	ounces cream cheese, softened
½	cup sugar
1	cup confectioners' sugar

1	(16 ounce) container frozen whipped topping, thawed
½	cup angel flake coconut

Preheat oven to 325 degrees. With an electric mixer, beat together cake mix, sour cream, eggs, oil, butter, sugar and milk for 6 minutes. Pour batter into a greased and floured 9x13-inch baking dish. Bake for 35 minutes or until a toothpick inserted into the center of the cake comes out clean.

Begin making the topping about 10 minutes before the cake is done. Put butter, sugar and evaporated milk into a saucepan and bring to a boil. Boil for 2 minutes. Stir in vanilla. When the cake is taken out of the oven, poke holes all over the cake using the handle of wooden spoon. Then spoon the topping over it, covering entire cake. Spread pineapple over cake. Cool.

With an electric mixer, beat together cream cheese, sugar and confectioners' sugar until fluffy. Fold in whipped topping. Spread over cooled cake. Sprinkle with coconut.

Note: This cake is better when made the day before serving.

Makes 12 servings

Chocolate "Good" Cake

Cake

1	box Duncan Hines® devil's food cake mix		⅓	cup vegetable oil
1	cup sour cream		1	stick butter, softened
5	eggs		¼	cup sugar
			¼	cup whole milk

Topping

1½	sticks butter		2	teaspoons pure vanilla extract
1¼	cups sugar			
1	(12 ounce) can evaporated milk		1	(20 ounce) bottle of fat-free caramel sundae syrup

Ganache

1	cup heavy whipping cream		2	cups semisweet chocolate chips

Preheat oven to 325 degrees. With an electric mixer, beat together cake mix, sour cream, eggs, oil, butter, sugar and milk for 6 minutes. Pour batter into a greased and floured 9x13-inch baking dish. Bake for 35 minutes or until a toothpick inserted into the center of the cake comes out clean.

Begin making the topping about 10 minutes before the cake is done. Put butter, sugar and evaporated milk in a saucepan and bring to a boil. Boil for 2 minutes. Stir in vanilla. When the cake is taken out of the oven, poke holes all over the cake using the handle of wooden spoon. Then spoon the topping over it, covering entire cake. Spread the bottle of caramel syrup over entire cake. Cool.

Microwave whipping cream on high for 2 to 3 minutes. Pour over chocolate chips and let set for approximately 5 minutes. Stir until smooth. Spread over cooled cake.

Note: This cake is best when refrigerated overnight after it has cooled.

Makes 12 servings

CHOCOLATE CREAM CAKE

CAKE

1   box Duncan Hines® devil's food chocolate cake mix
1   cup sour cream
5   eggs

¼   cup milk (or water)
⅓   cup vegetable oil
1   stick butter, softened
¼   cup sugar

FROSTING

1   (12 ounce) container frozen whipped topping, thawed (do not use light whipped topping)

2   (14.5 ounce) cans Duncan Hines® chocolate butter cream frosting, well stirred

Preheat oven to 325 degrees. With an electric mixer, beat together cake mix, sour cream, eggs, milk, oil, butter and sugar for 5 to 6 minutes. Pour batter evenly into 2 greased and floured 9-inch cake pans. Bake for 35 to 40 minutes or until a toothpick inserted into the center of the cake comes out clean.

Once the cakes are cooled, place one cake on a decorative cake plate. Split this cake through the middle and set aside the top half. Put half of the whipped topping on top of the bottom half of the cake. Put the top half of the cake (cut side down) on top of the whipped topping; spread 1 can of frosting on the top and sides. Split the other cake through the middle and put the bottom layer of cake (cut side up) on top of the chocolate covered cakes. Spread the other half of the whipped topping on top. Then place the top half of the cake (cut side down) on top. Finish the cake by spreading the other can of frosting on the top and sides of the cake.

Makes 10 to 12 servings

Chocolate Fudge Cake

Cake

3   cups firmly packed brown sugar
¾   cup canola oil
3   eggs
2⅔ cups all-purpose flour
2¼ teaspoons baking powder
2¼ teaspoons baking soda

1½ teaspoons salt
1   tablespoon pure vanilla extract
1½ cups milk
1½ cups water
1⅛ cups cocoa powder

Frosting

6   sticks butter, softened
3   cups sifted confectioners' sugar

2   tablespoons pure vanilla extract
Pinch of salt

Ganache

1¼ cups semisweet chocolate chips

¾   tablespoon light corn syrup
¾   cup heavy cream

Preheat oven to 350 degrees. With an electric mixer, cream together brown sugar and oil. Add eggs and mix on low. Let the sugar, oil and eggs mix while sifting together the flour, baking powder, baking soda and salt in a separate bowl; set aside.

In another small bowl, mix the vanilla into the milk; set aside. Bring water to a boil and pour over the cocoa and whisk until smooth. To the egg mixture, alternately add the flour mixture and the milk mixture beginning and ending with flour. With the mixture at a low speed, add the cocoa. Pour this mixture into 3 greased and floured 10-inch cake pans. Bake for 15 minutes or until a toothpick inserted into the center of the cake comes out clean. When cake layers have cooled, remove from pans and refrigerate until cold.

For the frosting, cream butter with an electric mixer on low speed. Add confectioners' sugar; mix well. Add vanilla and salt and let the mixer beat for 5 to 7 minutes on medium speed. Spread between layers and on top and sides of cake. Refrigerate for 10 to 20 minutes to set up the frosting.

For the ganache, place chocolate chips and corn syrup in a 2-quart glass measuring pitcher. Bring cream to a full boil. Pour the cream over the chocolate and whisk it until smooth; set aside. Pour ganache over the top of the cake and, with a cake spatula, smooth the top of the cake and allow ganache to spill over the sides. Refrigerate for 20 minutes or longer.

Note: Serve the cake cold or allow it to come to room temperature before serving.

Makes 10 to 12 servings

PRIZE CHOCOLATE CAKE

1 stick butter, softened	5 eggs
½ cup canola oil	2¼ cups sifted cake flour
2 cups sugar	1 teaspoon baking soda
2 teaspoons pure vanilla extract	1 teaspoon salt
4 (1 ounce) squares unsweetened chocolate, melted and cooled	1 cup buttermilk
	Frosting of your choice

Preheat oven to 350 degrees. With an electric mixer, cream together butter, oil and sugar until light and fluffy. Blend in vanilla and cooled chocolate. Add eggs one at a time, beating well after each. Sift together flour, baking soda and salt in a separate bowl. Add to creamed mixture alternately with buttermilk, beating after each addition. Pour batter evenly into 3 greased and floured 9-inch cake pans. Bake for 20 to 25 minutes or until a toothpick inserted into the center of the cake comes out clean. Cool in pans for 5 minutes. Remove from pans and finish cooling on racks. Frost with your choice of frostings.

Makes 10 to 12 servings

$300 Chocolate Sheet Cake

Cake

2	cups all-purpose flour	1	cup water
2	cups sugar	4	tablespoons cocoa
1	teaspoon baking soda	1½	teaspoons pure vanilla extract
1	teaspoon ground cinnamon		
1	cup vegetable shortening	½	cup buttermilk
1	stick butter	2	eggs, beaten

Frosting

1	teaspoon pure vanilla extract	1	(16 ounce) box confectioners' sugar
1	stick butter		
4	tablespoons cocoa	1	cup chopped pecans
6	tablespoons milk		

Preheat oven to 350 degrees. In a large bowl, combine flour, sugar, baking soda and cinnamon. In a small saucepan, bring the shortening, butter, water and cocoa to a boil. Pour cocoa mixture over dry ingredients and mix well. Add vanilla, buttermilk and eggs and mix well. Pour batter into a greased and floured sheet cake pan. Bake for 30 minutes or until a toothpick inserted into the center of the cake comes out clean.

About 15 minutes before cake is done, put vanilla, butter, cocoa and milk in small saucepan and heat until melted. Add confectioners' sugar and pecans and stir well. Pour over warm cake. Let cake cool in pan.

Makes 10 to 12 servings

Sharing our "table" with family, friends and sometimes strangers when God has added to our life.
Hebrews 13:2

MARBLE CAKE

2½ cups cake flour
1½ teaspoons baking powder
½ teaspoon baking soda
1 teaspoon salt
1⅔ cups sugar
¾ cup Crisco® vegetable shortening
1 cup buttermilk
1 teaspoon vanilla

3 eggs, room temperature
1 (1 ounce) square unsweetened chocolate, melted
2 tablespoons warm water
¼ teaspoon baking soda
1 tablespoon sugar
Frosting of your choice

Preheat oven to 350 degrees. In a large bowl, sift flour and add baking powder, baking soda, salt and sugar. Sift again. In a bowl, beat shortening until creamy. Add dry ingredients alternately with buttermilk and vanilla. Beat for 2 minutes. Add eggs and beat 1 minute. In a separate bowl, combine melted chocolate, water, baking soda and sugar. Add 1 cup of white batter to chocolate mixture. Pour white batter evenly into 3 greased and floured 9-inch cake pans. Drop chocolate batter by spoonfuls on top of the white batter. Using a knife, swirl the chocolate batter into the white batter to incorporate it in a marble effect. Do not over mix. Bake for 25 to 30 minutes or until a toothpick inserted into the center of the cake comes out clean. Cool in pans for 10 minutes. Remove from pans and finish cooling on racks. Frost with your choice of frostings.

Note: Add 2 tablespoons liquid coffee to your favorite chocolate frosting to add flavor.

Makes 10 to 12 servings

JANE CAPSALIS AND MARCY BOMBELYN

Marcy Bombelyn and her mother, Jane Capsalis, celebrated Marcy's birthday together at *The Lunch Bell.*

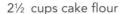

STRIPE-IT-RICH CAKE

1   box Duncan Hines® butter recipe golden cake mix
⅔   cup water
1   stick butter, softened
3   eggs
2   (3.4 ounce) boxes instant chocolate pudding
4   cups cold milk
1   cup confectioners' sugar

Preheat oven to 375 degrees. With an electric mixer, blend together cake mix, water, butter and eggs in a large bowl until just moistened (about 30 seconds). Beat at medium speed for 4 minutes. Pour batter into a greased and floured 9x13-inch baking dish. Bake for 25 to 30 minutes or until a toothpick inserted into the center of the cake comes out clean. When the cake is taken out of the oven, poke holes all over the cake (about 1-inch apart) using the handle of wooden spoon. After poking the holes, combine the pudding, milk and sugar in a large bowl. With an electric hand mixer, beat the pudding mixture for 1 minute on low speed (do not overbeat). Immediately pour half of the thin pudding mixture evenly over the warm cake and into the holes to make the stripes. Allow remaining pudding to thicken slightly; spread over cake as frosting. Chill for 1 hour.

Makes 10 to 12 servings

If you have a high calorie cake that you don't want to compromise by using low-fat products, simply serve slivers of the cake.

CAKE BALLS

1   box cake mix, your choice of flavor
1   (14.5 ounce) container frosting, your choice of flavor
1   (24 ounce) package of almond bark or confectioner's coating

Bake cake according to package directions. Remove cake from oven and immediately dump into a large bowl. Use a fork to break up the cake into crumbs. Add frosting to the bowl and combine well. Line a cookie sheet with wax paper. Roll mixture into balls and place on wax paper. Chill cake balls in refrigerator for 2 hours. In a medium bowl, melt almond bark (½ block at a time) and stir until smooth. Dip cake balls in almond bark to coat. Place back on wax paper until firm.

Makes 3 to 4 dozen balls

CANDICE CARPENTER

 # MILK CHOCOLATE BAR CAKE

CAKE

1 (18.25 ounce) package
   Duncan Hines® Swiss
   chocolate cake mix

1¼ cups water
½   cup vegetable oil
3   egg whites

FROSTING

8 ounces cream cheese,
   softened
1 cup confectioners' sugar
½ cup sugar

10 (1.5 ounce) milk chocolate
    candy bars with almonds,
    divided
1   (12 ounce) container frozen
    whipped topping, thawed

Preheat oven to 335 degrees. With an electric mixer, blend together cake mix, water, oil and egg whites on low speed until moistened (about 30 seconds). Beat at medium speed for an additional 2 minutes. Pour batter evenly into 3 greased and floured 8-inch cake pans. Bake for 20 to 25 minutes or until a toothpick inserted into the center of the cake comes out clean. Cool in pans for 10 minutes. Remove from pans and finish cooling on racks.

Beat cream cheese, confectioners' sugar and sugar at medium speed with an electric mixer until mixture is creamy. Chop 8 candy bars finely. Fold cream cheese mixture and chopped candy into whipped topping. Spread icing between layers and on top and sides of cake. Chop remaining 2 candy bars. Sprinkle half of chopped candy bars over cake. Press remaining chopped candy along bottom edge of cake.

Makes 10 to 12 servings

# Mound's Bar Cake

Cake

1	box Duncan Hines® devil's food chocolate cake mix	1	stick butter, softened
1⅓	cups buttermilk	⅓	cup vegetable oil
		4	eggs

Filling

1	cup whole milk	1	tablespoon coconut extract
1	cup sugar	1	(7 ounce) bag angel flake coconut
33	large marshmallows		

Frosting

1	(14 ounce) bag semisweet chocolate chips	2	sticks butter

Preheat oven to 350 degrees. With an electric mixer, beat together cake mix, buttermilk, butter, oil and eggs. Pour batter into a greased and floured 9x13-inch baking dish. Bake for 35 minutes or until set.

In a 2-quart glass measuring pitcher, mix together milk, sugar and marshmallows. Microwave on high for 3 to 4 minutes (no longer); stir until melted. Add coconut extract and coconut and mix well. Pour on top of cake while the cake is still hot.

In a 1-quart glass measuring pitcher, melt chocolate chips and butter in microwave on high until melted (no more than 2 minutes). Pour chocolate on top of coconut filling while still hot. Place cake in freezer until it is cooled and set.

Makes 12 servings

"The Lunch Bell is a delight and I so enjoy going. The food, service, and atmosphere are excellent. I feel like family when I'm there, as I have known Billy Swain since he was a little boy."
Mary Joyner

German Chocolate Cake

This is Joe Frank's special birthday cake, and if it's not made by Betty, then Joe hasn't had a special day! Joe was the first elected mayor of Newport News.

Cake

4	ounces German sweet chocolate	2	sticks butter, softened
½	cup water	2	cups sugar
2	cups all-purpose flour	4	eggs, separated
1	teaspoon baking soda	1	teaspoon pure vanilla extract
¼	teaspoon salt	1	cup buttermilk

Frosting

4	egg yolks	1½	cups sugar
1	(12 ounce) can evaporated milk	1½	sticks butter
1½	teaspoons pure vanilla extract	1	(7 ounce) package angel flake coconut
		1½	cups chopped pecans

Preheat oven to 350 degrees. In a 2-quart glass measuring pitcher, combine chocolate and water and microwave on high for 1½ to 2 minutes or until chocolate is almost melted, stirring after 1 minute. Stir until chocolate is completely melted.

Mix flour, baking soda and salt; set aside. With an electric mixer, cream together butter and sugar on medium speed until light and fluffy. Add egg yolks, 1 at a time, beating well after each addition. Blend in melted chocolate and the vanilla. Add flour mixture alternately with the buttermilk, beating until well blended after each addition.

Beat egg whites in small bowl with an electric mixer on high speed until stiff peaks form. Gently stir into chocolate batter. Pour batter evenly into 3 greased and floured 9-inch round cake pans. Bake for 30 minutes or until a toothpick inserted into the center of the cake comes out clean. Immediately run small metal spatula around cake layers. Cool in pans for 15 minutes. Remove from pans and finish cooling on racks.

For frosting, with a wire whisk, beat egg yolks, milk and vanilla in a large saucepan until well blended. Add sugar and butter. Cook on medium heat for 12 minutes or until thickened and golden brown, stirring constantly. Remove from heat. Add coconut and nuts and mix well. Cool to desired spreading consistency.

When cakes are completely cooled, spread frosting between layers and on the top and sides of the cake.

Note: If you don't have buttermilk, you can add 1 tablespoon of lemon juice or vinegar to 1 cup of milk. Let the mixture stand for 10 minutes before using.

Makes 12 to 16 servings

RICOTTA CHEESE CAKE

1 box yellow cake mix
1⅓ cups water
⅓ cup vegetable oil
7 eggs, divided

32 ounces Ricotta cheese
¾ cup sugar
1 tablespoon pure vanilla extract

Preheat oven to 350 degrees. With an electric hand mixer on low speed, mix together cake mix, water, vegetable oil and 3 eggs in a medium bowl for 30 seconds. Pour cake mix into a greased and floured 9x13-inch baking dish; set aside. In a medium bowl, mix together ricotta cheese, sugar, 4 eggs and vanilla. Pour cheese mixture evenly onto cake batter. Gently shake pan to mix. Bake for 1 hour.

Makes 12 servings

RUTH BREEGER

"The Lunch Bell is my favorite place to eat. It is clean, the food is fresh and well prepared and the service is pleasant."
Ruth Breeger

Ray and Ruth Breeger frequently enjoy lunch at *The Lunch Bell*!

PEACHES AND CREAM CHEESECAKE

¾ cup all-purpose flour
1 teaspoon baking powder
½ teaspoon salt
1 (3.4 ounce) box instant vanilla pudding mix
3 tablespoons butter, softened
1 egg
½ cup milk

1 (15 to 20 ounce) can sliced peaches
8 ounces cream cheese, softened
½ cup sugar
3 tablespoons peach juice
1 tablespoon sugar
½ teaspoon ground cinnamon

Preheat oven to 350 degrees. Combine flour, baking powder, salt, vanilla pudding mix, butter, egg and milk and beat 2 minutes with electric mixer. Batter will be VERY thick. Pour batter into a greased and floured 9-inch deep dish pie pan. Drain peaches, reserving 3 tablespoons of the juice. Arrange peach slices on batter. Combine cream cheese, sugar and peach juice and beat 2 minutes with electric mixer. Spoon cream cheese mixture over peaches to within 1-inch of edge of batter. Combine sugar and cinnamon and sprinkle over cream cheese. Bake for 30 to 35 minutes or until lightly browned. Filling will appear soft. Refrigerate leftovers.

Makes 8 to 10 servings

SARAH KAY ROWE

BANANAS FOSTER CHEESECAKE

CRUST

½   stick unsalted butter
9   (5x2½-inch) graham crackers

2   tablespoons granulated sugar
12-13 Italian Savoiardi® lady finger cookies

BANANAS FOSTER FILLING

¼   cup sliced almonds
½   stick unsalted butter
½   cup firmly packed dark brown sugar
2   tablespoons banana liqueur

2   tablespoons dark rum
⅛   teaspoon ground cinnamon
½   teaspoon pure vanilla extract
4   ripe bananas

CREAM CHEESE LAYER

5   eggs
24 ounces cream cheese, softened
1   cup sugar

2   tablespoons banana liqueur
1   tablespoon pure vanilla extract

PRALINE TOPPING

1½ cups pecans
2   sticks unsalted butter

1   cup firmly packed dark brown sugar
1½ tablespoons water

Preheat oven to 350 and butter a 10-inch springform pan. Wrap outside of entire pan with heavy-duty foil to waterproof.

To make crust, melt butter and cool slightly. In a food processor, finely grind graham crackers with granulated sugar and blend in butter until combined well. Press crumb mixture evenly onto bottom of springform pan. Halve cookies crosswise and arrange upright, rounded edges on top, around side of pan, pressing lightly into crust to stabilize them.

To make the filling, toast almonds in one layer in middle of oven in a shallow baking dish until pale golden, about 5 minutes. In a large nonstick skillet, melt butter with brown sugar over moderate heat, stirring until smooth. Stir in liqueur, rum, cinnamon, and vanilla and simmer mixture, whisking until sugar is dissolved, about 1 minute. Remove skillet from heat. Halve bananas crosswise and cut lengthwise into ¼-inch thick slices. Add bananas to butter mixture and cook over moderately low heat, turning them gently with a spatula, just until softened, 30 seconds to 1 minute. Sprinkle almonds over bananas.

"*I went to a restaurant in Houston, TX in 1998 and had this for dessert. It was DELICIOUS, but the restaurant had gone out of business by the time I visited Texas again. I searched for ten years and finally found it. This cheesecake is TO DIE FOR.*"
Candice Hilliard

For the cream cheese layer, whisk together eggs until just combined. In a medium bowl with an electric mixer, beat together cream cheese and granulated sugar until light and fluffy and slowly beat in half of eggs, scraping down side of bowl with a rubber spatula occasionally. Slowly beat in remaining eggs and stir in liqueur and vanilla.

Pour half of cream cheese mixture into crust and bake in middle of oven 10 minutes. Cool layer on a rack 5 minutes. Gently spoon filling evenly over layer, arranging bananas so they are not overlapping. Pour remaining cream-cheese mixture over filling and put springform pan in a large roasting pan. Add enough hot water to roasting pan to reach halfway up the side of the springform pan. Bake cheesecake in middle of oven until filling is set in center and top is golden and firm, 50 to 60 minutes. Cool cheesecake in springform pan on rack. Chill cheesecake, loosely covered, 1 day.

For the praline topping, preheat oven to 350. In a shallow baking dish, toast pecans in one layer in middle of oven until a shade darker, about 5 minutes. In a 2 to 2½-quart heavy saucepan, melt butter with brown sugar over moderate heat, stirring until smooth, and stir in water until incorporated. Stir in pecans and cool topping to room temperature. Serve cheesecake with praline topping.

Serves 10 to 12

CANDICE HILLIARD

PUMPKIN ROLL

CAKE

3	eggs	2	teaspoons ground cinnamon
1	cup sugar	1	teaspoon ground ginger
⅔	cup canned pumpkin	½	teaspoon ground nutmeg
1	teaspoon lemon juice	½	teaspoon salt
¾	cup all-purpose flour	1	cup finely chopped pecans
1	teaspoon baking powder		Confectioners' sugar

CREAM CHEESE FILLING

1	cup confectioners' sugar	6	ounces cream cheese, softened

Preheat oven to 350 degrees. In large bowl, beat eggs and sugar until smooth. Add pumpkin and lemon juice to eggs and beat until thoroughly mixed. In separate bowl, combine flour, baking powder, cinnamon, ginger, nutmeg and salt. Slowly add flour mixture to egg mixture and beat until well mixed. Pour batter into a greased 10½x15½-inch baking pan. Top with pecans and bake for 20 minutes or until a toothpick inserted into the center of the cake comes out clean. Immediately turn out onto hand towel covered in confectioners' sugar; roll up like a jelly roll.

Mix together confectioners' sugar and cream cheese. When pumpkin roll is almost cool, unroll carefully and spread with cream cheese mixture. Roll up cake again and sift with confectioners' sugar. Sprinkle with extra pecans, if desired. Chill. Cut into ½-inch slices and serve.

Note: Makes a beautiful and delicious dessert for Thanksgiving dinner.

Makes 8 to 10 servings

MARILYN HOLLAND

WELSH CAKES

3   cups less 2 tablespoons all-purpose flour
1   cup sugar
½   teaspoon ground nutmeg
4   teaspoons baking powder

2   sticks butter
2   cups currants
2   eggs, slightly beaten
1   tablespoon milk

Sift together flour, sugar, nutmeg and baking powder. Cut butter into flour mixture until crumbly. Add currants, eggs, and milk. Blend together. Roll out to ¼-inch thick, then cut into 2-inch rounds. (You can vary the size to make them smaller or larger.) Cook on ungreased electric griddle, heated to 380 degrees. Lightly brown evenly on both sides.

Note: The dough can be made ahead of time and refrigerated until ready to bake. The tea cakes can also be frozen after baking. They are especially good with brunch, as they are not too sweet. As a variation, you can use chopped golden raisins instead of currants.

Makes about 6 dozen cakes

MARY JOYNER

FANTASTIC FUDGE

2   teaspoons pure vanilla extract
1   (13 ounce) container marshmallow crème

2   (12 ounce) packages semisweet chocolate chips
4½ cups sugar
10 ounces evaporated milk
2   sticks butter

In a large mixing bowl, combine vanilla, marshmallow crème and chocolate chips; set aside. Mix sugar, milk and 2 tablespoons butter in a large saucepan. Bring to a full rolling boil on medium-high heat, stirring constantly to avoid scorching. Continue boiling and stirring mixture until candy thermometer reaches 233 degrees (approximately 8 minutes). Add the remaining butter to the boiling mixture and heat until melted. Bring back to a boil, stirring constantly. Immediately pour the hot mixture into the bowl of chips, marshmallow and vanilla. Mix until well blended. Pour the fudge into a 9x13-inch baking dish. Cool at room temperature until firm; cut into squares.

Note: Heat mixture longer for firmer fudge. Use 12 ounces of evaporated milk for softer, creamier fudge.

Makes 117 (1-inch) pieces of fudge

*"I have been eating at **The Lunch Bell** since they opened their first location in Oyster Point and enjoy the atmosphere as well as the food. We used to live next door to the Swain family and some of my children attended school with them. I have always felt very welcome."*

Mary Joyner

PEANUT BUTTER FUDGE

4	cups sugar	1	cup peanut butter
1	cup evaporated milk	1	cup marshmallow crème
2	tablespoons syrup	2	teaspoons pure vanilla
½	stick butter		extract

In a medium saucepan, cook sugar, milk, syrup and butter until a soft ball forms. Remove from heat. Add peanut butter, marshmallow crème and vanilla and stir well. Pour mixture into 9x13-inch baking dish and let set until firm.

Makes 117 (1-inch) pieces of fudge

MARGIE STALLINGS

 # EASY PEANUT BUTTER FUDGE

1	(12 ounce) package peanut butter flavored chips	½	stick butter, divided
1	(14 ounce) can sweetened condensed milk, divided	½	cup chopped nuts (optional)

In a large saucepan, melt peanut butter chips, 1 cup of condensed milk and 2 tablespoons butter; stir occasionally. Remove from heat; stir in nuts. Spread mixture into wax paper-lined 8-inch square pan. In small saucepan, melt chocolate morsels, remaining condensed milk and butter. Spread chocolate mixture on top of peanut butter mixture. Chill for 2 hours or until firm. Turn fudge onto cutting board; peel off paper and cut into squares.

Makes 64 (1-inch) squares

Measurements and Equivalents

1 tablespoon fresh herbs	=	1 teaspoon dried herbs
1 tablespoon fresh ginger	=	1 teaspoon powdered ginger
Dash cayenne or red pepper	=	few drops hot pepper sauce
1 teaspoon	=	$\frac{1}{3}$ tablespoon
3 teaspoons	=	1 tablespoon
$\frac{1}{2}$ tablespoon	=	$1\frac{1}{2}$ teaspoons
1 tablespoon	=	3 teaspoons or $\frac{1}{2}$ fluid ounce
2 tablespoons	=	$\frac{1}{8}$ cup or 1 fluid ounce
3 tablespoons	=	$1\frac{1}{2}$ fluid ounces
4 tablespoons	=	$\frac{1}{4}$ cup or 2 fluid ounces
8 tablespoons	=	$\frac{1}{2}$ cup or 4 fluid ounces
12 tablespoons	=	$\frac{3}{4}$ cup or 6 fluid ounces
16 tablespoons	=	1 cup or 8 fluid ounces or $\frac{1}{2}$ pint
$\frac{1}{3}$ cup	=	5 tablespoons + 1 teaspoon
$\frac{3}{8}$ cup	=	$\frac{1}{4}$ cup + 2 tablespoons
$\frac{1}{2}$ cup	=	8 tablespoons or 4 fluid ounces
$\frac{2}{3}$ cup	=	10 tablespoons + 2 teaspoons
$\frac{5}{8}$ cup	=	$\frac{1}{2}$ cup + 2 tablespoons
$\frac{3}{4}$ cup	=	12 tablespoons or 6 fluid ounces
$\frac{7}{8}$ cup	=	$\frac{3}{4}$ cup + 2 tablespoons
1 cup	=	16 tablespoons or $\frac{1}{2}$ pint or 8 fluid ounces
2 cups	=	1 pint or 16 fluid ounces
1 pint	=	2 cups or 16 fluid ounces
1 quart	=	2 pints or 4 cups or 32 fluid ounces
1 gallon	=	4 quarts or 8 pints or 16 cups or 128 fluid ounces

Source: The New Food Lover's Companion, Second Edition

INDEX